THE NEXT DEMOCRACY

THE
NEXT
DEMOCRACY

REIMAGINING HOW WE GOVERN OURSELVES THROUGH THE POWER OF DATA AND MARKETS

ERDEM OVACIK

WILEY

Published by John Wiley & Sons, Inc., Hoboken, New Jersey.
Published simultaneously in Canada.

For general information on our other products and services or for technical support, please contact our Customer Care Department within the United States at (800) 762-2974, outside the United States at (317) 572-3993 or fax (317) 572-4002.

Wiley also publishes its books in a variety of electronic formats. Some content that appears in print may not be available in electronic formats. For more information about Wiley products, visit our web site at www.wiley.com.

Library of Congress Cataloging-in-Publication Data Applied for:

Print ISBN: 9781394315383
ePDF ISBN: 9781394315406
epub ISBN: 9781394315390

Cover Design: Wiley
Cover Images: © CreativeCreations/stock.adobe.com, © VIK/stock.adobe.com
Author Photo: Courtesy of the Author

Printed and bound by CPI Group (UK) Ltd, Croydon, CR0 4YY
C9781394315383_290425

The manufacturer's authorized representative according to the EU General Product Safety Regulation is Wiley-VCH GmbH, Boschstr. 12, 69469 Weinheim, Germany, e-mail: Product_Safety@wiley.com.

To Robert and Julian who saw my passion for social change and inspired me to take the path off the beaten track.

And to Petra and dear friends who encouraged me to speak my mind even when I felt vulnerable and held me when the path felt too long.

CONTENTS

CONTENTS

Contents

INTRODUCTION

We are living through a turbulent age with democracy at a crossroads. On one hand, it struggles under the weight of growing global crises such as climate change, disinformation, mental health epidemics, and geopolitical tensions. On the other, the system itself seems increasingly ineffective in tackling these challenges. Public disillusionment with governance is spreading, sparking debates about the sustainability of democracy as we know it. Is the democratic model outdated, unable to manage our interconnected, complex world? Are authoritarian systems like China's or even an AI-powered governance models the answer?[1] Or can democracy find its necessary new forms to be the way we govern ourselves? The question around what kind of governance can deliver the kind of future we seek has not been more pressing in the last few centuries.

We seem to talk about various issues from the rise of populism, to climate inaction, biodiversity loss, economic inequality, and the mental health crisis as if they are unrelated. They are essentially the symptoms of the deeper issue: our public governance systems cannot deliver. Our democracies were designed in the nineteenth century and only slightly adapted in the twentieth, are simply not fit to solve twenty-first-century challenges.[2]

Politicians are incentivized to focus on short-term popularity, not long-term solutions. Transparency and accountability are often afterthoughts. We do not have a way of linking policies to the results they create, or mechanisms to follow through. The art of governance has turned into a spectacle, where narratives, often twisted or outright fabricated, matter more than facts. Adding to the dysfunction is the influence of money and media in politics. Major media outlets are politicized, and focus on click bait over truth in public discourse. Our representatives focus on securing re-election and respecting party lines, whilst dancing between narrow interest groups and the story that resonates with the public, instead of what is in essence in public interest.

This misalignment between governance and societal well-being is fracturing our social contract. And innovation in governance is virtually nonexistent.

This is the "metacrisis," the common thread that lies beneath our environmental, social, and political crises. It is a crisis of democracy itself in failing to protect and serve the collective good. The democratic systems that once facilitated human progress now appear outdated, unable to generate the leadership and vision we desperately need.

In this book, I present Merit Democracy, a radically different framework to reimagine governance. Merit Democracy is not just about tweaking the existing system but proposing a comprehensive overhaul. It draws inspiration from the organizing principles of the data-driven marketplaces and innovative powers of tech companies, and merges them with the need for public service. It bridges the gap between private incentives and the public good to draw individuals in crafting legislation and companies in delivering public service. In Merit Democracy, citizens aren't merely voters; they are active participants and are rewarded based on their contributions to society. Similarly, companies are not merely catering services to us as consumers, but also as citizens, and get compensated for their impacts. In Merit Democracy, data and markets become powerful tools for collective benefit.

THE PRESSURE FOR CHANGE

Time is running out in order for us to realize a new kind of public governance. Our social troubles show in various statistics. In the past three decades, inequality has reached unprecedented levels in the west. In the United States, the richest 1% now own as much national wealth as the bottom 92%. At the same time, homelessness tripled and adult depression and anxiety rates doubled to 10% and 20% of Americans, respectively. Half of Americans report feeling lonely, which is a worldwide trend despite the digital connectedness and material abundance some enjoy.

This system also trashed the environment like there is no tomorrow: Climate change is accelerating with latest Intergovernmental Panel on Climate Change trajectories showing a trend toward 2.2 to 3.5 Celsius warming by 2100 (IPCC, 2023). But let's not get stuck in on the climate issue, as there are many others that are also more local. The United States lost about 75 million acres of forest in the past 35 years, an area equivalent to Poland, about 50% its insect and 30% of its bird populations, while plastic waste went up a whopping 20 times to 42 million tons a year. In our cities, we let cars take most of available public space, and deal with their noise and pollution as if they are a given. Not to mention nitrification of soil due to fertilizers in agriculture, or acidification of oceans.

Meanwhile, technological innovations continue to accelerate. We are entering an era of AI which is already enhancing human capabilities significantly. Many seem to expect tech innovations will fix our public governance issues. They can't: Technology is an enabler; it accelerates the dynamics already at play. Social media can connect us with loved ones, while also making us lonely and insecure. AI can be our assistant to guide and solve problems for us, just as it can manipulate us. No, new technologies on their own cannot save us. They need governance; the incentive structures and regulatory frameworks to ensure their capacities are directed at solving our collective challenges, not adding to them.

REIMAGINING DEMOCRACY

The next democracy we create must be at least as strong in creating an economy for the public goods as the neoliberal system we created that focuses on the private. To do so, it must leverage the most powerful technologies, just as the companies it intends to regulate, do. More specifically, this book proposes experimenting with a set of ideas towards a completely new public governance structure:

1. **Pricing and Measuring Public Goods**: Public goods like clean air, safe streets, and social trust are difficult to quantify but vital. In our future democracies, we can define these goods and measure them through metrics that citizens can directly engage with, creating a transparent framework for tracking progress.

2. **A Marketplace For Legislations**: Laws and policies could be developed and evaluated through prediction markets, which we know do well in aggregating opinions and knowledge from commodity futures to sports games. Proposals with highest value would be presented for a (liquid) vote. Successful policies that yield measurable benefits would result in rewards for their creators, aligning personal motivations with the public good.

3. **Aligning Companies' Incentives with Public Outcomes**: Using data analysis, the impacts of products and services on public goods could be clearly linked to financial incentives. Companies would need to consider the societal and environmental consequences of their operations, as these would directly influence their profitability. This transforms companies' focus from merely consumer value to social value, harnessing their innovative powers.

4. **Data as Core Competence of the State**: State would generate, aggregate and process data, ensuring privacy, integrity, and security of it. When we trust our governments, we must also equip them

with the most valuable asset of all, our data, just as we do with the leading tech companies.

5. **Continuous Improvement**: Unlike our static, outdated political systems, our future democracies would be agile and iterative, constantly refining itself to deliver better outcomes. It would monitor its own performance and adapt as needed, embodying the principles of agile governance.

The power of markets lies in their efficiency and adaptability. Capitalism has demonstrated that markets are excellent at allocating resources for private goods, where consumer demand and producer supply are in a dynamic balance. Yet, when it comes to public goods, markets have failed us. Neoliberal capitalism has driven extraordinary wealth creation but did so at the cost of: social fragmentation, environmental degradation, and political instability.

Similarly, data-driven companies like Meta and Alphabet have mastered the art of prediction, using data to know us better than we know ourselves. Data is the power fueling tech companies, enabling faster innovation through experimentation. Yet, such data capabilities have not been a part of our legislative processes or public service.

Our next democracy needs to harness these powerful concepts, and redirect them at the service toward solving collective problems. The dysfunctional democracy we have is our heritage, but not our destiny. We can design democracy where markets and data can enable societal advancement.

A CALL TO ACTION

This book argues that the solution for a sustainable future isn't in returning to some nostalgic past but lies in creating something radically new. We must design a governance system that rewards evidence-based decision-making, fosters long-term thinking, and aligns individual success with societal well-being.

We are at a crossroads: innovate or watch democracy further erode. Ideas behind what I call "Merit Democracy" could provide us with inspiration for necessary evolution. This book is a call for a democratic vision where governance is as responsive, transparent, and efficient as the companies and markets it needs to regulate. Where we are empowered not just to vote but to actively and transparently shape the future and be rewarded for it. Where our governance technology evolves constantly to meet new challenges.

The west, who traditionally has been the spearhead of democracy, might not be at the forefront of the new democracy. For various reasons, the United States and Europe might be simply too slow to act on this governance metacrisis. It may be other countries and cities where leaders dare to try new methods for democratic governance may well provide the hotbeds of the future of governance as the example of Taiwan shows us.

This is a journey of transformation, not incremental change. It may not happen overnight, but we need to make changing governance our main agenda, and learn by experimenting with various components of a promising future democracy.

CHAPTER ONE

EXODUS FROM POPULISM

I t was 2006, and I was spending time around the campus of UC Berkeley, studying for my masters degree in public policy. I was having goosebumps almost on a daily basis as we delved into a new area of policy and read about social studies that are showing causal links between well-being and various social policies. This felt like real enlightenment, and I was very excited, for I didn't know such knowledge even existed! Here were the people with the tools to collect and analyze data that would show the links between early childhood education and health, as an example, or the impact of access to affordable transport on earnings. It seemed like the world was possible to understand through science, one step at a time. I was thrilled by the wisdom.

Just about a year before that, I had been seeking such conversations on the dinner tables of McKinsey colleagues. I would question how our work would impact the industry and society, whether the project was in telecom, banking, construction, or energy. I was 23 when I started at McKinsey and brought with me a lot of idealism and ambition and thought I could be a part of fixing things, while enjoying lucrative social status. Yet, despite the fantastic learnings on analysis methods and structuring arguments, the sense of meaningful work evaporated one expensive dinner at a time, where the conversation went from the loyalty points one had on their Hilton Diamond card to what car they would get next year when promoted.

It was in ex-Secretary of Labor Robert Reich's class on leadership and society, where we discussed how movements started and ended. The class was much about understanding leaders that brought about social change, and the dynamics surrounding them. Professor Reich had transferred recently from Harvard's Kennedy School of Government to UC Berkeley's Goldman School. Some months into his presence at Berkeley, which was when I had started the program, he noticed something odd: Goldman School's motto was "speaking truth to power," which he realized by definition was not in power. In contrast, Kennedy School prided itself on their motto of "preparing public leaders."

Truth needs power, Professor Reich insisted. We live in Western democracies, where truth has lost its power in public space. The reason behind this is deeply rooted in the design of our system itself, and not the personal features of specific leaders. Lobbyism and spin doctoring are also not the deepest root causes. They've arrived as an outcome of the shortcomings of our governance system. The way forward to embrace the future is not going back to something we romanticize, but putting our forces to build something new, and, possibly, radically different, so long as it excites us and brings us together.

In my late second year at Berkeley, I was yet again venting to Adam, my friend, about my frustrations about how so many things needed to change in the United States. Sure enough UC campus was a beautiful place to be, despite its many homeless. The campus hill oversees the golden gate bridge, where the sun sets. Most days are sunny where I would run into people throwing frisbee on the streets, as they wouldn't give in to the pressure of demands of grades. In the middle of the campus is the circle that marks the free speech movement in the 1960s, which is the root of many social movements that unfolded in the decades following: civil rights, anti-war, environmental protection, academic freedom, gay rights, feminism. In this space being curious is encouraged, the professors take their time, you can see them hang out between breaks or in cafés with students having debates of sorts. As I hit the hills for my regular runs through the oak and eucalyptus trees with their distinct smell, squirrels stop and look at me, just as I stop and look out to the bay when I get to the top.

Yet, a few miles away from Berkeley campus toward Oakland or Richmond, I would start to note the private trucks replacing the fuel-efficient and discrete Prius of Berkeley's streets. The inescapable marks of crime and pollution enter the picture with fear and frustration on faces in the BART trains. Richmond has a brown suspended cloud over when the wind is light thanks to its coal plant, with pollution warnings forcing people driving through to close their windows. "But we do know better, why isn't that happening?" I would refer to lack of bike lanes or a preventative public health system, complaining to Adam.

He challenged me to leave. "Why stay if you are so upset about things?" he said. Many of the studies we had gone through were actually related to northern Europe. And many of my friends were also from there. After a few nights of sleeping on it, I knew he was right. I didn't feel it was my fight to fix America. I wanted to go somewhere where I would not get as frustrated with the status quo.

On the first day of my move to Copenhagen, Denmark, an October afternoon in 2007, I took a long walk. I was curious about the country I ended up moving to. And I immediately fell in love with what I saw. It was cargo bikes being ridden near the city center, with kids having blankets on them. I didn't quite understand why so many people would be on the bikes at around 16:00. Was this a special day, I asked back in the office. It wasn't. This was the rush hour in Copenhagen. In fact, it starts around

15:00 and is already over by 17:00. The people on the bikes seemed not to be the poor ones who couldn't afford luxury cars. Quite the opposite; they seemed well-off and cultured. I knew I landed in a good place. And I've called Copenhagen home for the past 17 years.

Meanwhile, the time that has passed shows me that similar problems of populism are also present in Denmark. The truth doesn't easily make its way into shaping policy, our mechanisms for public decisions, and for delivering public goods, becoming unforgivingly dysfunctional and outdated. Even with best intentions, and bright people working on them, I see Denmark, and the rest of Europe walking slowly down the slopes of populism, just like the United States, dividing into the political far right and far left. I am not going to leave anywhere now. There is a battle democracies have to fight.

For the first time in history, today's 30-year-olds feel they are worse off than their parents. This is a trend in the democratic west, despite the explosive and exponential technological development in these past three decades. Scott Galloway, a business professor at NYU and celebrated entrepreneur, sees that there is less hope for the young to earn enough for owning a house and to secure their future financially (Galloway, 2024). It also puts pressure on the idea of finding meaningful work and making time for human connection. Uncertainty of one's financial future, as it is very much coupled with one's job, means the paycheck of work takes precedence over relationships.

We can't blame that on democracy, you might say. It's just how markets have behaved, housing became more expansive, while salaries didn't go up the same rate. But that response would be missing the point that *markets are nothing but a construct of our social contract* as Prof Reich would correctly state. We can and must change its rules to fit our collective needs.

We define how many more housing permits are issued, which manages the supply of housing. We also manage how much we tax financial gains on housing, thus making it a more or less attractive investment object.

In Denmark, where I lived the past 17 years, normal income is taxed up to 58% (for annual incomes exceeding $80k annually) to support delivery of public goods. Yet, income from gains in trading one's house is – guess what – tax free, and most people here find wealth not through their income savings, but through the increases of their housing prices. This means there is more pressure on buying homes, which contributes to increasing housing prices. This makes real estate into objects of investment, and more difficult for new potential owners to enter the market.

When it comes to salary levels, it is a similar story. Our democracies define not only what the minimum income is, but also what kind of social security needs to be paid along with it, rules about vacation, job terminations, and social security. I have been on the side of running a business and know how costly it is for a business to provide vacations and other securities. A liberal argument usually goes along the lines of making markets free such that supply and demand for workers meet most naturally. Indeed, there is something that seems natural about this process. However, the rules of that liberal system itself are not so natural as the research shows how it impacts our societies. We must have a system where policies are changed regularly to tilt the balance of income and wealth to our collective benefit.

These are all problems related to our social contract. What is being questioned is not how we behave individually, but as a society. If we look at society as one entity, and personalize it, we could say it is engaged in self harm.

To be fair, governments used to work. Historically, they addressed many societal challenges rather successfully. For instance, they effectively tackled the smoking problem through effective regulations including bans and special taxes. The rates of smoking are thus now far below those of the 70s, when "markets were free" (UK Government, 2024). They managed to mitigate the impact of ozone-depleting substances (UNEP, 2021). They introduced safety regulations for air travel making it much safer.

In the decades preceding, our governments led our societies out of all sorts of issues with back then new and enticing approaches: from setting limits to firms for possible environmental damages to administering licenses to drugs, creating K-12 public education, ensuring stability of financial institutions to protect public savings and many more.

So, our governments have been capable of solving our issues, back in the day, before the world became as complex as it has become. It was never a rosy picture, but the *trend* was a positive one. People had better lives and opportunities than the generations before them. My argument is that our governance technologies fell behind in relation to the sophistication of markets in the past 40 years, and they can no longer deal with the issues created in the modern economy from loneliness to biodiversity with the organization and governance technology they have.

Where and how did this change? Adam Tooze, a historian at the European Institute, has identified the neoliberal course that Western consensus has taken in the past 50 years as the one responsible for crises we face today (Tooze, 2021). They essentially denied any limits to markets in relation to ensuring a sustainable environment and society. Because for neoliberal thinkers, government interventions are simply seen as unnecessary. Former US Federal Reserve Chair Alan Greenspan had replied, when he was asked about his candidacy for president, that he didn't see the point of politics because not public authorities but markets, according to him, set the course for society.

Nobel laureates Daron Acemoglu and James Robinson documented their work on elite capture of democracy (Acemoglu and Robinson, 2012), how the rich are influencing political parties and policy makers and controlling information. They explain how the elite can form coalitions with bureaucrats, offering them high salaries or job security, and create a more loyal class of bureaucrats than the general public, undermining the democratic system's accountability (Acemoglu and Robinson, 2006). Lobbyism and election campaign financing served as a part of this elite capture. It is also not a secret that much of the media are owned by a handful of corporations and have coverage that favor corporate and elite agendas. In return, our institutions did not have fail-safe design against these developments. They did not manage to reform to prevent the trend accelerating.

In *The Great Regression*, famous contemporary philosopher and sociologist Zygmund Bauman tells us that neoliberal policies and economic globalization have dismantled traditional structures of community and solidarity (Geiselberger, 2017). As the bonds that once united people have weakened, societies have become more individualistic and competitive.

People are encouraged to see themselves as autonomous agents responsible for their own successes or failures, which exacerbates feelings of inadequacy and helplessness. They are asked to find refuge in consumerism, which falls short of overcoming feelings of isolation and vulnerability, fostering a climate of fear and mistrust. This worldview makes it difficult to build the kind of collective movements needed to push back against neoliberal policies and defend democratic norms.

Meanwhile, Bauman asserts that the economic insecurity created fertile ground for populist movements that exploit people's fears. They gain traction by promising to restore a sense of security and order, presenting themselves as champions of "the people" against a corrupt elite. They offer unrealistic yet simple, emotionally resonant narratives that tap into voters' fears and frustrations.

Populism, in Bauman's view, is a symptom of deeper social and economic dysfunctions that must be addressed through thoughtful and comprehensive reforms instead of scapegoating marginalized groups. Reversing democratic decline is challenging due to a media environment driven by emotion and sensationalism instead of rational, evidence-based discussions. He calls for more participatory forms of democratic engagement, exploring opportunities that digital platforms can offer to empower us, the people.

The problem is that our democracies have stopped being effective or efficient tools to provide collective goods. More specifically, it is the institutions and processes we've built around our democratic governance structure that don't deliver what we need from them. When it comes to democracy's fight to defend collective benefit, our discussions are more about perception management than they are about solving problems.

We do not measure the various policies' impact on our economies, and do not link compensation or power we give to politicians to the success they achieve in meeting our collective goals. We give them power and reward them for telling us stories we want to hear and speaking and looking like how we do. If we measured what kind of thinking we apply in our politics, in behavioral economics terms, I fear we would find that most of our policy making is driven by an emotional connection (system-1[1]) to a story or policy instead of critical thinking and reasoning (system-2) in the words of behavioral economist, Daniel Kahnemann (Kahneman, 2011).

Let's face it: our technology of democracy does not deliver and cannot respond to the complications we need it to respond to. For the past few decades now, it did not succeed in creating or maintaining a social and environmental balance that is sustainable. It increasingly falls short of producing outcomes that convincingly improve our nations' and humanity's chances of long term survival. That is because governments now need to deal with increasingly sophisticated businesses and technologies, and concentration of power. We are not able to regulate effectively, let alone handle the upcoming AI and biotechnology revolutions, or, the now decade old social media and business models based on click bait content, data gathering, and monetizing our addictive behavior at our cost (Bhargava and Velasquez, 2020).

Also, increasingly, our democratic institutions have lost their legitimacy.[2] The Democracy Index, often considered the best measure of democratic integrity, has taken a global downturn in the recent decade.[3] We live in a time where most prominent intellectuals question democracy's capacity to be the most viable system to govern going forward. Many wish that we go back to the good old days, before governance became too complicated. We seem to lack visions to move on to new directions.

I believe what we need is a transformation of democracy that goes deep, does not settle with changes in the surface, and goes back to the simple idea: how can we best take collective decisions for our best interest?

Big changes often happen at a time when everything else seems impossible, i.e. when there is a "burning platform." The United Nations was founded on the ashes of the Second World War. We now live in a time again where challenges pressing us are big enough that we can see our platform for governance is in dire need of change.

We shall not need a big war, or a bigger, unprecedented economic crisis or pandemic, or deeper ecological threats than those we already have or had. We shall not need more human suffering, people on drugs, on anti-depressants, in jails, or committing suicide in order to realize transformational change is needed.

THE GROWING MISTRUST IN PUBLIC GOVERNANCE

There is increasing evidence that democracy is under threat. According to the Economist Intelligence Unit (EIU), over the past 13 years, all five key indicators except political participation have been eroded (Figure 1.1). Those include the electoral process and pluralism, functioning of government, political culture, and civil liberties. The report in 2022 reads that "trust in government has plummeted" and "people's attachment to democracy is weakening." But the attachment has been strong enough that we had "an upsurge of popular participation and protest." Having been raised in Istanbul, Turkey, and being at Gezi protests in 2013, I can relate to the civic upsurge that in return results in not more but even fewer civic liberties.

Figure 1.1 Democracy is globally in decline the last 15 years.

Source: The Economist Intelligence Unit, Democracy Index 2023: Age of Conflict, 2024 / INDVSTRVS / https://indvstrvs.org/eiu-democracy-index-2023-age-of-conflict/, last accessed on 14 December 2024.

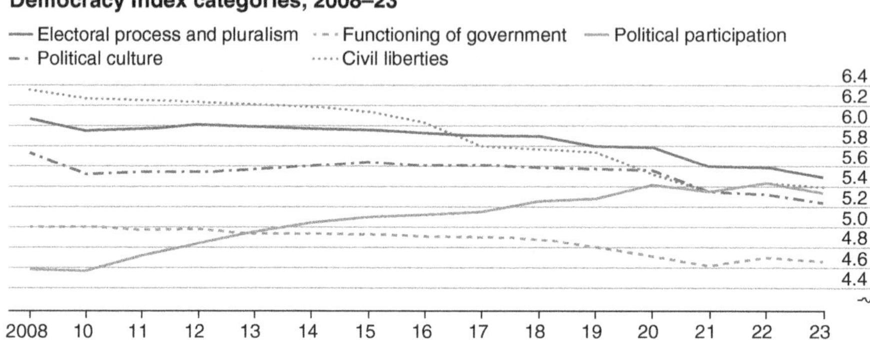

According to the EIU again, only 8% of the global population are now living under full democracies. While countries like Germany, Canada, Australia, the United Kingdom, and Japan remain full democracies, the United States, Italy, Portugal, and Poland are not considered full, but "flawed" democracies.

The erosion of democracy is happening mostly in the emerging economies, or global south, the BRICS moving the average down. But it is also the trend in North America (Figure 1.2), and in some European countries, especially in Eastern Europe. The EIU names various factors as to why democracy is in decline (Economist Intelligence, 2024):

- Perception of corruption, and government's inability to address societal challenges such as inequality, health, environment.
- Polarization and feeling stuck in a gridlock.
- Populists exploiting public dissatisfaction by presenting themselves as outsiders who challenge the "establishment."
- Rhetoric and threats that undermine democratic processes from free speech to elections.
- Erosion of democratic norms, such as respect for the rule of law, checks and balances, and judicial independence.

Figure 1.2 Public trust in US government remained very low during the past decade.

Source: Trust in government: 1958-2015 / Pew Research Center / https://www.pewresearch
.org/politics/2015/11/23/1-trust-in-government-1958-2015/, last accessed on
14 December 2024.

Public trust in government: 1958–2015

Trust the federal government to do what is right just about always/most of the time ...

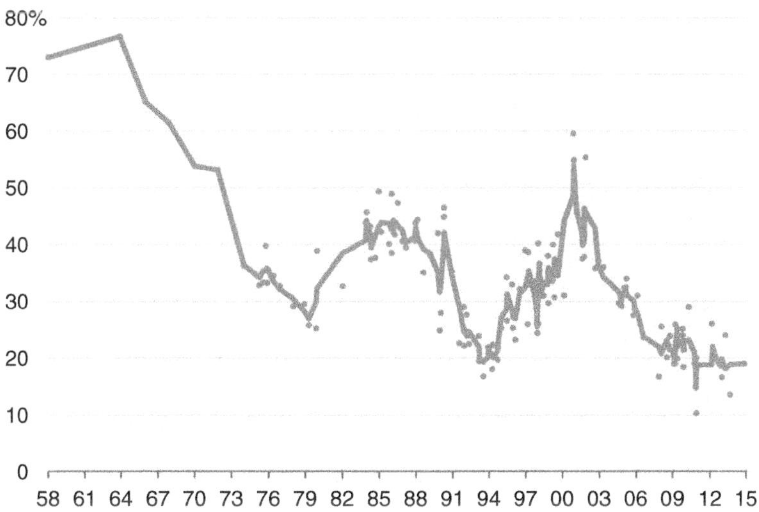

Trust in government is a key indicator of how democracy is doing. Unfortunately trust in government has been on a decline in the US and many other democracies. In the United States, less than 20% of the citizens trust "the federal government does what is right most of the time." Further, various surveys show that people trust companies more than they do their governments. Also interestingly, the best performing companies are digital platforms, like Google, Amazon, and PayPal, who rank better than other companies and brands (Figure 1.3).

Throughout this book, I will be promoting a system that is transparent and enables data-driven decision-making. OECD's analysis on use of evidence to drive public policy seems to help build trust in public institutions, where citizens understand the evidence behind decisions (Figure 1.4).

Figure 1.3   Americans trust tech companies more than their government.

Results of Morning Consult survey, in which 16,700 individuals were interviewed at the end of 2019.

Source: Nicole Lyn Pesce, 2020 / https://www.marketwatch.com/story/people-trust-amazon-and-google-more-than-the-police-or-the-government-2020-01-14, last accessed on 14 December 2024.

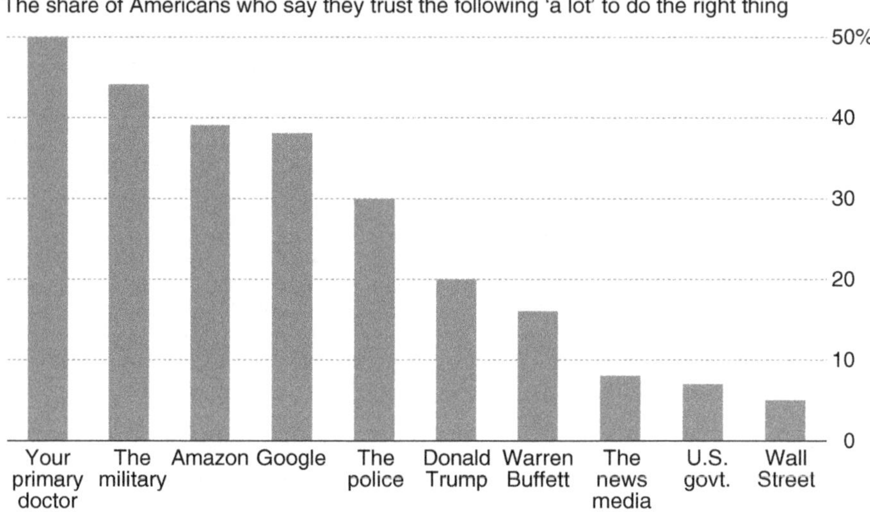

Why can governments not reduce this decline in trust and democracy? The PEW institute has been reporting on government trust on a yearly basis since 1955. One reason for this decline in trust could be that many government structures are not adapting or reforming quickly enough to meet modern challenges. As I will explain in Chapter 3, our governments made a lot of progress up until the 1970s in the United States, and 1990s in Europe. Nevertheless, thereafter, the act of state building and innovating government has stalled. The government reform was to get out of the way of business as much as possible. The neoliberal philosophy led by economists like Friedman argued successfully that the government was ineffective in its ways to achieve results and progress. He famously said, "The government solution to a problem is usually as bad as the problem itself."

Figure 1.4   Trust in governments correlates closely with how much people believe governments use evidence in their decisions.
The Organisation for Economic Co-operation and Development (OECD), surveyed citizens on their beliefs for government decisions being based on evidence. The result showed a strong correlation: when citizens believe governments make decisions based on evidence, they trust them more.

Source: OECD Survey on Drivers of Trust in Public Institutions – 2024 Results / Organisation for Economic Co-operation and Development / https://www.oecd.org/en/publications/oecd-survey-on-drivers-of-trust-in-public-institutions-2024-results_9a20554b-en.html, last accessed on 14 December 2024.

Percentage of population who trust national government and percentage who think government uses best available evidence, 2023. *Each data point on OECD's survey of countries indicates an individual country.*

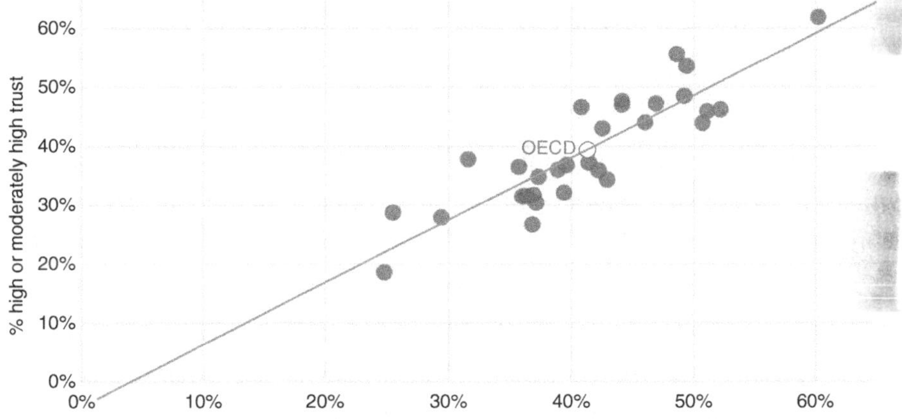

We started expecting changes from the private sector. The government lost its role as an agenda setter, and instead assumed the role of maintaining the status quo. It only stepped forward when its action was obviously required. The 2008 financial crisis, however, highlighted the limitations of the free-market approach, with governments stepping in to stabilize economies through large-scale interventions. This was a massive intervention, where the US government alone allocated $700bn to stabilize financial institutions, and another $800bn to stimulate the economy. So much for Milton Friedman's free market.

In the 15 years that followed, other noteworthy government intervention was again necessitated by a crisis, namely the COVID-19 pandemic. The pandemic proved the importance of wide-reaching, coordinated efforts, and the ability to govern. Government interventions during crises like the COVID-19 pandemic extended beyond health measures, also encompassing economic support, such as financial relief for businesses and individuals. Government borrowing increased: the United States, the EU, and Japan all had large-scale programs to provide financial support to citizens and businesses. The US federal government alone spent $5 trillion in various stimulus and relief packages to keep the economy going.

Yet, these interventions were, in their nature, not focused on reforming markets or our social contract, but maintaining the status quo. They did not change the challenging long-term trends of increasing inequality, or other social and environmental pressures. We did not see new regulations coming into action, or the way regulations were imposed happen any better, or any significant means providing citizens with more agency. Many people remain concerned about the future, reflecting widespread anxieties about economic stability, inequality, and the efficacy of government action.

In the meantime, shortcomings of current democratic governance practices become more apparent. Thanks to digital technologies, our experience of how the world *could* work changes. With the introduction of social media and now recently AI in our daily lives, the way we consume and seek information is very different from 20 years ago. The shortcomings of the democratic decision process, whether its quality, lack of transparency, engagement or pace, become more apparent (Figure 1.5).

There is a trend among tech entrepreneurs in Silicon Valley – buying land in New Zealand – to seek refuge in a system that is doing better. Others are looking to move to northern Europe, where things seem stable.

Figure 1.5   As of 2023, significantly fewer people think representative democracy is the way to govern their countries compared to 2017.

Source: Richard Wike , et al., 2024 / Pew Research Center / https://www.pewresearch.org/global/ 2024/02/28/representative-democracy-remains-a-popular-ideal-but-people-around-the-world- are-critical-of-how-its-working/, last accessed on 14 December 2024.

Fewer people now say representative democracy is a very good way to govern in many countries surveyed

*% who say a system in which representatives elected by citizens decide what becomes law would be a very **good way** of governing their country*

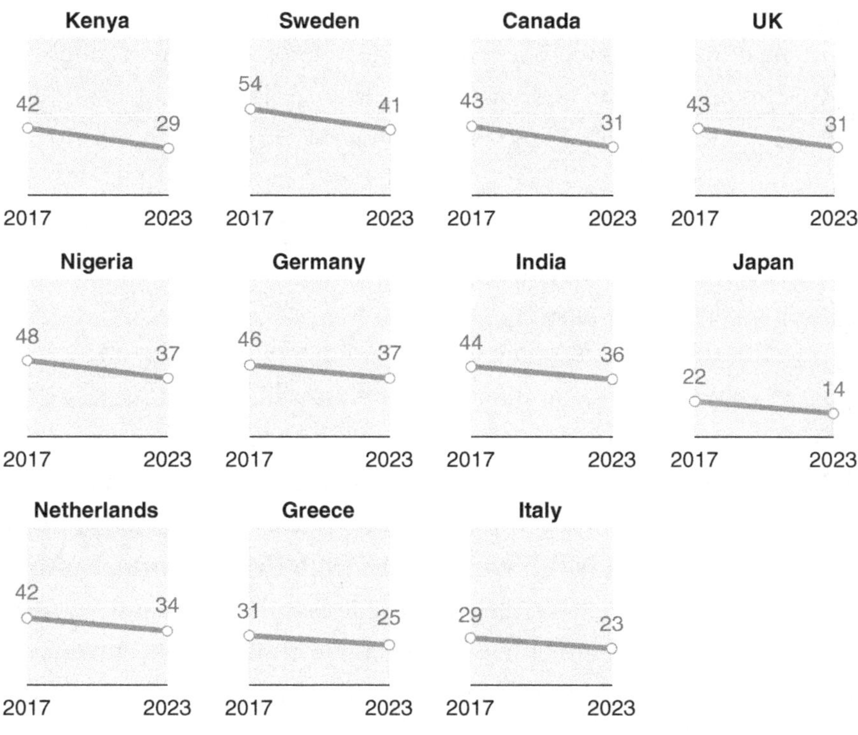

Surely, there are many pockets of public trust and prosperity where one can ignore the bigger trends. Copenhagen, where I live, is one of them. For me, bicycles have become an important symbol of what I think is a good life. In this so-called cycling capital, about half of trips of Copenhagen residents happen on a bike. And I came to see that one could meet powerful people in Copenhagen on their bikes. The mayor of Copenhagen would be on his bike. Ministers are on their bikes. Just a month ago, I saw the world-renowned vice-commissioner of European Union, Margrethe Vestager, on her bike.

This nearly six million people nation has been shaped by grassroots movement toward democracy through the nineteenth century, a high level of trust in one another, and low power distance. The social trust levels in Denmark and northern Europe are among the highest in the world. One of the indicators to measure it is the wallet test. Researchers have dropped wallets in public spaces and observe the return rates. Denmark is one of the top scorers, with +80% being reported back. That's against about 50% in the United States, and about 30% in Turkey (Cohn et al., 2019).

Denmark surely has some of the ingredients to be a strong democracy, and the state of democracy in many aspects is in better shape than other Western states. Denmark has even been subject to democratic debate between Bernie Sanders and Hillary Clinton, quite famously in 2016, where the two debated how the United States could become more like Denmark. And what lessons to learn from this state, which also has been repetitively selected in the past decade as one of the happiest nations in the world. The country has a high amount of GDP in government spending at 48% estimated for 2024, which is in line with many Western European nations (Statista, 2024), whereas the United States spends about 35% of its GDP on government expenditure. And its cultural heritage drives a low hierarchy where people feel their agency. Denmark has one of the lowest in the world, according to Hofstede's measure (Clearly Cultural, n.d.).

But things aren't as good for Denmark as it may seem. The trust in politicians has been in decline (Wang, 2023). While +60% of Danes trusted the government in the first decade of the twenty-first century, now less than 40% do so. The decline in trust in government is paralleled by the increasing income inequality in the country. It had one of the lowest income inequalities in the world with a Gini below 25% in 2000s, and exceeded 30% as of 2021. A report by Oxfam shows that from 2010 until 2020, the income for the bottom 40% in Denmark grew by 2% per year in comparison 13% for the top 10%. This means that the top 10%'s earnings have increased 200% in 10 years, while the bottom 40%'s earnings have increased only 20%.

No part of the democratic world is immune to the challenges lying ahead. We live in an interconnected world, not only by trade, but also our political and economic culture. In many ways, European institutions have been influenced by the United States' free-market approach and have not produced other bold alternatives. These are challenging times for Denmark with the rise of populism, and deteriorating public trust, among other national assets, such as the environment, mental health, and even its cycling rate.

The erosion of democracy is a result of wide-ranging trends that undermine our capacity to govern. It is not only a matter observed in BRICS, or the United States or Europe. It is observed in all modern democracies; we are no longer believers that governments can deal with the challenges of our times as they are. If we do not act, things are going to keep getting worse, before they get any better.

Moving away from home to another, more promising land and system could be a solution for a while. Moving away from a difficult regime can provide much needed fresh air and hopes for the future. Ultimately though, the struggle for better governance will catch up in the new home unless we have figured out a better way to govern ourselves.

Everywhere there is a global fight to be fought for democracy. We need to create a vision of democracy that can deliver for all of us. In this interconnected media and culture environment, our biggest asset will be uniting around powerful new rhetoric that can fuel an awakening of the democratic ambition.

Before talking about the new visions, I will now dig deeper into the problems and set the stage.

DIGGING INTO THE REPRESENTATION PROBLEM

I've met Filip Watteeuw toward the end of the conference about cycling in cities called Velocity in 2024. Even though it is a business conference, it has the vibe of some kind of festival. Most people here share a passion for creating a better world through cycling. This year's big star was Filip, the deputy mayor of Ghent, the city that hosted the conference. I asked him for a short interview, between a performance of monocyclists and a DJ humming with rhythms, while people rushed to fill themselves with healthy snacks. Filip is humble and unpretentious. He didn't mind me recording. He is one of the few who dared to implement some policy decisions that were immensely unpopular for some people for a short period. He wanted to reduce car usage from 50 to 60% of trips in Ghent to less than 20%. And he managed to do that within four short years, with almost no budget! He did so, by banning driving and residential parking on most of the streets, and dropping the speed limits below 30 km/hr (19 miles/hr) in many others. There were rewards for car owners to let go of their cars, and alternative parking just outside of the city. Still, many car owners and shops were initially outraged, he said. But now, the result is that the city and shops are thriving.

The city keeps attracting more inhabitants, and people are spending more time out and about in local shops. The city is also attracting more local and international visitors. Real estate prices increased in the city center, driven by demand for housing in less noisy and environmentally friendly neighborhoods. Somewhat to his surprise, Filip has remained popular in the elections following the changes, with broad support from especially the youth.

When I asked him what the hardest thing in this journey was, he said it wasn't the threats he received and people being angry. It was that the majority he assumed enjoyed the changes remained silent, he said. That made him and his team doubt themselves as they needed to push forward with changes despite the clashes with the loud few who did not want the changes. And to my question, why so few politicians dare to lead social changes as he did, he said, "they are afraid of losing power, of being ousted by their party." And he added: "I accepted to lose it all, if it comes to that."

Such an attitude of personal integrity is rare in any kind of leadership, especially in government. The stories like Filip and the mayor Mathias De Clercq, who backed Filip, are unfortunately exceptions to the rule. Most politicians are focused on keeping a popular face in public where they react to negative media attention instead of defending their values and the need for change. They frequently poll the popularity of their policies, and quickly yield to media pressure mounted on various interest groups against changes they would otherwise defend. This is not a feature, but a bug of our current democratic technology. Such adherence to media pressure and popularity undermines all democracies, even the small and relatively well-functioning democracy of Denmark.

An example is the housing tax bill in Denmark. In 2015, Social Democrats had introduced a bill to tax net gains from real estate. That tax adjustment was needed as real estate gains are free of tax, unlike any other form of income that is taxed at a high level. The policy fed the increasing inequality as it negatively affected a large part of the population. Forty percent of the households did not own their home, and most of the real estate value is kept in the hands of the wealthiest few percent on top (Hansen, 2018). When the bill was introduced, real estate professionals and homeowners' associations led a media outcry, backed by political opponents. After the negative media pressure, the government took steps back on this very key issue feeding inequality.[4]

Another reason representatives' view of the world is so blurred is lobbyism. Lobbyists are influential people, many ex-politicians, with strong networks connecting them to campaign financiers and corporations. They "help" politicians understand the issue at hand by framing the debate, of course from the lens of special interest groups. According to OpenSecrets.org there are approximately 13,000 lobbyists in Washington DC as of 2023, generating a (record) spend of $4.3bn in 2023. This means there are around 24 lobbyists per representative in the federal government who are paid an average of $330k annual salary for their lobby work. It also means $8m is spent per representative annually to lobby them. To put the figure in contrast, a member of the house has a salary of $174k, while about 46 times that amount is spent on lobbying them. Unsurprisingly, lobbying is powerful, and the history of its success paved the scale it has reached today.

The problems facing our governance technology are numerous. Below is a recollection of challenges we experience with our current systems. While the challenges are common, their strength varies across jurisdictions given their culture, social-economic and political context.

- **Self-interest (a.k.a. principal-agent problem)**
  In the case of representative democracy, citizens are the principals represented by the agent, the politician. One member of national or federal parliament represents 100,000 to 1 million people in our Western democracies. The problem is that the further the agent gets from the principal, and lacking the alignment in the contract between them, the agent acts on their best interest, not on the interest they are supposed to serve. A politician often wants re-election, to belong to a party group, to cultivate business relations to serve for possible future career. Many talk about the concept of "elite capture": a small,

well-networked group that shapes important political decisions that they deem right, biased by their own interest. The outcome is lack of transparency, and reduced quality in decisions.

- **Short termism**

When elections are repeated every few years while many public goods require a long-term effort with pain to be endured before projects bear their fruits, we do not see the focus on what is important, but what is visible within a short amount of time. However, many worthy public projects take a much longer time to undertake, decades even. That is why China has development plans that extend well beyond the 3- to 5-year policy frameworks that most democratic governments operate with. Chinese plans include the Belt And Road Initiative, which is planned to occur over several decades. The Chinese Communist Party expects to be in charge of the country for many decades to come, and the constancy of party leadership allows them to undertake long-term projects and commitments, and follow them through. Compare that with the US policies around green transition: it entered and exited the Paris accords (twice!) amid presidency changing hands. Similarly support for fossil fuels versus green energy seems highly dependent on the government in charge. Short termism compromises the quality of our decisions; preventing us from focusing on long-term and important priorities.

- **Information asymmetry**

I would rate this as the most severe problem we deal with. People in power have more information than the rest of us. They have information about their own interests, and interests of various groups who lobby them, that the rest of us do not know. They have access to polls and data that we don't. The rising job of spin doctoring and public relations work proves the point – representatives are concerned with spinning the story. Governments also have a default tendency not to share information that concerns public well-being – basically all of their work, as such publishing, can bring accountability questions to politicians and civil servants. As a result, governance is concerned more with how things look, the cosmetics rather than the outcomes, and we lack transparency.

- **Populism and polarization (a.k.a. identity politics)**
  Polarization is enhanced by a number of trends. A system where we talk down others in order to promote ourselves creates divisions. The business model of media placing focus on click bait prioritizes flashy news over important facts or discussions. Arguments should not be about who we are, but merely about the policies we propose. We divert from the subject of public policy when we start making personal attacks in politics. Focus on personal identities can be dangerous in alienating the other, whether gender, race, profession, etc. Quality of decisions suffers.

- **Corruption and regulatory highjacking**
  If you work for the public sector, your salary is managed by a schedule; your performance is hardly reflected in your salary. There is no bonus or equity. Many public workers are naturally drawn to obtaining better means – we all do – by leveraging their positions. One of them is imagining potential future careers in the private sector, where wages are far higher. So, the person who is supposed to manage an industry for the behalf of all of us earns a fraction of the people whom they indirectly manage. They network through their jobs and want to build bridges. Their actions are naturally impacted by their personal interest in these companies and industries. Again, the impact is lack of transparency and reduced quality.

- **Lobbyism and election finance**
  This is often what many activists call out politics on – businesses with vested interest in specific regulations will spend money on

professionals, often ex-politicians now lobbyists with a good network, to shape regulations in their direction (Figure 1.6, Figure 1.7). The arguments will be packaged in beautiful slides, delivered with expensive suits and perfected smiles.

Not only do the quality of decisions suffer when it is focused on a narrow group interest, but so does also our feeling of agency. With more than 10 paid lobbyists per politician in Brussels and 20 in Washington, DC, where all of them specialize in protecting certain industry interests and have deep networks; it is no surprise that we feel politics are somehow corrupted (Figure 1.6, Figure 1.7).

- **Serial (and limited) processing capacity**
  Stock markets handle share prices for thousands of companies in the United States alone, through buys and sales – the price setting for companies is processed in parallel. Compare that with how we make

Figure 1.6   Citizens suspect political favors are the norm.
OECD Trust Survey, Perceptions of Undue Influence, 2021.
Source: Adapted from Trust in government, http://oe.cd/trust, last accessed on 14 December 2024.

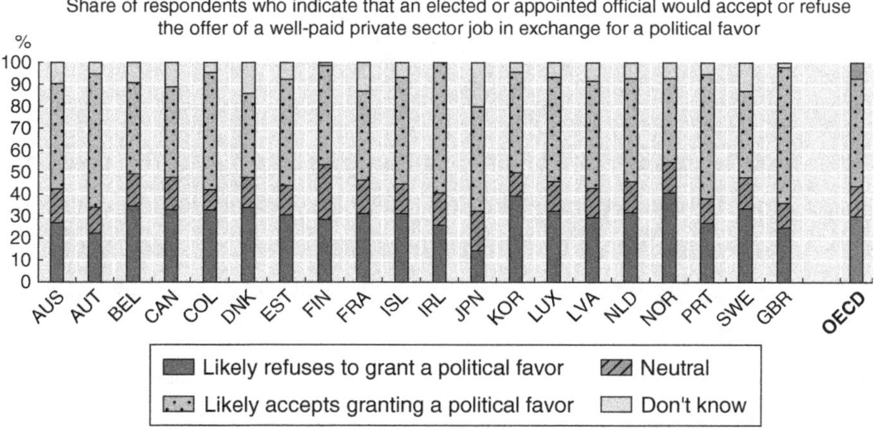

Figure 1.7   Many democracies allow anonymous campaign donations.
Inner ring: ban on anonymous donations, and all contributions made to political parties and/or candidates must be registered and reported. Middle ring: ban on contributions from publicly owned enterprises. Outer ring: ban on contributions from foreign states or foreign enterprises. Note that many countries that prohibit anonymous political donations also experience low levels of trust in government.
Source: Adapted from OECD (2022), Public Integrity Indicators.

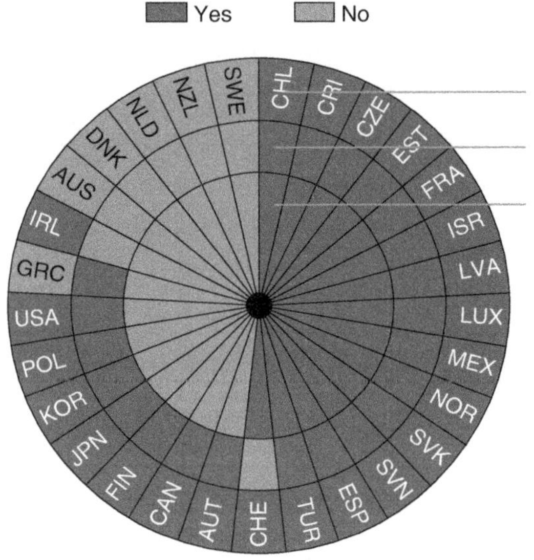

policies: quite cumbersome with one legal proposal discussed at a time, in one physical room. Yes, there are commissions that do some parallel processing, yet the actual decision process happens one at a time, and in one space, and filtering through the same few representatives. This greatly limits how fast we can take decisions compared to a parallel processing design. The result is slow decision-making. I recently heard one consultant in Denmark speaking to the minister for transport about the country's transport spending, each year in the billions of dollars. How much time were they discussing in the government about the transport plans and spending? Less than an hour per year. The consultant shared the frustrations of the minister, that getting the time – even of his own party members' let alone other parties – needed to make a decision in coalition for a meaningful conversation on the topic was simply too difficult. Serial processing and simply lack of time in the increasingly complex world reduces our agility the quality of our decisions.

An August 2017 survey (Stein, 2017) by the Congressional Management Foundation finds that "overwhelming majorities of senior congressional aides believe Congress is not equipped to execute its basic functions." The most cited areas of concern deal with the lack of both the skills and abilities as well as adequate time and resources "to understand, consider, and deliberate policy and legislation" (Thierer, 2020).

- **High cost of entry**

Say you have a policy idea that you think would work really well in improving some area of public life. Your policy could be transport policy, education, or taxation, bridging what we want collectively. The way we aggregate knowledge from the many experts we are, as we gain expertise through our jobs and everyday life in some area of public life, is very weak. Compare that with how businesses work: we made it increasingly easy to start a new business, we have businesses that cater for niche markets.

Creating a political initiative around a policy proposal is much harder. It requires one to build wealth to lobby, or build a political network, or to become a politician. Getting into politics became more demanding on one's material wealth, and one needs to spend a long time in their career to become affiliated. A study by Harvard political scientist Brian Feinstein (Feinstein, 2010) found that family connections in Congress made one 13 times more likely to join the

Congress (Ting, 2017). Engaging in political decisions doesn't seem to be so easy as doing some teaching as a side job, or selling some goods on Amazon – no it is far from it. Therefore, the current system is deprived of aggregating the knowledge that sits with all of us, we fail in collecting the wisdom that markets are so good at. This deteriorates the quality of decisions and creates a lack of agency.

This is not a knock on our politicians. This is a knock on our system. It is a knock on all of us, especially the older generation, for not having taken steps toward reforming it. Political leadership and new regulations are lagging in many fronts, from AI and social media – some global in nature, others more local. The issues are increasingly complex, and the decision structures we have are not designed to deal with the sophistication of the industries they intend to regulate.

As of 2025, at an age with great data capabilities, and sophisticated information technology infrastructure, and a track record of stock markets for investors and consumer markets of endless products and services, I have a hard time believing that we still govern ourselves with such an old fashioned democracy model.

We have, effectively, abandoned our citizen hat behind our consumer hat and focused on ensuring we are privately fine. The argument has been that if we each focus on ourselves, we will be just fine collectively. That argument has been proven wrong. We need a well-functioning governance technology.

QUALITIES OF GOOD GOVERNANCE

Humanity's future, as well as each nation's and even city's future, is tightly connected to the performance of its governance technology. Our future is tied to our ability to defend ourselves, how we treat each other and our environment, and if we are able to produce things others want, in order to trade them. Yet creating those abilities, and providing ourselves with an internal order that brings stability and a sustainable platform and enables us to focus on the common aims are ultimately all subjects of the governance technology.

What are the qualities of a good governance system? If we want to reform our governance technology, we need to define what makes a compelling public governance. We need such metrics to be measurable, just, as I will argue, as we need every other public good to be measurable. While I have not found much literature on this topic, the metrics I argue for are in line with the ideas behind the Economist Intelligence Unit's evaluation of democracies (Economist Intelligence, 2023) and the decentralized autonomous organization (DAO) movement (https://daoscience.org). The absence of literature and experimentation on this topic speaks to one of my main points in this book: we have not understood the importance of innovating our governance technology and have greatly underinvested in exploring other, innovative forms.

I identified four metrics as the markers of good governance technology. They are quality, agility, transparency, and agency.

Quality is perhaps what we talk about most when we think of good governance. It is how good the policies are that the governance technology generates, at solving our (collectively agreed on) issues. When quality is high, we would make policy initiatives that properly address the issues at hand.

I think this is where representative democracies have a score that is mediocre. I zoom in on local (city-level) or national issues for a moment to see how well we are doing to respond to our collective well-being. We have many challenges that could have been solved with appropriate policy but are not: the obesity epidemic, loneliness and depression rates, public (city) space filled with cars, staggering income inequality. These are not even international challenges that require global collaboration.

No, our systems are not good at delivering policies that work. At best they are mediocre. We have the knowledge of solutions that could work – I have studied them and met the people that generate the knowledge. From environmental regulations, to childcare, from public transport to taxation, we often have good reasons to believe what could work.

It was, for example, well-understood that the investment in children had the highest returns when they were youngest, and parental leave was one of the key ways to provide that. I had naively asked my professor how we could know such a thing while it would not be the policy nationwide in the United States, or in a state such as California.

The answer is pure disappointment. The knowledge we have doesn't turn into policy because it doesn't appear popular, and decision-makers' main concern is to remain popular. This is far from how science and technology works and advances. There, knowledge shapes actions.

The decisions we make today are about maintaining popularity, and not about generating results. We do not even track the actual goal of our legislations, or their performance. A system that harms itself, because it cannot turn insights into actions, is not a healthy one. Quality in our decisions therefore is a key goal for our governance system.

Agility is about how fast we respond to new issues. Think of the COVID-19 epidemic. Think of the Ukraine war. Think of a disaster approaching. How fast can we decide? And how fast can we revise our decisions? In a good governance technology, it shouldn't take us months to respond to an urgency that has material impact within days or weeks.

Our current governance systems are not agile enough. The United States has some mechanisms to cater for urges, via "presidential orders" but the scope of those is limited while their use is contested. Federal laws take on average 12–15 months to make on both sides of the Atlantic (EPRS, n.d; Govtrack.us, 2023). Most public institutions make budget allocations once per year. Besides making new laws, agility is about how fast we can revise them and improve them. Laws become old, not fitting current-day's issues as time goes by, and they need to be revised.

Our agility in acting is compromised by the capacity of decision-making by few individuals in a centralized fashion. The decision bottleneck is enhanced with the meetings that need to happen in a narrow time and space, while aiming to optimize. The bills introduced in the meanwhile get longer and more sophisticated, and we get more and more laws that need to be cleaned and simplified.

Compare the agility of stock markets, or foreign exchange markets with the agility of public governments. How long does it take for foreign exchange markets to respond to an earthquake in a given country, or a new government being elected? It is minutes if not seconds. How about a new product launch or release of an annual report of a company – how long does it take for its stock price to adjust to the news? By the end of the day, most of the adjustment will have taken place. Markets are dynamic and are engaging millions of experts globally who take into account different factors to respond to a new situation. Can we be inspired by that in how we govern our commons?

<u>Transparency</u> facilitates trust. What are the biggest arguments behind Bitcoin or other blockchain based Web3 initiatives? It is transparency, of course, in how they are governed and transacted. The institutional design does not allow specific interest groups to influence the decisions, nor can there be corruption or theft. Processes of decision and administration are absolutely transparent.

The ideas behind transparency is that we need not to trust the intentions or declarations of individuals in power. The success of Bitcoin, and Ethereum, is thanks to transparent governance behind them. Their code is open. Decision process in terms of updates to the code are delegated to miners in the network (Fracassi, Khoja and Schär, 2024).

A system that is not transparent in its steps is vulnerable to corruption, and even if it doesn't happen, people can start mistrusting power structures. Indeed, we have a political culture with many behind-closed-door discussions and considerations. There are promises of future (campaign) support, or trades of favor that the public never hears about.

A lawyer by training and a researcher of government, politics and entertainment industry, Martin Kaplan argues that truth does not matter much any longer in politics. He says, "It used to be, the myth was; if you tell the truth, you'll be appreciated" (Kaplan, 2009). He refers to the presidential candidate Walter Mondale's confrontational plan to raise taxes back in 1984 (Joyce, 1984). He tells us that confrontation resulted in a backlash and was a turning point where it became obvious that it wasn't the truth but popularity of arguments that mattered in politics. Kaplan adds that "the truth does not have a constituency because the truth does not have a meaning across the board. People care about what their tribe says. The person speaking the truth is seen as lying." He interprets the TV coverage of politics as trivialization or ignoring politics. However, he says, in an open society, the truth, or falsifiability should drive generations of truth.

We can also turn the growth of spinning in politics. The term spinning refers to techniques such as cherry picking, non-denial denial, non-apology apology, distancing language, avoiding the question among others (National Press Foundation, 2022). The profession of spin doctors coming into politics goes back to the 1990s, when politicians started to use specialist communicators to spin the truth to tell something more popular or desirable from the perspective of retaining power.

The desire to maintain power over the desire to uncover the truth seems to be a key challenge that derailed our democracies. George Soros, founder of Open Society, says in one of his lectures in 2009 (Soros, 2009):

I discovered a flaw in the concept of Open Society. Popper was concerned with an understanding of reality. He provided an epistemological rather than a political argument for an open society. He said 'Only the democracy provides an institutional framework that permits reform without violence. And the use of reason in politics.' But his approach was based on a hidden assumption: The main purpose of thinking would be to gain a better understanding of reality. But that was not the case. The manipulative function could take precedence over the cognitive function. Indeed, in a democracy, the primary objective of the politicians is to get reelected and stay in power.

[...] Our view of the world is deeply rooted in an intellectual tradition that either ignores the manipulative function, or believes it is subservient to the cognitive function.

So, Soros says that our cognitive function has to battle away the manipulative function for a society to become and remain open. He speaks of "enlightenment fallacy," a basic assumption that the truth will win. However, it will not if we do not specifically design and improve our democratic process to seek it. In Soros's words, "we need to stop avoiding unpleasant realities and reward deception, as long as it remains convincing. These tendencies must be resisted and remain open to flourish."

Surely democracy's challenges are not the same across the board. Societies with higher levels of personal wisdom, or critical thinking, seem to resist the tendencies of manipulation better. However, besides the education that is needed, we also need to recognize the same manipulative tendencies are rising in all democracies, including seemingly the best ones in the Nordics. Denmark has experienced its fair share of manipulation of the public with increasing role of spin doctors, and deals cut between political actors that often have a personal element such as withholding and threatening information on someone's personal life that could diminish their political power.

The need for transparency and truth to maintain trust in our social contract remains a key challenge and criteria for democracy to thrive.

<u>Agency</u> is the last key building block. And probably the most important and divisive one. Without agency, you could have, for example, a Superintelligent AI making decisions on behalf of us, or that could as well be a (for some) benevolent dictator. Agency is the difference between us humans having a shot at steering our future versus being imprisoned by either our own inventions, or our greed for power.

The argument for why we need to have agency on our collective governance calls for a discussion on the meaning of life.

Does it matter where we end up as humanity? Does it matter for each and every one of us? Can we define a collective goal that is always better to have more of? Shall we chase an ever growing GDP as our collective mission? Or is it a higher global happiness index that we should optimize our collective resources? What is the end goal for us, as humans, if there is one? Could we imagine a north star for human well-being? Something that makes humanity better off, even when we have lots and lots of it as we know markets will do? Perhaps this is also the principal discussion of aligning the goal of humanity and the general AI.

The simple answer could be that there is no such common goal for humanity. That we are lost souls swimming in a fishbowl. But I will argue that a shared common goal, a north star, is there and is a necessity to function as a society, to align us as fellow humans, and to find meaning and seek agency.

The lack of such a concept means we don't have a simple way of linking our collective national and global goals and weigh them against one another. Globally, we have defined SDGs, and we talk about many different goals. How important is one goal compared to another? And if one project improves one of them and worsens another, shall we do it? What are the trade-offs? And what are they all serving, collectively seen? Human happiness? Compromises are difficult to make, when our goals are not subgoals in a greater outcome.

For companies, achieving a decision in the face of complexities involving multiple goals is simplified in that they all boil down to one goal. If we could do the same for the sake of humanity, it would help us achieve a much more productive decision process.

Unfortunately, our system currently seems to place GDP as that ultimate goal, when it is challenged to produce one. That seems far from representing our well-being. So, what could be another goal to align ourselves?

In his book, *The Moral Landscape*, Sam Harris argues that if we imagined a state of total suffering, the worst imaginable for everyone, that would be a universe we all can agree to avoid. He also speaks about the opposite; a state of the universe that makes each person as happy as they possibly can become. These are then the two ultimate ends of the spectrum in his definition, and we want to move furthest away from one and as far as possible toward the other. Making everyone as happy as possible, or as little miserable as possible, can sound like a plausible option.

I'd like to argue for another one.

I think we need to see a human as a living creature, an animal, and see what drives living creatures in general. Evolutionary biology offers many examples of how animals sacrifice their individual benefit or even life in order to sustain the benefit of their species. Richard Dawkins's *The Selfish Gene*, as its title reveals, provides plenty of examples of how it's the genes that are sustained and protected over time, not the individual animal. This notion gives us a perspective on seeing the behavior of animals – or even their intuition – in a new light. The purpose of their life seems to be the sustainability and longevity of their species. They may or may not have feelings which we call happiness, but they act in ways that sometimes materially harm them, yet in the larger picture, the set of actions they take serves their collective good. It would be fair to say that animals have a common feature that they have evolved to secure the continuation of their genes, not their individual selves. Such evolution makes sense, since evolutionary pressures favor behaviors that are better for the species, not the single individual. Thus, humans as a species, we care de facto about our species' future. We might not be conscious of it, but we all care about our future intimately, and that is the core purpose of all humans.

We used to achieve this primarily by our mating preferences in providing stronger physical conditions for our kids.[5] The better physical conditions could be resistance to diseases, a greater intelligence, etc., which made their survival more viable. Over time, we evolved to develop tools and technologies to shape our well-being more than our physical conditions. Nowadays, improving the security of our species has more to do with spreading our values (or memes), not our genes. This is so because the threats surrounding us are not threats we overcome by running faster or maintaining warmth in cold weather. The threats to our collective challenges now depend on how well we coordinate and convince one another to overcome them.

The way we try to secure sustainability of our species is thereby through influencing others, our surroundings, and ultimately our society and humanity. We do so by spreading our values (a.k.a. our memes, a term coined by Richard Dawkins as a unit of human memory) using different channels that are available to us. We feel the lack of agency when we are not heard, and even if we are fine, economically seen (i.e. not in poverty etc.), agency is a core need for us. Our strategies to spread our values is comparable to what bankers do with the portfolio of money they are managing: you spread the risk across many vehicles of influence, some are high-risk high-return attempts (such as this book), some have lower risk and return profile given how much influence and risk you are taking (for example, teaching a class, or gathering friends for a nice long evening of talks).

And arguably, all humans with a functioning mind and psychology are aiming at making humanity better off – even if we don't interpret their behavior in that way. We may think there are ill-intentioned people who have some opinions that seem insane to us, from the firearms rights advocates to those willing to kill or die for religious dogma. Even if so, my argument is that they also instinctively try to make humanity more sustainable from their perspective. The same is true for leaders that we might find especially inspiring: For me, that includes Margrethe Vestager who led EU regulations on data privacy and a competitive digital market. Or Julian Assange and Edward Snowden whose focus on transparency efforts elevated the debate on our governmental practices.

We are in a world where memes are being exchanged and executed in an attempt to figure out what will survive. We feel agency to the extent that we are a part of the conversation, how we shape it. Such need for influence (and feeling of agency) seems well aligned with what Maslov would refer to as the highest level of self-realization. It seems also in line with what Martin Seligman, a leading positive psychology researcher, identifies as the most important thing that makes us sustainably happy: belonging and contributing to something that outlives us. Another happiness researcher, Laurie Santos, tells us that wide social relations[6] is a key contributor to what makes people happy. Those are people who are interacting with many individuals, making meaningful connections all the time.

As humans, we have a deep need for influence, for a wide range of meaningful interactions that contribute to shaping our environment in ways that will outlive us. When we discuss with friends, bring up our children, volunteer at an event, or when we look for meaningful work, there is more than the economically narrow animal that wants self-pleasing and maximization of utility.

We belong to nature and are inherently seeking to make our species sustainable. Sustainability of humanity, thus, could be thus our north star, giving each of us the opportunity to contribute. That contribution, our gift, is also our deepest burden, and hence our need for agency.

EXCESSIVE INEQUALITY UNDERMINES DEMOCRACY

We must make our choice. We may have democracy, or we may have wealth concentrated in the hands of a few, but we can't have both.

—Louis Brandeis

Brandeis, an American lawyer born in the mid-nineteenth century, was a leading figure in the antitrust movement at the turn of the century. He particularly resisted the monopolization of the New England railroad. He criticized the power of large banks and monopolies and made a name for himself as the social justice crusader. He was appointed to the Supreme Court and became one of the most influential figures of his time. One disappointment about him remains that he did not vote against racial segregation despite his otherwise strong flair for fairness.

Where does the concept of fairness come from? Is that a modern human invention, or have we evolved to live in a fair society?

Primatologists Frans de Waal and Sarah Brosnan were curious about the question. They conducted their first experiment with capuchin monkeys in 2003. Monkeys are placed in cages next to one another, where they can see the other. The experiment starts with monkeys receiving a coin in their cage, one at a time. When they bring this coin to the window, they receive a slice of cucumber. This process is repeated several times, until both monkeys are quickly and swiftly grabbing the coin dropped into the cage, bringing it to the window and eating their cucumber. They do so joyfully and watch each other carefully. Then, all of a sudden, one of the monkeys starts receiving a piece of grape same size as a cucumber slice. The grape, being sweeter, has a higher value for monkeys. One receiving the grape is enjoying that quietly. The other one expects to get a grape as well, and when he doesn't he gets very upset immediately. Then this cycle is repeated. The cucumber receiving monkey is totally outraged by the third cycle, shaking its cage, screaming, having an outburst of emotions. The unfairness is absolutely unacceptable. And the monkey with the grape? He quietly keeps munching on the grape (Brosnan and de Waal, 2012).

Such studies have been repeated many times since, also involving other monkeys. The conclusion is that our close relatives in the mammal world do not tolerate well that similar tasks or efforts are rewarded differently. Being exposed to such treatment in return creates forms of anger, sadness, and resentment.

The Ultimatum Game is another famous experiment to mark the importance of sentiment of fairness in human behavior. In this game, two players are involved, who are to share a sum of money. One is asked to propose how they should divide this sum, while the other needs to accept or reject the offer. A rejection means neither of them receive any money. Researchers find that the commonly accepted split gives the responder between 50% and 30%, while a proposed split that gives the responder less than 30% is typically rejected (Oosterbeek, Sloof and van de Kuilen, 2004).

The economists are surprised by this. In their view of the world, any split that gives the responder something more than zero makes them better off, and hence should be accepted. But that is not how "our utility curve is shaped" – for a good reason. We have the deep, inner wisdom that understands power and influence. We have the inner need to defend what we believe is fair.

Another interesting experiment by Katherine DeCelles and Michael Norton from 2016 shows that when people enter airplanes through the first-class gate, they get a higher level of testosterone, the marker of aggression, compared to if they entered it through the economy class. The passengers who were exposed to inequality appeared to increase tension, and the economy passengers were found to be 3.8 times more likely to act out when there was a first-class section present, and particularly if the economy passengers passed through the first-class section (DeCelles and Norton, 2016). Similar to this, I feel the direct impact of inequality on me and others every day on the streets. It happens when looking at the drivers of expensive cars, or people dining at a ridiculously expensive restaurant. I am more easily provoked in these situations. No, we are not evolved to obey extreme inequality.

The idea behind neoliberal capitalism is that all wealth goes to the earner, who deserves it due to their ability to create it, and will be able to do so again with more wealth. This is how we end up with one of the highest levels of inequality of modern history, and arguably all human history, which is matched only by the late nineteenth century levels, according to famous French economist, Thomas Piketty. One of the most interesting aspects of his research is showing how periods with high rates of return on capital (real estate, stocks, etc.) exceeding overall economic growth automatically increases inequality, creating a perpetual, divergent cycle, in which wealth creates more wealth. Piketty tells us that we are headed for even more extreme and disastrous levels absent serious policy changes (Piketty, 2014).

Indeed, income and wealth inequality are shooting for historic heights. In the United States, the top 1% owned 32% of national wealth in 2021, receiving close to 20% of the national income (Figure 1.8). Statistics show us that the rise in equality started in the late 1970s (Figure 1.9). This collides with the rise of neoliberal capitalism, and a shift in mindset for the government's

Figure 1.8   Inequality in the United States rose fast since 1980s to historic peaks.

Such high inequality was last reported in the 1920s, just before the Great Depression.

Source: ECONOMIC REPORT OF THE PRESIDENT / The White House / https://obamawhitehouse.archives.gov /sites/default/files/docs/cea_2015_erp_complete.pdf, last accessed on 14 December 2024 / CC BY 3.0.

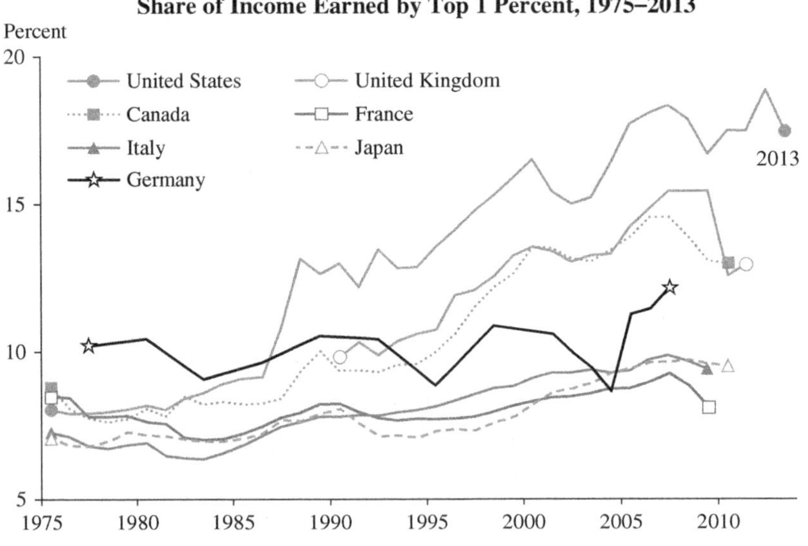

Figure 1.9   Bottom 80% earners' share of income kept reducing since 1980s.
(Left) From end of 1970s the real household income for bottom 80% of Americans remained similar or dropped while top 20% and especially the top 1% received all of the gains.
(Right) Accordingly, share of national income continued to drop for 80% of the population.
Source: Congressional Budget Office, 2009 / Mother Jones / https://www.motherjones.com/politics/2011/02/income-inequality-in-america-chart-graph/, last accessed on 14 December 2024.

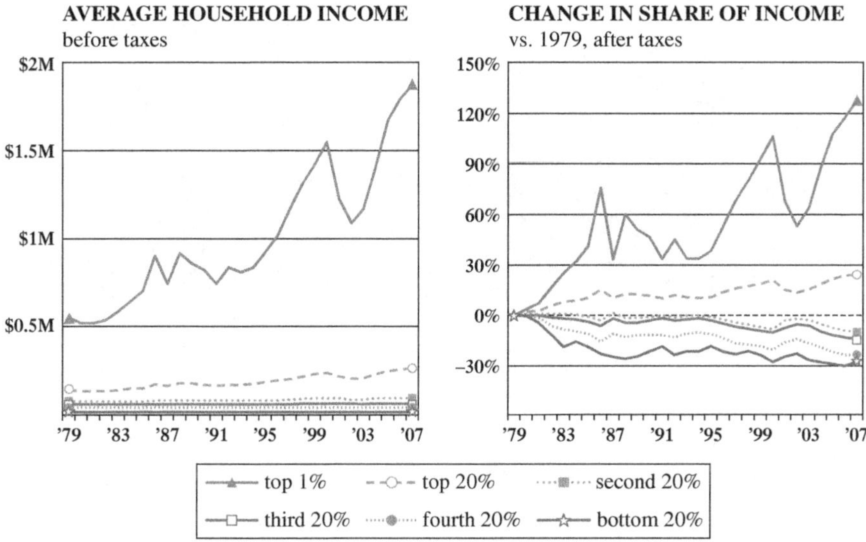

role: to secure the free-markets and get out of the way. In the coming decades, the bottom 80% of Americans did not see an increase in their incomes, while the top 20%, and especially the top 1% collected all the increase (Figure 1.10). The average American CEO now earns around 300 times of the minimum earning employee in their company (Kerber, 2024). Sixty percent of Americans have no significant savings, and live from paycheck to paycheck (PYMNTS, 2023). When surveyed, people show interest in much lower levels of inequality (Figure 1.11).

Figure 1.10   Inequality of wealth is similarly staggering.
Often in the discussions of income inequality, wealth is forgotten. As of 2021, top 10% wealthiest owned about 70% of US wealth, where top 1% owned more than 30%. In 2024, top 10% ownership of wealth rose to a whopping 92% of US national wealth.
Source: Federal Bank of St Louis / Statista / https://www.statista.com/chart/19635/wealth-distribution-percentiles-in-the-us/, last accessed on 14 December 2024.

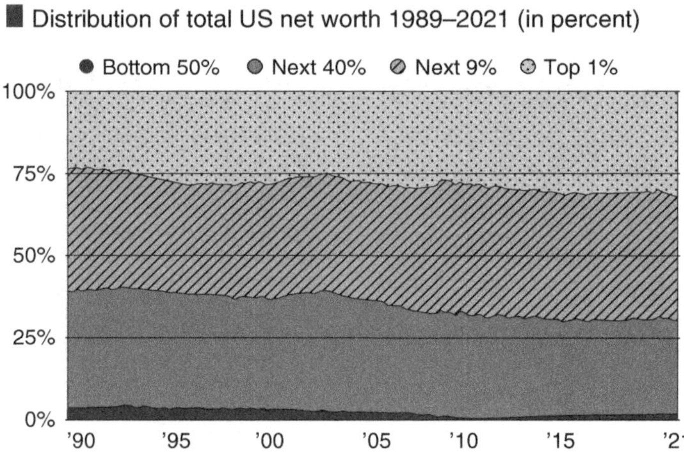

That is not surprising: wealth does not only translate into material well-being, but also social status, and that, in turn, into political power. The few becoming extremely wealthy means loss of political agency for the rest. We see that translation of wealth to political power play through mechanisms of media, lobbyism, election finance, regulatory highjacking, and also through merely networking. This is where the political and business elite meet and blend: they are the elite and hold excessive power.

This book is not about inequality, but democracy. I dig into the inequality debate as I am convinced that it is a core driver of democratic crisis. I do not argue for a complete equality or communism, but that excessive inequality undermines democracy. I will make three arguments why a too high inequality is undesirable for a society: one is about its negative

Figure 1.11   Economists found that Americans would like much less (but some) inequality of wealth.

Instead of the top 20% wealthiest owning 80% of national wealth, Americans think they own around 60% and would like that to be around 30%.

Source: Norton, Airely, 2011 / Association for Psychological Science / https://www.hbs.edu/ris/Publication%20Files/Norton_Michael_Building%20a%20better%20America%20One%20wealth%20quintile%20at%20a%20time_4c575dff-fe1d-4002-b61a-1227d08b71be.pdf, last accessed on 14 December 2024.

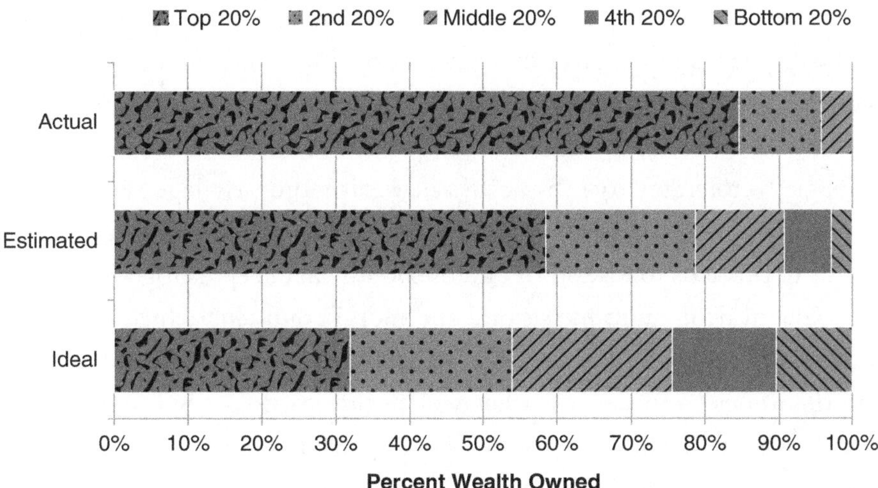

consequences on our well-being. The second is about the morality of it, when we question the validity of "free will." And the third point argues that it is unfair, not-so-free market rules that favor the interests of corporations and the wealthiest.

Starting with our well-being: we know that humans are greatly adaptive animals. We have adapted from nomadic life to settled life with the agricultural revolution, and then a few thousand years later, to living in cities with the Industrial Revolution. But our adaptation is not limitless. Gabor Maté, Canadian physician and author, explores the broad and clear linkages between socioeconomic status and health. He finds that wealth and income inequality are major contributors to negative health outcomes due to chronic stress. Psychology of shame and inadequacy leads to alienation and disempowerment, resulting in low social trust and violence. People then rely on coping mechanisms of all kinds of addiction and end up with adverse childhood experiences. He also points out that the inequality affects the entire population due to increased competition, fear of downward mobility and reduced social cohesion (Maté, 2022).

Wilkinson and Pickett, authors of *The Spirit Level* (2010), also provide extensive data (see also https://equalitytrust.org.uk) showing that greater inequality leads to negative outcomes in health, crime, and social cohesion. They argue that extreme inequality is detrimental to both individual well-being and societal stability, implying that human beings naturally struggle to tolerate large disparities in wealth and privilege. They point out that we are social primates, and inequality exceeding some threshold seems to cause us to lose spirit and the bonds that keep us together.

Now moving on to my second and moral argument, which has to do with questioning the idea of the "free will." In his book, *Free Will,* Sam Harris argues "You can do what you decide to do — but you cannot decide what you will decide to do." Harris tells us what science is providing increasing evidence for: while people feel they are making choices, the underlying factors – such as genetics, environment, and unconscious processes – are beyond their conscious control.

The main argument justifying high inequality is about creating incentives for innovation and hard work, and thereby reflection of one's merit. If one is able to create value for others, then they should earn more. But this view undermines all the factors that played into the person's ability to achieve success, while ignoring the disadvantages of the others.

Imagine that for a moment we accept what brain researchers are telling us, that all that happens to us, what we feel and think, is related to our biology, the environment, and then (perhaps) some level of randomness. We experience the illusion of ourselves making decisions at any moment of time, and even controlling our thoughts. Instead, the truth is we are floating in time with history taking its course through us, and we need to accept that our firsthand experience and consciousness is not necessarily a basis for declaring what we deserve. Nor, in this light, is it wise to punish someone who committed a crime, except for sending a signal of high cost to others to control them.

We can stop viewing the gifted people who achieve material success as those who deserve to keep it all, and instead view them as people who were lucky to have many enablers in their life to achieve success.

We can see how ancient wisdom displays such understanding of "deservence." Like many Native American communities, the research into the Blackfoot community is telling: they have no hierarchy, and the respected person is not the one who accumulated the most, but one who has been most generous. Everyone born is given the trust and respect – without having to prove they are good enough. If someone is struggling, they are supported to become their better version of themselves. The whole tribe sees not self-actualization as the ultimate goal but the actualization of the tribe, and not only now, but over time (Ravilochan, 2021).

My final argument is about pointing out design elements in our social contract, which some view as "free-market" to point out it is not free after all. Among others, Robert Reich's work *Saving Capitalism* (Reich, 2015) explains several mechanisms that favor the wealthy, from bankruptcy laws to how we regulate intellectual property rights. Patents are granted for 15–20 years to companies filing them and often extended with marginal changes on them. In the age of digital information and development, is that perhaps too long a period? Bankruptcy laws enable companies to put most of the burden of restructuring on employees, ahead of their debtors. Should employment contracts matter more in resolving bankruptcy? Why should capital gain income be taxed at a lower rate than income from labor? And why should corporates have the right to deduct cost of interest from their taxes?

Then we have the issue of inheritance (Figure 1.12). Piketty's work shows that inheritance counts for 50–60% of private wealth in the 2010s,

Figure 1.12   Today, like beginning of nineteenth century, most of Europeans' and Americans' wealth are not earned by themselves but inherited.

Source: Alvaredo et al., 2017 / John Wiley & Sons / http://www.piketty.pse.ens.fr/files/AlvaredoGarbin-tiPiketty2017.pdf, last accessed on 14 December 2024.

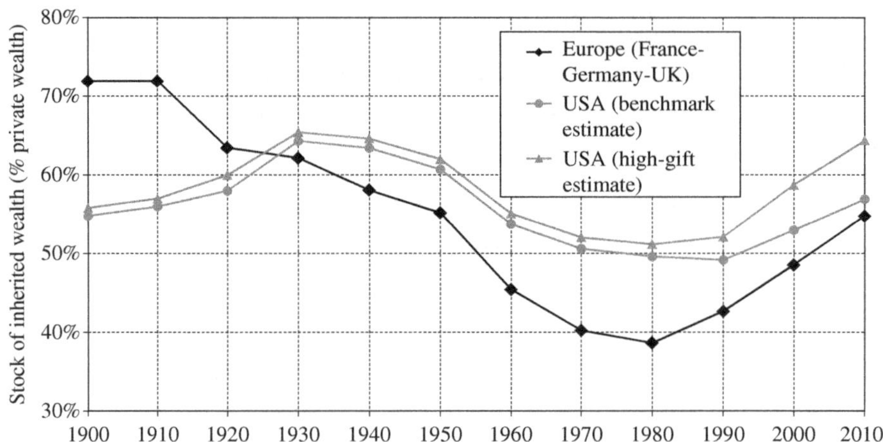

both in the United States and Europe (Alvaredo, Garbiniti and Piketty, 2017). Such wealth transfer over time raises the obvious question: where is the merit and fairness in handing someone wealth who has not done anything for it?

Can our value system absorb these ideas, and re-think not only that we need to share the gains more collectively, while also supporting each other.

PUBLIC GOODS: WHAT MONEY CAN'T BUY

Can you buy yourself into being safe, secure, and happy?

I've heard this from several friends, especially those in finance and entrepreneurs, who told me of a similar future plan: once they will get to a figure of wealth, somewhere between $5m and $10m, they will stop worrying about their financial future. They will stop focusing on wealth accumulation, and start focusing on other things that matter, and live off the return of their wealth. We live in a time where the main story is that pretty much everything we care about is up for sale, and all we need to do is to gather enough money to buy it.

In Denmark and Europe in general, this rhetoric is a little less common for now. For many who have grown up in a strong social security system, life is much less about securing financial freedom, and more about meaning in everyday life. Nevertheless, increasing inequality and pressure on social systems and their struggle to perform is putting the European model in question. We are increasingly focused on wealth accumulation in a competitive setting.

Ray Dalio, a famous financial investor and author of several books, who was among world's richest 100 persons in 2020, wrote in a recent article that he did not think his rich friends were particularly happy (Dalio, 2024). They were troubled with concerns about getting their kids to good schools, security of their family and friends, the societal situation they find themselves in with much suffering. Similar messages are seconded by researchers (Beyer, 2022; Stonehage Fleming, n.d.) – there are limits to obtaining happiness through accumulating wealth.

The thinking that we can accumulate enough wealth to protect us and keep us happy is misleading. Individual wealth cannot make up for the public goods. A societal feeling of safety and security is a public good. People trusting each other and not fearing one another is a public good. Clean air and calm streets are a public good. Forest nearby with a clean river to jump in is a public good.

We can and must change the underlying perceptions about "wealth," to account for what we have in our lives not only privately, but also collectively, in all of our circles; our neighbors, city, state, nation, and globally. Trust, security, belonging, inclusion are some of the public goods that are perhaps harder to account for, and perhaps the most valuable.

Further, understanding and acknowledging the value of public goods is crucial for us to build a stronger social contract. Public goods are not things we can buy individually, because they need to be achieved, or paid for, collectively. Public goods define "us," in the sense that they are the expression of our social contract.

Much public goods have to do with coordination. In a classroom, one public good is that we are quiet, so that all can hear the main conversation, the teacher or whomever else is speaking. The contract, that we won't speak during the course, that we make with each other and our teacher, secures that good.

We live in a world where we try to fix public goods problems with consumer solutions. If the streets are getting too congested, we want self-driving cars so we can work while driving. If our tap water starts to lose its quality, we can establish a subscription service to a clean drinkable water provider.

Why do we live in a world with so much suffering that we don't need sophisticated technology to address, while we are constantly developing new products and services that don't prevent the suffering but try to cure it?

My thesis is that the reason is we – and especially the elite who accumulated wealth – do not yet fully understand the importance of public goods, and we have lived with the illusion that those goods are plenty and well secured. We have taken them for a given, and also stopped expecting we could do any better.

An interesting feature of public goods is that they apply to everyone in the group. There is no opting out while remaining in the group. The idea of optionality itself is the marker that the good is not a public one, but private. If you live on this street, you will collectively suffer from road damage. If you remain in this city, you will be breathing the same quality of air. In this nation, the social trust levels are more or less the same. And in this world, there is no part immune to climate change.

The nature of what is public and private goods is changing, through technology that creates levels of optionality. Over the past few decades, we saw privatization of many goods that were perceived to be public goods before. Access to TV content used to be a public good before the introduction of cable TV: anyone could catch the signal with a simple antenna and watch the content. Gated communities are emerging promising enhanced security and even some green space within the street level. Private schools and private insurances promise better education and health treatments for those who can afford them.

Yet, trying to save oneself, or one's family, privately in a broader community where public goods arc perished is, at the end, a hopeless exercise. No matter how rich you are, you cannot make up for the diminishing democratic infrastructure, including a dysfunctional justice and financial system. The effort to isolate ourselves ends up with dystopian visions like an elite living on their ocean island. But such escapism cannot offer long-term security. Nor does it bring desirable long-term consequences to humanity as a species. In the end, we and our children will have to live in the same world, and we must find ways to agree and collaborate to fix our collective problems. We are deeply and humanly interdependent, through what we call public goods.

* * *

Another noteworthy feature of public goods is that their provision is not only top-down delivery, but often linked to private actions or transactions. Each little activity often represents implications for both the private person and the different public circles they are in.

A beautiful garden in one house makes the whole street look more interesting, they will enjoy higher value of their estate due to a better looking building. When I ride my bicycle in order to get where I am going, not only serving my interest to get there quickly and healthily, but I am also contributing to safer streets, and I help air quality and traffic congestion by not choosing the car instead. When you attend college, it doesn't only mean that you later get a higher pay in your job, but the public also enjoys higher economic activity, and arguably that you are in a better shape in performing critical citizenship. When my company provides a generous paternity leave, it is not only helping the employee to be more motivated but is also helping the child have much higher prospects in the future, and the mother whose chances in the labor market are increased.

On the other hand, a theft in a neighborhood makes everyone worry about their security although it only struck one house who experienced the losses. One person smoking in the room reduces the quality of air for everyone. A noisy truck driving by can wake up everyone around. One person's worsening health impacts everyone in the form of public health insurance and care we provide for the person. One person being exposed to a certain kind of media and believing in alternative facts challenges the public conversation in the whole jurisdiction, especially at times of elections.

What seems to be an act of individual freedom and a private transaction between two people or entities almost always has some form of consequence for the collective.

Further, the impact of an activity for the sake of private interest can often challenge the public interest: having a larger SUV makes you less vulnerable in a crash at the cost of everybody else. Having a gun may make you feel safer, however, everybody having guns makes everybody less safe. Paying your employees the lowest possible salary means you can have more profit, but where the salary starts to put pressure, it means no savings and little financial resilience, low education, poor healthcare for the kids, which in turn means loss of talent pool for society.

We derive value collectively when we can get individuals or companies to act in alignment with the public goals. That means the situations where we manage to coordinate our actions optimally.

My message is not going to be that we need to think about our private actions to mind the greater good, inviting everyone to do their bit. No. Because in the civilizations we live in, it is no longer possible to naturally account for everyone's actions as we did in our tribal past. We cannot create the public goods by simply acting privately in line with collective interests on a *voluntary basis.* The reason is simply that we are too many people to keep each other accountable, which is called the free-rider problem. Even with the best intentions, people test the boundaries of what is permissible, and eventually exploit the public goods, where others will follow suit, if there is no enforcement against it.

Thus, we need sophisticated coordination of our collective actions. This is the role of what we call the government. This is why we have set many regulations and rules, from paying taxes, redistributions, minimum salary, special taxes on cars and gas, CO_2 emissions, fines linked to environmental violations, labor market fringes, and so on. In other words, our laws and public budgets are designed to change the individual actors' actions in accordance with the collective optimal.

Now, let's talk about how we account for public goods versus private goods, and see if we can imagine a future where money doesn't only translate to value for the private person but also for the public.

WHEN MONEY NO LONGER MEANS VALUE

I cofounded and ran as the CEO of Donkey Republic, a city bike share service, from 2015 until 2022. The company aims to make city life better for everyone by offering an affordable and sustainable transport option with our bikes and ebikes. While no longer working there, I remain a member of the board of the company, which today employs around 250 colleagues. I founded the company with great ideals and the urge to improve the city life, by creating a strong alternative to the car with the easily available bike. The purpose alignment with the founder team has been strong from day one, and our team really enjoyed being part of such a purpose-driven company. We spoke about our social impact frequently as a team and made first-in-industry efforts to measure it in detail.

What I see today is that people do not only define the value of their work by how much money they make. Nor do they value others' work for how much money they make, because today we have *an underlying intuition that someone making a lot of money nowadays does not mean they are generating value for society.* Experiences of the past half-century showed that much of the rent-seeking behavior of companies and individuals came at the cost of others and the environment. The transaction between the company offering goods and the consumer does not include the impacts to the people not taking part in that transaction, yet indeed impacted by it.

David Courtwright in his 2019 book *The Age of Addiction: How Bad Habits Became Big Business* talks about our global system where industries are leveraging human vulnerabilities with addictive products, exploiting our deeply ingrained pleasure–reward pathways. And that is not only about tobacco or alcohol, but also streaming social media or YouTube, watching movies, playing games, and any other experiences that bring temporary satisfaction. Aza Raskin and Tristan Harris talk about the addictive design of tech products on their podcast, "Your undivided attention," that are shown to contribute to the loneliness epidemic. Ride hailing services such as Uber increase overall car trips, contributing to congestion, noise and air pollution in cities (T&E, 2020). Unregulated, Airbnb rentals have been found to undermine local life and affordability of housing in city centers (Fast Company, 2024).

Eventually, we come to understand intuitively that what seems to be a relationship between the seller and buyer almost always has an element of impact on the collective, that is currently not accounted for in that transaction.

The impacts of products and services are not always a net negative. There are many companies who add value to society and/or the environment. A club that brings people together to play a sport or share a hobby is a good example. That helps us connect with others. A bike share service like Donkey Republic creates a lot of value for society, such as better public health, and fewer car trips. These situations represent another problem: when the social value is not accounted for and the companies are not paid for it, we end up in sub-optimal delivery of such services. Were these paid even a fraction of their positive impacts, they will become vastly more attractive businesses and will play a bigger role in our economy, creating a virtuous cycle for the society and environment.

The attribution of positive and negative impacts is tricky. The social phenomena they impact are not one-dimensional, and we often need complex analyses to understand the true impact of a product or service on our social and environmental goals. Tesla replacing combustion engine cars, all else equal, may be a positive externality, given its EVs emit less CO_2 in their lifetime. Yet, the impact of cars driving autonomously is less clear. While we may save driver time from actually doing the driving, and parking, absent regulations, the social consequences may be tricky due to creating possibly many more car trips in urban areas, making our cities less livable (Zipper, 2023).

Take some of the most valuable tech companies of our day: Apple, Google, Amazon, Facebook. Do their products have a strong bias toward positive or negative externalities? Does Amazon enable a healthier, more sustainable humanity? What about Facebook and Instagram knowing what we know about their effect on one's psychology and well-being, can we say they help a more sustainable humanity? Does Google help us live better lives when all its products are considered as a whole? Famously, Steve Jobs was reported to restrict his kids' play use of the iPad, worried about their mental health and addiction to the device (Bolton, 2016). Facebook knew about its products contributing to teenage anxiety, with 32% of girls feeling worse about their bodies after using Instagram (Graber, 2021). The answers are not trivial, and one can imagine that if we did the math, some of the companies may be detracting value from the things we collectively care about but have not found a way to place a price tag for.

We might have lost account of companies' products and services side effects, but companies are not the ones to blame. *They never signed up to secure our social and environmental well being. That is not their task.* It is and always has been the task of our governments and our democracies. If governments cannot regulate markets effectively, and companies start to take advantage of lack of legislation, or exploit new markets that are not yet regulated, then our frustration should be channeled to challenging our democracy's efficacy, not expecting the companies to self-regulate.

In the past half-century, the image of man making money through hard work and creating social value has been replaced by a new image of man making money by taking advantage of humans' most vulnerable aspects, often using new technology and data science.

As a result, we created a system where porn sites are some of the most visited websites, and OnlyFans is one of the most successful startups. Its performers go through Brazilian butt lift operations in order to increase their monthly viewers highlighting the rationality of their investment given the returns (The Guardian, 2021). Would we have different economic incentives for OnlyFans if we linked social impacts of such services, and public health implications of plastic surgeries (Masterton and Evans, 2024)?

We need a democracy that regulates markets, effectively, that ensures externalities are accounted for, where they are a part of the effective price of a product or service. In Chapters 5 and 6, I will take you through ideas to redesign accounting in order to align money with value for society.

TECH WILL SAVE US: THE TECH-NAIVE STORY

I was at a friend's birthday party at a cozy Copenhagen apartment. I'm introduced to his friends, many from the bubble of internationals living in the city. We talk about the state of the world. He is from Argentina, like my friend. Things are not looking very good, we agree. Not only in Argentina or Turkey, but really, globally. We want to change things. Hearing about my past as an entrepreneur, he says excitedly that he really wants to start a tech company to help make the world a better place. That is he would, if he just had a good idea. I tried to dig into his wish – was it really driven by purpose, or was it more about him wanting to be his own boss, or wanting to enjoy the hyped status of a tech entrepreneur? That was a question I had kept asking myself when working with Donkey Republic. He actually seemed to be genuinely driven to make a positive impact on the world.

Then it dawned on me that what he sought for was perhaps a political movement, changing the way society works. When I later that evening asked him about why not start a political organization instead, he said "There is no way to change anything with politics – that's just a dead end." "But tech solutions can pave the path to change." I wanted to tell him then, that given what I saw, all companies end up part of the system, serving its profit maximizing. That is, unless we are focused on changing the government, and ensuring effective regulations and price mechanisms to protect public benefit.

Seeking refuge in a tech startup to change the disturbing trends we see in our democracies is itself a trend. We want to create a company that fixes this and that specific problem. I see the story resonate with many, as it did with myself.

I find this trend frustrating: Working with governance and politics is increasingly seen as a dead end, losing the most idealistic and talented people who actually want to change things. The story of our time is that if you're ambitious and want to be a part of creating the future, you should create or join a tech company.

Does the solution to our problems really lie in inventing the next big technology, the AI for humanoids or genetic engineering? Do we really expect that the next invention will solve our collective problems, or that it might add to them?

Well, unfortunately, technology seems indifferent to the way we govern ourselves, and simply exacerbates our challenges. According to Daniel Schmachtenberger, a contemporary American philosopher and systems thinker, the technological advancements make our economic machine work even faster toward its goal of wealth creation, misaligned with the goal of humanity's sustainability or thriving. He calls our system the "superorganism," which he likens to the concept of Moloch, a mythological figure that is trapped in a cycle of self-harm due to short-term gains at cost of long-term well-being.

Expecting that some technological innovation can fix some of our problems on its own is a dangerous mistake. Technology is an enabler, a tool, a catalyst. When nuclear technology was developed, it was used both for generating electricity as an alternative to dirty coal, and to exercise power via nuclear weapons.

Even the most innocent looking technologies can often create unintended second, third, nth order social consequences. A protein design technology, for example, can be used to design beneficial drugs, but also for bioweapons. A new but expensive drug can end up exacerbating social inequalities and access to care.

The three-decades-old wave of digital technology and internet provides a great example. What many saw early on as an opportunity to bring us together, and make us free, and democracy stronger, is also making us lonelier, more anxious and confused. We experience social media being turned into a platform to spread conspiracy theories and harm social trust, in the meanwhile aiming to make us consume more (Centre for Mental Health, 2018).

Nick Bostrom, a Swedish-born philosopher with a background in theoretical physical, computational neuroscience, logic and artificial intelligence, talks about how technology could bring an end to the world in his "vulnerable world hypothesis": an evaluation of each technological innovation's potential to do harm versus their availability (Bostrom, 2019). As an example, he refers to a possible innovation which would be similar to creating a nuclear explosion by placing sand in a microwave for 10 minutes. This would be a black-ball technology in his definition, due to scale of damage being very large, while high ease of access. Other technologies we discovered are shades of gray – they can do harm if not deployed with care.

I like to call those who assume technology alone can make us achieve a sustainable future "tech-naives." As true believers, they may be constructive, optimistic and well intended. They would like to contribute. But they are also in a comfort zone as this philosophy conveniently fits the story of impact investment and entrepreneurship, and allows for following a career path of success and status rather than confrontation. Moving out of this path means compromising one's social recognition as well as letting go of pleasures of material wealth.

I consider my earlier self a tech-naive as I studied mechanical engineering. I thought I would work on technology to enable a more sustainable humanity. I was interested in green tech such as solar and wave energy and fuel cells. This was the turn of the century and much work lay ahead to enable a possible green transition. Later, during my internships and attending conferences I realized that while developing green technologies made them more cost-competitive, it was not only the problem with lack of new technology solutions that kept the status quo. It was the lack of willingness to recognize the cost of coal power on environment and climate that prevented us from making the switch as well.

Looking deeper into engineering jobs, I sense that most engineering resources today go toward making us consume more, not to make us more sustainable environmentally or socially. That is, for example, work to make your car accelerate faster, or make you click just another time on that social media channel. It is not at all the case that the goals of tech companies, and their engineering minds, are working toward achieving humanity's goals, as much as narrow, short-term financial goals linked to selling more at whatever cost.

Take the case of the car industry: despite the seeming great comfort they offer, cars in cities today actually represent an abuse of human interest. I liken cars in cities to indoor smoking. We surely need cars in rural areas, and also some in cities. However, our level of car use is in cities is far from a social optimum. Cars are dangerous and are one of the largest causes of death with 1.35 million people dying annually due to road accidents (WHO, 2023a). The cost of road crashes is estimated at 3% of GDP for most countries. But this is only the start of bad news of our car addiction: our quality of living in urban areas suffers from noise pollution, particle pollution, from lack of public space due to using most of our public space to drive and park cars. Cars enable a society where we live further from one another, and travel on our own. Due to traffic congestion billions of productive hours are wasted each year. As citizens of Paris nowadays experience, We need to get around our dirty car habit, and looking back, they will seem as absurd as smoking cigarettes in airplanes that some may remember.

Technology, of course, could work toward advancing the human condition. The solution to ensuring technology serves human sustainability is through governing the markets effectively so that companies are properly incentivized to protect our collective goods, and not harming them.

The smartest artificial intelligence engineers, the brightest genetic engineering teams need to have the incentives to make humanity better off, not just generating profits that do not account for broader impacts. We can make technology serve humanity as a collective, while creating more convenience for us individually. When working with bike sharing my company focused on delivering a great individual experience, to achieve desirable social outcomes. The goal of ensuring collective sustainability doesn't mean forgetting about the individual. The goal is balancing the individual value and the collective values.

Without such governance, any company, including tech companies will by default prioritize its narrow commercial interest at the cost of public interest, that is ignoring its negative footprint on the environment and society. Therefore, without a change to the structure of our markets, a focus on technology cannot by default deliver goals for our society.

To get things straight, we first need to define our collective goals, and re-wire the economy to ensure that companies stand to benefit or pay for their impact on them. Currently, we are like boxers who work on their punching in all directions so long as we hit something. Getting stronger will not help punching where we need to aim it. We need to work on the aiming bit. When that is more balanced – as it will never be perfect – then we can once again focus on creating new technologies that will contribute to achieving collective goals.

When we think of how we would live a century from now, we don't seem to imagine what kind of governance and democratic rules we will set up. We don't really have exciting visions for that. Our perception of democracy and how society can work seem stagnant. Instead, our focus is on tech-driven fantasies in the form of gadgets and algorithms shaping our lives. It is understandable: after all, it's only been a little more than a decade since the first iPhone was sold, and we now have a hard time spotting a person not looking at the screen in public transit. We were trying to sequence the DNA at the turn of the millennium and now we have the possibility to engineer our kids.

We have plenty of annoyingly dystopian science fiction (have you watched Black Mirror?) as a result. In contrast, we are yet to experience sci-fi that shows a world where public governance blossoms and we manage to create a world we want to live in with more harmony and belonging. Have we lost our ability to fantasize about positive change? Did we run out of utopian visions for how we can run our societies for the better?

FILLING THE VOID? CHARITY, IMPACT-INVESTING, CORPORATE SOCIAL RESPONSIBILITY

I am at the Wellbeing Economy Alliance conference, the launch of the organization in Denmark. Discussion topics include how we should work with sustainability thinking in our governments workplaces. I joined a discussion track on the role of foundations. Some larger, international foundations are present in the room, and present proudly how they have placed funding into some areas of concern. They are represented by older women, who deliver all the right words fitting to the popular norms of our time; impact, inclusion, long-term thinking.

Many participants, including myself, are keen to build bridges with foundations. They represent money and power, which can of course help fund the projects we want to execute on. Personal relationships in the world of donation are very important. Halfway through the event, a younger woman raises her hand. She is a journalist. She asks them why they think they have the right to have a say in public matters, using large amounts of private wealth. She asks them about the source of their legitimacy. And further, she questions the linkage of the wealth earned by their founders exploiting various tax avoidance schemes. How much of the foundations' money should have been public funds? And wouldn't it make sense that they delegate the decision mechanism of which projects their money supports to some democratic mechanism, i.e. a citizen panel?

I breathe in, with joy. Now the session has become worthy of my time, hot air replaced with real talk.

Altruism is a part of human nature. We have evolved to help one another, without expectation, and to have empathy. As many who work in the not-for-profit sector, especially in fundraising, may also know that we are not rational when it comes to our altruistic instincts. But we do want to feel good about ourselves and feel that we made our contribution.

I will argue here why charitable acts by neither individuals nor companies or foundations can or will match the needs of our societies alone. We must have strong public institutions to create sufficient public goods. And we shall not rely on charity or (impact) companies to save us.

Let me offer a few arguments. First, imagine that we had no taxing of income or wealth at all: we would only have charity to rely on for social services. In this scenario, we end up not raising nearly as much money for public purposes, because of the free-rider problem and lack of enforcement. We need coordinated and binding taxing of income and wealth to raise the optimum social amounts we need to run our public systems.

Second, foundations or impact companies may each do their own actions, but they lack broad coordination. Schmachtenberger explains that it is problematic to imagine you are solving the world's problems by focusing on one of the issue area (i.e. climate change) at a time, without knowing its effects in other areas. This can easily result in supporting causes that help one agenda, while worsening another. We need a holistic picture of impact, and not be trapped by the narrow impact focus of various agents that shoot uncoordinatedly.

Further, even if foundations and companies wanted to create sufficient and holistic impact on all relevant areas, they would need much more data to understand such impacts. Companies typically have access to their direct operational data, but not the data to help them interpret second, third, or nth order of effects. If you produce digital media content, you will know how many eyeballs you have looking at you, and what your audience sounds like. But you will have little idea about your media's effects on their short-term habits, let alone long-term outcomes. That kind of analysis requires access to data that we have in public accounts. Further, such analysis would need sophisticated and large analysis efforts, dwarfing the individual organization's abilities.

Finally, private entities are not legitimate organizations to define what the most important agenda is for the world, or how the different public goods shall weigh up against one another. Is Saudi oil worse than Canadian oil? One violates human rights, the other one is dirtier to dig. How do you compare those two? A foundation might hire some experts that are famous and respected, but that still doesn't make them legitimate. Legitimacy about shaping the world and society lies in the democratic decision process, where we together need to weigh the goods we want up against one another.

You may be wondering why we couldn't build an economy with impact companies. This is a highly trendy topic at the moment. More and more companies seem to report and focus on their impact, and there are more impacts sought in investments nowadays.

Here again, I enjoy Daniel Schmachtenberger's framing of the debate: impact companies cannot really focus on impact ahead of profits, because if they do, others will come and only focus on delivering the services without the impact, and do so cost competitively, driving the others out of business.

A company may be working on creating better impact as a long-term strategy if they seek new regulations, which justifies their changing focus. That could explain why shipping companies as well as airlines look into new, sustainable fuels for example. Importantly, though, this is not companies driving change, but regulations instead. The move toward positive impact in this case is a strategy with the purpose of maximizing profits. Companies are not evil, quite the opposite: they are run very logically, by a well-founded system of capital markets and accounting rules.

Besides the competitive forces, companies are even bound to focus on profits beyond anything else through explicit laws that explain (for listed companies) that they have fiduciary duty to shareholders to maximize shareholder returns (Rhee, 2017). The concept that companies only work for its shareholders is being somewhat broadened by a recent focus on stakeholder governance, but here again, the focus is long-term well-being of the company, not the stakeholders (Palladino and Karlsson, 2019). Therefore, we cannot criticize companies or executives, for not undertaking benevolent acts on their own initiative.

On the other hand, other companies make (some and doubtful) efforts toward impact so long it pays as a marketing (a.k.a. branding) effort. That is because there is a market for conscious consumers who are trying to choose the right thing.

Back when I was at McKinsey, we had an internal competition for new ideas where the firm could grow capacity. Being an early enthusiast of impact business ideas, I initiated a project around potential premiums that sustainability focused companies could charge by tapping into consumers' consciousness. This was the year 2004, and there was little talk about impact business. The most outstanding products we found were fair trade coffee, chocolate and bananas, as well as green (renewable) energy. After some research we concluded that about 10–20% of consumers are willing to pay about 10% extra price on average, for a quality of a product (i.e. fair farming paying minimum wages, green energy emitting less GHG) where the consumers themselves were not gaining value, but creating value for others. The finding we had matched another interesting research I've heard about recently: it shows companies with strong ESG scores were able to receive debt at 1% reduced cost of capital (ESG News, 2024). That 1% is the same as 10% of 10%.

Therein is my point: a consumer-choice driven impact world will create very limited resources for the impact, which will not move the bulk of the economy. The free-rider problem here requires a coordinated effort, a.k.a. a regulation, as consumers who buy "consciously" will over time get frustrated with paying the bill for the rest.

The money available for impact is through consumers and through (impact) investors is far below the levels we need in order to change the way our economies work. The inconvenient truth is companies have become the address for many of us to seek positive change, either as laborers, or as investors, or as consumers, even though the whole economic structure we have prevents the outcomes we wish for.

Similar to the story of consumer-choice driven change, I do not believe impact investments can drive change. As I mentioned already, I worked with bike sharing over some years and studied the impacts of the trips we facilitated for society. These impacts, by rather simple calculations, amount to not less than 2–3 times our revenue. But when it comes to growing the company, one needs to raise funding, and such impacts have little financial meaning. As mentioned, research shows an ESG company could expect to raise debt at 1% lower annual interest rate compared to non-ESG peers. This was also our experience; being an ESG company brought some very slight advantages. Such reduced debt would translate to about 0.5% of the revenue of my bike sharing impact company. When a company's impact on society is more than 200% of its user revenues, a 0.5% of revenue as reward for being an impact company is simply laughable. It falls clearly short of incentivizing impacts, and impact investment is not the appropriate approach to really measure or reward impact.

Given the right incentives, we can see companies as positive change agents, as they are able to bring about radical technological innovations. In this book, I argue for much more reliance on companies delivering public goods. Companies are the institutions that can deliver the green transition, or institutions that can deliver the social innovations needed to help overcome various problems from obesity to mental health. Companies' ability for innovation, and the social need for such innovation is not understood well enough by public institutions, especially in Europe. Through such innovations, companies could strengthen an economy and develop export opportunities while making the society better off.

But they can only do so effectively and sufficiently, if they are in the context of making good business for creating those impacts. If we want companies to create the impacts, we need to give them the correct incentives to achieve them – actually and properly measuring their impact on public goods, pricing those goods, and reflecting their result appropriately.

One reason why we have so much focus on bringing about change through businesses without public incentives could be that we have many well-intending people with a business background who see that the world is not going in a good direction and want to be a part of changing that. There is a saying that if you only have a hammer, you treat everything like a nail. This may be true for those with MBAs: everything can be done simply through a business. For them, the world revolves around the company, which is central and free. The reality is they are profit maximizing agents that must have the right set of incentives toward social benefit to be able to contribute.

Corporate social responsibility and stakeholder capitalism could have been fine concepts, if they acknowledged the central role of the state as the regulator instead of treating the matter of social impact as a free and voluntary choice of the company and its consumers. I think few things have harmed our collective governance as much as the well-intended but ill-founded idea that we can bring about the changes we need through our free and voluntary choice merely as consumers or as investors, and not as citizens.

Let me also debate the impact we could expect or wish for, from the ultra-rich. They come in very different ideologies and values from Bill Gates and Warren Buffet to Elon Musk and Michael Bloomberg. Indeed, the wealthiest can throw billions after the various issues we see. The problem is that they have neither the mandate nor the legitimacy to do so. Just like everybody else, they feel that a coordinated effort is needed, where all rich people contribute together into causes around some kind of consensus, not singling themselves out. Otherwise, they understand that their effort alone will end up being a drop in the ocean, and they may risk being marginalized.

I see an important role for the wealthiest, and their foundations, to play: that is to help improve our social contract. They have to find ways to make such efforts utmost legitimate, arguably by donating to causes that have a broad, transparent and democratic decision body, and by supporting experiments tied to research and public knowledge, and helping our knowledge for options of better governance. More on this in the last chapter.

OUR FOUR ECONOMIC HATS: THE CONSUMER, INVESTOR, LABORER, AND THE CITIZEN

We recognize the increasing number of issues and public concerns, from climate change to democracy's retreat, overfishing in oceans to loneliness. The way to take care of this mess these days, we are told, is by purchasing various responsible products, by buying stocks of companies we believe are doing good, and even, by working for a company at a less than market salary to work for a cause.

As I tried to argue in the final chapter, uncoordinated efforts by us as consumers, investors or laborers will fall short of addressing the problems at the scale necessary. Unless our efforts are specifically directed at system change, and with that I mean how we govern ourselves, the changes we seek cannot be large or sustained sufficiently enough. Our efforts will remain futile.

Essentially, we want to feel good about ourselves by doing something that seems responsible. We want to feel we have done our personal part when we sort our trash or choose the secondhand shirt. However, as long as these are voluntary actions, we as a society will not make them sufficiently. Altruistic actions cannot provide sufficient response to our collective needs. Take climate change: in absence of any financial incentives, can we see people changing their habits around what they eat or how much they are willing to fly or drive cars?

Economists have called the issue "tragedy of commons." When there is a common good such as sustainable climate, and when it is costly to contribute for various agents, they will not commit the cost on their own – in lack of a collective agreement to do so. The consumer, investor and laborer in us are all powerful entities from the economic point of view (Figure 1.13). However, if we try to realize our collective goals through these personas, we are not likely to succeed. The only remaining hat we have that can bring the change we need is through the citizen hat.

The citizen hat is our economic identity that is a part of a collective negotiation – be it our apartment building, street, neighborhood, or city council, our nation, continent, or the whole globe. We are used to exercising it mainly through our vote once every few years. This is the

Figure 1.13   A representation of our four economic identities, and how they interact.
All of these four economic identities – the consumer, laborer, investor, and the citizen – are displayed by all of us to some extent.

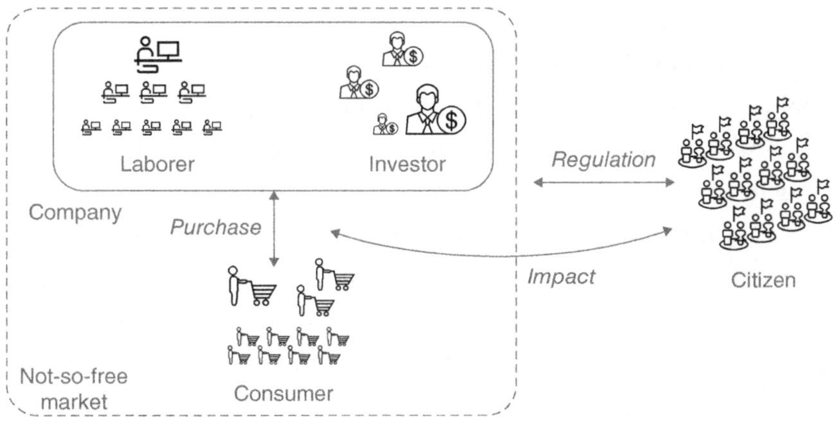

identity, I believe, we shall utilize far more in the future by reimagining our democracies.

Does this mean that it doesn't matter to buy the socially responsible product? Or, to work in an organization that seems to have a positive impact on an important cause? Not really.

Individual actions matter as well, they each make a small dent in the universe. However, more importantly, they inspire us to alter our collective direction, or influence our collective decision: we are in constant flux of influencing one another's opinion, and by taking certain individual responsibility (be it animal rights, greenhouse gases, or volunteering to educate immigrant youth), we demonstrate to others what is the preferable course of action for our collective. Such individual actions help us convince others with the aim of one day striking a collective deal.

Nevertheless, too often we take actions as individuals with the idea of "if everyone acted in this way." History and economics shows that we cannot rely on that assumption. Instead, when we make our voluntary contribution, we should do so acknowledging this does not give us the right or expectancy for others to do as we do. That right is born when we manage to turn our expectancy into a social contract. Calls for acting responsibly can create backlash as they can signal identities that alienate "the other," creating divisions. The ESG investment category, for example, has led to such divisions.

The same can be said for impact companies and impact investments. If they truly seek the impact to be at the forefront of the business, they need to lobby for that impact to be economically meaningful through regulation. Otherwise, other companies who don't care about such impact will eventually out compete them.

In a sneaky way, the individual action of an impact investor or responsible consumer can create the opposite message of what we need: that broader, coordinated change is not necessary, because that change is already happening through individual actions of consumers, companies and investors even in the absence of any changes to our laws and regulations.

So, next time you are buying responsibly, volunteering, donating funds or doing a similar giving action, let's figure out how this action is enabling a coordinated effort that helps necessary regulations to come about, or that it is not intending to change any rules and regulations, and accept that it remains a limited measure.

It is good to note that the scale of the issue calls for action at different levels – depending on which stakeholders have legitimacy to decide over it. It doesn't make sense to make a regulation in the city if you can have pets or make noise late into a Monday night in your apartment – that's an issue that needs to be addressed in your apartment council. Similarly, climate change actions aren't something your apartment council can significantly influence – it's a global issue and needs global governance to address.

The citizen in us represents our role as the participants in striking a new collective decision. As citizens, in a truly democratic system, we are equally far from power, it is up to us to pursue a coordinated change. Change makers have always been able to inspire others to take action, and redefine the social norm, which is translated in some shape or form into the social contract. The most obvious and effective way to establish a new social norm *should be* via legislation and budgets, not through laboring for an impact company, or buying responsible products. It is time we awaken the citizen in us, and demand a democracy that allows that citizen to breathe.

CHAPTER TWO

DEMOCRACY'S CROSSROADS: INNOVATE OR DIE

"Our scientific power has outrun our spiritual power. We have guided missiles and misguided men."

—MLK, Strength to Love, 1963

I t was not only MLK, but Einstein who also talked about how our tech advancements have gone faster than our ability to make them work to benefit us. Can we make our governments smarter using data-driven feedback loops as tech companies do? And what happens if we cannot innovate and improve our governance technology?

When we founded Donkey Republic in 2014, we were the first company globally that offered bikes for rental on a mobile app, without physical stations. Getting access to a bike on the street and unlocking it with your phone truly seemed magical to any first time users, with a big wow moment. The company continues to grow as one of Europe's largest bike-sharing services, and a listed company on NASDAQ First North.

While bike-sharing may not sound like a tech company, thanks to the ability to collect a lot of information, we actually ran the company very much as a tech company, using data-driven learning loops.

For example, we used data-driven learning to find out which of our bike models were more attractive to rent for new users. Similarly, we learned about which locations were better performing in generating user-ship, the kind of registration flow that would enable onboarding more customers, and pricing models that would yield higher returns. Perhaps one of the more interesting experiments we ran was around how often we should inflate our bikes' tires. We knew how much it cost us to inflate a tire, through estimates of time spent by our mechanics. What we didn't know was the value of it. Being an avid cyclist I sensed that inflating tires often is a good thing for the rider experience. But how often should that be? And if it is an important cost-driver, could we find an easy way to drive an answer using data?

Many services use Net Promoter Score (NPS), to measure their customer satisfaction. The company simply asks the customer "How likely they are to recommend the service to others." Five out of five is considered a "promoter," whereas a four out of five is neutral, and anything less is considered a "detractor." You may have run into this when you used Airbnb, Uber, or one of our Donkey bikes. So, in order to figure out the value of how inflated a bike tire should be we looked into its impact on the NPS. We prepared some bikes to have 2 bar, others 2.5, and others 3 bar of tire pressure. We left everything else random. After some time there were enough data points to give us a statistically significant level of difference between the NPS among the different pressure levels. Thanks to this experiment, we were able to create a curve for how much more customer value we generate with each decimal bar we put into our tires and compared that with the effort and created an optimal frequency with which we could inflate our tires. This is a decision made using data and not guts.

Tech companies like Facebook, Google, and Amazon each have been running more than 10,000 experiments annually on their digital platforms, many engaging millions of users (Kohavi and Thomke, 2017). I have not worked at one of these, but I have discussed the methods with contacts and have been coached by consultants that worked with some of the tech companies in Silicon Valley, facilitating such learning processes. The experiments mentioned here mean smaller or larger changes introduced, in a page or design, which are usually served together with its alternatives, to verify a hypothesis. For example, let us assume that Facebook would like more events to be facilitated through its platform. One of the experiments they may be running is to make the creation of events faster. They may be creating different versions of the event creation page, one that involves capturing more information than the other. This will likely have an impact on how many people end up creating events. Next to that, they can also see how the event input impacts the attendance to the event. So, by playing with the fields concerning event creation, they can optimize for the number of events, and at the same time, optimize participation in the events. They will naturally need to weigh these two – more or fewer events, and stronger or weaker participation. They most likely will have a higher goal, which other sub-goals serve. For Facebook, time spent on the platform is an important goal, likely directly related to how many ads they can successfully serve to their visitors. So, the balance of number of events, and participation in the events will also be weighted for serving this higher goal: total time spent on platform.

The experimental nature of decision-making at Facebook is also demonstrated by how they sell ads on their platform: clients upload ad alternates – images, title, videos, etc. Then the platform displays these ads toward the target consumer group to identify which ones perform best in terms of click-throughs. Instead of guessing which visuals or statements would work best, they put it to the test. Compare this highly scientific method to catch our attention with ads online, to the way we had been running ads on TV, when there was no direct data feed. It is much easier for companies to spend money on Facebook because they can test ideas and scale those that actually work.

The Silicon Valley style data-driven innovation is now the norm for all tech companies, and increasingly for all companies who understand the importance of data-driven learning to become a truly powerful business.

It should be obvious that our governments need the same change of culture. There is a strong case for arguing that our governance technology needs to actually remain ahead of other technologies in order to keep them in check, ensuring they create social value. From space exploration to the study of atoms or DNA, the way companies exploit technologies can do favor or harm to our society and environment. These might be unintentional, and not direct (a.k.a. first-order) or obvious impacts as we see with social media. It is our governance technology that we must trust and find comfort in, above all other technologies to keep them at our service.

Nick Bostrom, a philosopher and technologist at Oxford University, points out that technologies carry a destructive danger, when used against humanity (Bostrom, 2002). Nuclear bombs are an obvious example. According to scientists, humanity faces 3–30% chance of extinction due to an asteroid hit within the next one billion years (Salotti, 2022), while an 0.5% chance of extinction due a nuclear catastrophe already by 2100 and a 3% chance of extinction by 2100 due to misaligned AI, which is ranked the highest risk factor for possible human extinction (The Economist, 2023). There are many other human technology induced risks, including bioweapons.

But we don't have to go so far with the "intentional" technology risks. There are many risks posed by technology without being intentional. When we introduce a new crop, for example a genetically modified crop that is resistant to heat, this can alter the ecosystem in ways that create unintended consequences, killing the trees or crops we actually need.

Climate change is the prime example of unintended consequences of use of technology. We did not aim to heat the planet but it is a consequence of our way of energy production. According to Nate Hagans, we are using 250 human-equivalent energy units per person (Hagens and White, 2017). That is, if we rewind history, back to where humans did not even make fire but only consumed energy through their diet, they would be using 1 human-equivalent unit of energy – this is what all other animals do. Don't get me wrong, this is not a bad thing. Actually, it is a great thing, the amount of energy we harvest and control is arguably a key signature of the greatness of our civilization in securing and expanding life – if provided in a sustainable manner. However, by causing climate change, humans are making the planet less habitable for themselves and are doing so despite its increasingly clear cost and future dangers.

Some other challenges unintended yet enabled by technology are:

- Cars in our cities, reducing quality of life with accidents, noise, and pollution.
- Social media exacerbating polarization and loneliness.
- Production of cheap alcohol, tobacco, and sugar, enabling addictions.

To sum up, technology is power, it is a tool. It is not necessarily good or bad. It is the context, as well as our ability to understand and measure its consequences that determines its impact on humanity. The more disruptive and powerful the technology is, the greater their consequences for humanity will be. And if we grow technologies in an environment where we are not able to govern them, we can easily see great harm done, as we experience with our environment and societies.

Therefore, innovating our governance technology is key for our survival as species. If we don't manage to do that, we can get stuck in power structures that reduce the potential of humanity and that are not democratic nor in the interest of humanity.

INNOVATING COMPANIES WIN, BIG TIME

We have seen a great leap of innovation in technology, especially related to everything related to data, since the birth of the internet in the 1990s making communication easier, and since smartphones have become commonplace in the late 2000s interfacing users and collecting data. We now have systems that carry a lot more data, and process data quickly.

More of our economy is now reliant on tech and increasingly more value is created by tech companies. When we say tech company we mean a company on the cutting edge of technology. It may or may not hold patents, but it is working with a product or service that is not commoditized and can be scaled with the help of cutting edge technology.

Looking at the top 50 companies by market capitalization in June 2024 (a.k.a. by company valuation), 36% of them are made up of tech companies. This is a rate significantly higher than 8% as of 2004. Further, all of the top five are tech companies, while 20 years ago there was only one, Microsoft (companiesmarketcap.com, 2024; visualcapitalist.com, 2024).

This is not a coincidence. Tech companies tap into fast learning loops, whereby they gather data and run tests continuously as a part of their daily decision-making process (Figure 2.1). Their learning is substantiated by the basic rules of scientific inquiry. The pace at which they grow and improve their products outpaces others who are slower to. Tech companies typically spend 10–30% of their revenues on research and development, a level much higher than traditional companies at around 1–4% (International Energy Agency, 2021; Sather, 2021). This is a cost not associated with their current operations and production, but preparing for new products or services to create more value in the future. And that strategy has brought them a great advantage over others in a short time.

Figure 2.1   Lean Startup: an iterative, data-driven cycle of innovation.

Source: Why we love the Lean Startup (and you should, too!), 2015 / Equidam / https://www.equidam .com/why-entrepreneurs-should-apply-the-lean-startup-business-valuation/, last accessed on 14 December 2024.

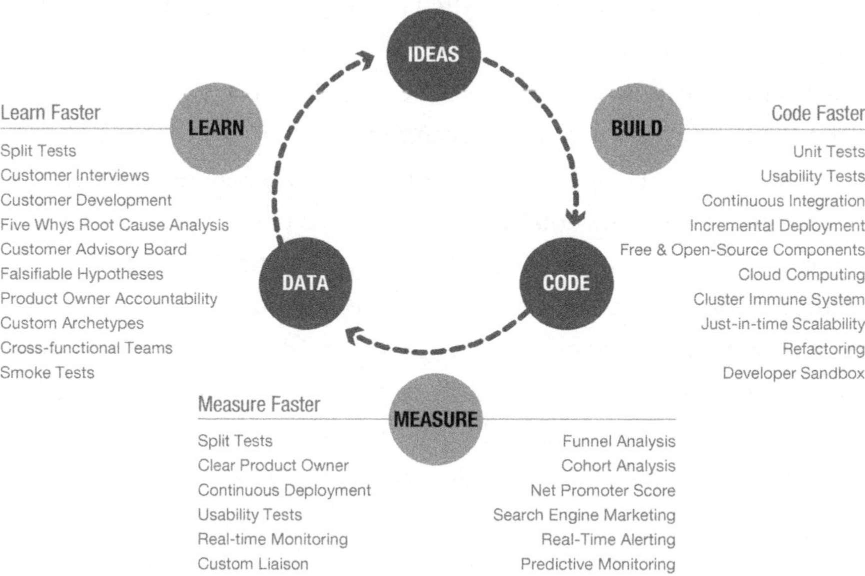

The concept of data-driven iterative learning loops has been visualized and popularized through Eric Rees's "the lean startup" back in 2011. The concept of "lean" has been and is a part of the business dictionary in various contexts, from industries to services. The idea of lean focuses on reducing mistakes and inefficiencies, but Eric Rees's application of it in startups has more to do with using the least effort to obtain the most learnings. Accounting for learnings is an important concept also: to support innovative culture, it would be perfectly fine to set aside a budget to run tests and to obtain learnings.

At Donkey Republic, the speed with which we learned the value of having sufficient tire pressure was of course directly related to how many bikes we put into the experiment, hence our effort. And while running such tests sounds beautiful, it does take resources to run them, thus one has to pick and choose institutional capabilities to target where they make most sense.

Note that running experiments on our customer onboarding, which is a fully digital experiment, versus experiment that involves preparation of hardware is different in cost. The digital experiments can be pushed to a large audience with a relatively small effort thanks to scalability of code. Nevertheless, the more we integrate our world of hardware with data collection, the more we learn about it and can run tests about their nature. Applying the lean learning loops into cars is what made Tesla stand out so quickly.

The ability to make good and speedy decisions is what has set tech companies, and especially Silicon Valley, apart. We must understand the importance of merit in this context: some decisions are better than others, objectively, serving certain common goals. The decision-making process must be one that enables such *merit* to come to the forefront, ahead of personal opinions and biases. The companies that succeed are the ones that have been open minded about how they cultivate their response to challenges and link that to data.

The superiority of tech companies' ability and methods to innovate through data-driven learnings must be a part of our thinking as we reimagine democracy.

EVOLUTION THRIVES WITH EXPERIMENTATION

At the policy school of UC Berkeley, we studied much about Scandinavian countries' way of handling education, healthcare, transportation, labor market and so on. One example is early childcare. Already by 2005, there had been a strong body of research supporting the long-term value of providing early childcare, in terms of indicators such as lifetime earnings of the individual, or their estimated lifespan. Given such a body of research,

I had assumed that knowledge would turn into legislation. I was naive. Our legislative practices are shaped by our beliefs, and popularity of certain claims, and not the data. Neither do we have a system of measuring the impacts of our legislation.

What should be the role of morality versus science in determining our collective decisions? It is not new that scientific methods of working with data, and driving decisions by that, is superior to non-experimenting, i.e. a random response. It is also superior to a convincing story, a moral argument, when it comes to the success of the decision serving its purpose.

Perhaps I don't need to convince you that data-driven decision-making is a superior mechanism of learning about the outcomes of a public policy compared to intergenerational survival of traditions and dogmas. Nevertheless, popular culture and the need to belong and find meaning in the everyday can easily facilitate cultivating dogmas – truths that do not allow questioning. I grew up in Istanbul, Türkiye, where Islamic dogma and related concepts of morality still reign over many peoples' lives. Also, as an exchange student of 17 years, I experienced similar dogma reign over large groups of people in the United States. This can also be said about traditions in Europe, where the lines against questioning are not as obvious but are still there. The everyday experiences of dealing with dogma around me made me question whatever is being imposed on me. Critical thinking and truth seeking has been the way to deal with dogma, in addition to finding belonging and spirituality that did not feature dogma as a part of the package.

I believe our current social media driven popular culture offers new hotbeds for dogmas to spread. Many young people seem to believe in astrology, for example, and other traditional practices. A shocking number of Gen Zers and millennials have been dumped over their zodiac sign (Wigle, 2024). Imagine your character being judged based on your birthday. In fact, there have been studies to verify claims of astrology, resulting in rejection of its claims (Pulu, 2024). Many conversations with my friends and acquaintances have been impacted by my persistence in challenging dogmas. "What information do we trust?" is the question we need to ask, and we need to maintain a critical view of all sources we are receptive to. It falls on the side of the people making the claims to provide proof supporting their theory, and not the other way around.

We ran an aggressive form of capitalism in the past 40 years, especially in the United States, ignoring the externalities of products and services. Can we overcome the dogma of free markets and critically ask what it is we want from markets, and how to get it? We talk about free markets as if it is a natural thing. As Robert Reich (2015) said,

> *Few ideas have done as much harm as the idea of the "free market," detached from government. The "free market" doesn't exist in nature. It is a human creation, and its rules are set by governments.*

We shall remember that markets are subject to laws, from intellectual property and bankruptcy to consumer protection. And markets cannot exist without those laws. The next thing is to decide how to steer those conditions to best serve our collective interests. And to do such steering well we need to run experiments and use data to figure out how those experiments perform to create the behaviors we want in the market.

As dry as it may sound, data-driven experimentation is actually beautiful, and it is the essence of nature seen with the lens of interactions that enables evolution. Every organism represents some kind of structure, which represents data, and life is constantly serving a series of interactions with other organisms. And over time, their interactions create some kind of balance between their survival in that environment. It is the mutations in nature that then creates random changes that turn into experiments played out through their survival. Usually, a small minority of such mutations are successful in serving the interest of the species, and they then grow to dominate the species to become the norm. The mechanism of evolution itself is a large data experiment.

Science and the Industrial Revolution created a framework for learning faster than evolution, using experimentation. Before we endorsed scientific revolution, our cultural evolution took much longer time. We used to learn through generations of people suffering or dying, or surviving based on their traditions leading them to their existing circumstances. That was anything from what they consumed as food (Muslims not drinking alcohol or eating pork) or what they acclaimed immoral (Christians punished homosexuality or premarital sex).

The scientific method of learning is powerful: it is about forming hypotheses, conducting experiments, and analyzing data to draw conclusions. Our capacity to formulate hypotheses after collecting and analyzing data enables us to use that data. It is precisely the use of that method that made the west rich after the long and dark Middle Ages. And it is now that is giving rise to the new powers of tech companies with use of these methods on steroids thanks to digital data collection and processing techniques internalized into decision-making methods.

For better or worse, while our scientific methods drove our technological progress they have not been for shaping our social realm. Even though we have social sciences that investigate our well-being, they have not trickled down to policy. Public policy has remained a realm of morality, where religious dogma and other values and memes carry more influence than our scientific methods. With regards to using scientific methods of learning for developing technologies, we have very clear market structures with financial incentives. With regards to using the same methods for developing our social policies we have little or no incentives. This book is about changing that.

Going back to tech companies and what we have learned from them: We could have a dozen companies, producing similar goods. If companies are taking decisions based on "expert opinions" which are naturally biased, the survival of these companies will be based on a lot of luck, and they will do worse than companies that exploit every opportunity for experimentation with data.

The same thing applies in public governance: governance mechanisms that are better in learning will do better in achieving various public goals and will be the stronger ones to dictate to others. If we are slow learners we will give in to the basic rule of life, our values will bow and give way to others whose civilizations do better.

The pace of evolution is increasing rapidly and exponentially in line with our data capabilities. What used to be considered fast 100 years ago, or even 10 years ago is no longer good enough. We, and our governmental structures, seem fully ignorance of this as our governance technology remains mostly unchanged in more than a century. And if we do not manage better we will give way to those who are pushing the boundaries of what is possible.

Therefore, the way we run our collective decisions, the way we govern ourselves, is the most important factor in determining our survival, or at least as important as the disruptive technologies that it allows and enables, such as AI, quantum computing, fusion power and so on. That is why we need to invest heavily in our (democratic) governance technology development.

GETTING INNOVATION INTO THE GOVERNMENT

Innovation is a buzz word that politicians like to use, but usually do not think needs to apply to the workings of their office. Innovation has become fashionable thanks to the ways our lives have improved in the last century, and especially in the last 25 years, moving us into a (consumer) abundance economy. At the same time, innovative companies created more jobs and economic prospects through their exports. For most governments, innovation translates to a stronger economy and therefore it is a politically desirable concept.

Innovation is not, however, understood as evolution of our public policies or democratic system. The realm of innovation stops at the office of the IT guy who will provide the latest model computer or mobile device, or perhaps the car that will drive the politician around. When it comes to how the parliament or overall democratic decision system works we don't think innovation is a relevant word.

This is perhaps due to a self-fulfilling prophecy: we needed governments to be stable and did not create ways to measure what government bodies achieve. Working for government became a safe job, attracting people and culture that did not seek change but more of the stability and risk reduction. People with more risk appetite chose other directions and often end up with private companies.

In my experience of about two decades interacting with public and private organizations, I see a stark difference in cultures. A civil servant will be fired if they made some grave mistake or offended someone in the system. More likely they will be not promoted if they are not seen as effective while also being obedient. In contrast, in companies, dissenting voices are welcome if they are about improving the business. There is tolerance for risk in companies, but public institutions prioritize stability, compliance, and strict risk avoidance. Good ideas are shot down for being too risky in public institutions far more often than in companies.

Public organizations seem to be far from understanding how tech companies operate and vice versa. The reasons for that are perhaps also about how the Silicon Valley culture evolved. The "Cluetrain Manifesto" published in late 1990s gave clues to this ideological break, calling for cyberspace to operate as a self-regulating realm free from government intervention. Over time, Silicon Valley's ecosystem evolved around a free-market ethos that champions disruption over regulation, solidifying a culture that often views government as an obstacle to rapid technological progress.

Indeed, tech companies and strong innovation in the United States worked without government intervention, except for strong support for scientific research. In return, the government also did not experience much of how innovation happens. The culture that drove innovation in the private sector remains largely away from the realm of public authorities. Despite the high pace of innovation in companies, the methods and ideologies did not define how we innovate our public governance.

Democratic government has two important legs: legislation – that is new decisions and budgeting, and execution – organizing and administering the delivery of public goods. We need to innovate in both realms. Legislative process is inherently something the government needs to sit with and work on improving. This is where we need to introduce new, data-driven iterative learning methods, and broad participation.

In terms of delivery of public goods, I believe governments need to innovate not the individual products and services, but instead, the way they work and incentivize markets. Instead of taking on the task of improving the services themselves, governments really need to focus on how they engage the markets and leverage the companies' abilities to innovate to create the services. We are, unfortunately, quite far from where we need to be, on both ends.

First, on the legislation side, the process takes much too long: average duration for new legislation in the United States is 12–15 months during the past decade (Govtrack.us, 2024), and the process in the EU is not any shorter. The process is long because of the committee work that goes on among the (few) representatives and party leadership to take positions, hear out various stakeholders, including the businesses. The process is very much centralized around a few people, whose time becomes a bottleneck. These key decision makers need to find time in their calendars to meet various stakeholders – remember the lobbyists? – and consider changes through back and forth dialogue (Figure 2.2).

Not only does it take too long to pass new legislation, but also our ability to consider multiple pieces of legislation is constrained by the availability of the centralized design of decision makers who need to coordinate.

Figure 2.2   Federal legislative process in the United States.

Source: University of Minnesota. The Legislative Process / University of Minnesota / https://open.lib.umn.edu/americangovernment/chapter/12-7-the-legislative-process/, last accessed on 14 December 2024.

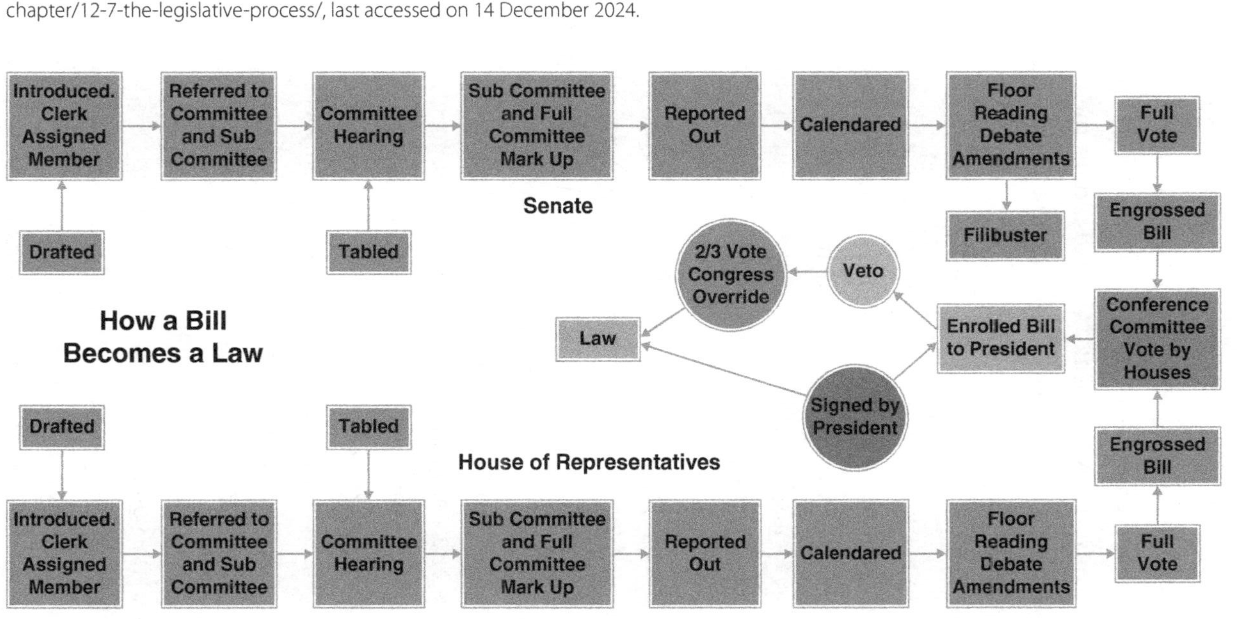

Unexpected developments needing attention and related fire-fighting have taken an increasing portion of the legislative efforts in the past decade making it even harder to focus on the proactive public agenda.

There are obvious opportunities to decentralize the legislative process, bring it to digital platforms, and make it much more agile to allow parties to consider various options real time, and reduce the time it takes to bring about new legislation, as well as the amount of new legislation. More on that on Chapter 6.

Second, we do not have any specified metrics assigned to our legislation, nor do we action in any systematic manner the level at which legislation fulfills the goals to assess their quality. The process of feedback in the legislative process happens mostly behind closed doors where a decision to back a legislative proposal is negotiated up against backing of other proposals among various stakeholders, which reduces transparency of the whole affair.

If we were to legislate similar to the ways tech companies make decisions, we would make some "cheap" experiments, which means experiments that test out specific hypotheses in a narrow scope and setting and iterate such experiments in order to gain more insight into the hypotheses. Instead of spending a lot of time and effort with a lengthy process of discussions and compromises, we would agree to grow the scope of our experiments and roll them out to the whole group once we have evidence we can achieve what we want.

Today, we declare a legislative success when there is a new law that is *assumed* to bring about certain effects. The world is much more complex than our pre-assessment models suggest, and unintended consequences will come up with each legislation.

Let me give you an example. Helmets are supposed to be good to wear when biking in case you have an accident. Biking is good for your health, except if you have an accident, and especially if you hit your head. In some cities, governments made helmets mandatory in order to improve health.

It turns out, requiring helmet-wearing makes people bike far less, both because they don't always want to bring their helmet, or don't have access to one, or the perception of helmet requirement makes it feel dangerous (de Jong, 2012). The overall health impact, that is fewer people biking, and fewer percentage of bikers get involved in an accident, turns out to be a negative one.

Politicians are interested in data, but they relate to it as a measure of popularity. Data entered politics a couple of decades ago through estimating the popularity of politicians' positions with regard to various policy proposals. Now there are advanced tools that read the sentiment on social media to provide an overview of topics that would resonate with their voters, or potential voters.

Yet we are shy of using data to ensure we actually attain the outcomes we want through new policies. The political system we have does not facilitate the kind of innovative process that companies engage in: companies don't ask their users what products they want. They ask them what their problems are, and they create products and services that solve the problems. Steve Jobs would have made the iPhone with bigger buttons than the Nokia phones if he surveyed people about what the iPhone should look like.

If you ask people about how they want to move around, they all want a big car for themselves, empty streets to go around, an otherwise green and safe environment, and rich human connection when they go out. That's simply not going to happen, yet what our politicians seem to end up promising is just that. Instead, if you focus on people's biggest problems, wasting time in traffic, unhealthy environments, including air and noise pollution and traffic accidents, and even loneliness, then it becomes increasingly obvious we should rethink cities around far fewer cars, and rather around bikes and public transport. Innovative thinking must start with assigning value to problems and testing solutions to fix them with data-driven validations. It is not a popularity contest.

Our capacity to collect and evaluate the data in order to judge legislative performance is challenged. Even in Denmark where the government has access to a lot of data, the use of such data is intentionally made difficult even for its own agencies due to privacy concerns. Further, politicians want to share the actual performance of various policies only if there are results they can brag about. The issue is management of perception and not actual results as it is the media stories that create public opinion.

"Leadership is not about the next election, it's about the next generation" says Simon Sinek. And unfortunately, this is very rarely the case. For politicians, their decisions are substantially – if not mostly – influenced by winning the next election, as well as winning the minds and hearts of companies and organizations that can pay them good salaries in their next jobs.

So much for legislation. If we look at the execution of government services, we have created large organizations that deliver services to public and companies, from education and health services. Some of the key features of these organizations are top-down control and risk averseness. Aversion of risk is not only about being at odds with complex public law, but also about giving way to a news story that will harm the popularity of the political layer. Often, even smaller budget activities need permission from top levels for clearing, especially if they are new and untried.

When it comes to buying goods and services from the markets, governments have to use tenders. Unfortunately, these contracts often define the goods they aim to buy quite narrowly leaving little room for innovation on the company's side in order to avoid problems with the purchased goods. Yet, the world is complex, and what is purchased often does not live up to the expected results.

In other words, governments struggle with innovation not only in law-making, but also in their service delivery. They struggle with it both internally and externally. If we were to mimic some of the methods from the private sector and especially tech companies, we would want to decentralize decision-making inside the organizations to project teams and allow and endorse experimentation to achieve certain success metrics. We would also reward the teams accordingly. Externally, we would want to contract companies based on their broader outcomes and allow multiple companies to deliver a service at the same time, instead of focusing on contracting one at a time. We would not want to define the solutions when we are buying the goods and services, but instead to define the problems, and let the markets try to solve them.

What kind of resource would be needed to innovate with our democracies?

As mentioned, top-tier tech companies spend 10–30% of their earnings on innovation. This is a comparable kind of spending to major wartime efforts; for example, Ukraine's war efforts are an estimated 20% of its economy (TheGlobalEcomomy.com, 2022). Mario Draghi's report recently talked about the EU's need to place 5% of its GDP to support its economy becoming competitive on critical technologies vis-à-vis China and the United States in the coming decade (Draghi, 2024). Let's not mix that with the innovation of the government. This would be funding of technology projects and companies in order to give rise to competitive industries.

Can we see democratic and governance reform as a critical technology? If so I believe we can justify spending 1–2% of GDP per year on innovating government in the coming few decades, and perhaps less thereafter once we have caught up with our innovation debt in the space of governance. I am not sure 1–2% of GDP is sufficient, but I think such an amount is a good starting point to save our democracies.

This money would be spent on implementing experiments for legislative processes, as well as new public goods delivery models. We would also need to improve our underlying data structures to enable better learning. Later in this book I will explore the possibilities for democratic innovations in both legislation and execution of services. But first, a discussion of what awaits us if we fail to innovate with democratic governance.

DYSTOPIAN OUTCOMES OF DYSFUNCTIONAL DEMOCRACIES

So, what are some scenarios that can play out, at least for a period of time, if we don't manage to improve our democratic technologies?

We have plenty of dystopian governance futures made into various films, from *V for Vendetta* to *Blade Runner*. They give us good clues, shaping our understanding, and culture.

My favorites in this genre are the "Black Mirror" series. It is the series that the BBC originally produced, and released, starting in December 2011. The series features one-hour shows that have their own plots that are unrelated to one another, except for the greater theme of all of it: the possible dystopian futures waiting for us with the growth of technology without the balancing governmental interventions. While the technologies featured in the shows are interesting, and increasingly accurate, the main focus is the undesirable social reality. A general theme in the show is the absence of a functioning democratic government. Each show explores a different dynamic in society being disrupted and turned into ways many find dystopian because they work against justice and agency.

Two futures stand out for me that can fill the gap of democratic empowerment.

One is a future with a strong state power governing us, in the style of China's governance today. In this future, the power is concentrated in a dictator-like government, controlled by powerful people at the top through state agency. Decisions are guided presumably with help of AI and big data. Such a government can have well-established top-down performance indicators for its tentacles, reaching various geographies and areas of governance, delegating power to local governments in areas that are not critical for centralized power. It does not worry about privacy and collects and exploits data to secure its power. In a hypothetical not-corrupt version of this state it could make decisions of decent quality without the worry of short-term election campaigns or remaining popular, especially if it truly uses the power of data for learning. It can act in an agile manner, even though the centralized control mechanisms represent a bottleneck. It can be transparent; in the sense that all decisions are made by one party, possibly also disclosing the reasoning behind them.

Citizens in this scenario can expect to live in some comfort, minding their work. However, they cannot expect to have agency or the possibility of dissent. There is no room for criticism or social movements, or freedom of expression. In *Nosedive* episode of "Black Mirror" (premiered 2016), there is a story told of a citizen trying to fit in, where social ratings have the power over one's life (Wikipedia, 2016b). Critics' evaluation is that this show represents a reality not so far from the Chinese social scoring, or what it might eventually evolve in to (ABC News, 2018). From what you buy in the grocery store to whom you speak to or where you go in your free time can determine your score. That score is in turn linked to your access to finance, job market and even mobility, hence it is highly critical. You are ever under surveillance and stopped from objecting to the framework conditions that shape your life. In a way, the experience of China and its surveillance society will show us how sustainable such a governance future will fare.

Another future could be a global or regional convergence toward a "fake democracy" with a very high inequality of wealth, where the vast majority of people believe they have some kind of power, but in reality do not. In this future, people owning and controlling companies with critical technologies such as AI or quantum computers generate a very large amount of wealth, moving our inequality levels far beyond anything we have experienced. As a result, they have access to data and information in order to control the beliefs and actions of the rest in a consumer oriented society, where political action is made intentionally impossible through control of politicians, public knowledge and opinion, and decentralized communication platforms (social media, YouTube, and the like).

Fifteen Million Merits is the Black Mirror show that gives an overview of how society could look like in the far extreme of such a situation (Wikipedia, 2011): people living and dying to consume in their cells day and night, besides turning pedals when they can. Survival is always a serious concern, and meaning is to be sought in the short-term pleasures of our animalistic senses. Another Black Mirror episode is the *Hated in the Nation* (Wikipedia, 2016a) where through control of technology platforms, public information and opinions are manipulated, to undermine legitimate voices of dissent.

Some may think we are already stuck in one or other of the scenarios. I don't think so, but we are not very far from such scenarios either. The technological, economic, and political trends at play give enough concern to doing something to place humanity and its governance on a new path. If we do not like the idea of such dystopias we must find ways to innovate governance at once.

We shall explore new paths of governance, so that we can find democratic mechanisms that satisfy our needs away from the dystopia in line with the four values I defended as requirements of a future system: quality, agility, transparency and agency. No mechanism will ever be perfect, but we can steer far from the dystopian scenarios if we start innovating the democratic technology, and make the innovation of the system itself a core internal mechanism and dedicate a healthy amount of budget to it.

CHAPTER THREE

BREWING CHANGE FOR LEGISLATION

In this chapter, I will take you through how we got to the form of democracy we have, and the experiments that are taking place.

Researchers have suggested that humans have lived for the longest time of their evolution in small groups of 20 or sometimes up to 100, in quite an egalitarian manner (Lin and Schank, 2022). In such groups, they see little signs of hierarchy, and decision-making was communal, involving all members (The Conversation, 2022). Leadership often had to do with age, experience, and trust placed by others in the group.

For many thousands of generations, we have evolved to live this way, in flat organizations, where our opinion mattered, and where we could see how the group itself was making decisions.

With the Neolithic Revolution, we transitioned to a settled life working with agriculture. The agricultural economy created surplus and gave rise to opportunities for new forms of governance. We were not in tribes of dozens any longer, but in tens of thousands. This meant we no longer had direct experience of one another, to keep one another accountable. And we needed some form of rule set that everyone needed to obey, which made the group functional, and able to survive. The lack of such a rule set and lack of enforcement – anarchy – means we over time are fighting to exploit the common resources over one another, and that is worse off for everyone (Rehal, 2024).

In my late twenties, I've traveled to Türkiye and Africa frequently, while living in Denmark. One of the things I've noticed was the similarities of the problems in Türkiye and in Kenya and Uganda – much had to do with lack of trust in institutions. Such lack of trust meant one needs to find their own tribe, and build a protective circle in terms of security, care, trade, and so on. This is perfectly fine for many social goods, and in fact, what we need in the west, is the co-living groups, taking care of many of one another's social needs.

However, I also saw that the development of further public goods: justice, roads, financial structures, education, and so forth were lacking as a direct function of social trust in the system. It is the trust that the system is not corrupt that enables people to pay their taxes in good faith. In absence of such trust we all look for loopholes to reduce our exposure to a taxing authority that has become the enemy. We start playing the "defect" route in the prisoner's dilemma.

This is in my opinion the biggest asset Nordic countries have – the social trust. Such trust enables them to leave their bags unattended in public, trusting others won't steal them. Enforcing deals is not too time-consuming, because a handshake is worthy. Sharing data with authorities is also much easier, once we trust that it is used to our benefit.

So, in our transition to settlement, there were a lot of civilizations that failed due to lack of trust in the system, where people did not cooperate, but defected to one another, which economists call the free-rider problem. Those that managed to survive often found the strong leader, a dictator or ruler, as the balancing form of government. This type of institution often suffered from successions and transition of power, corruption, and broad public dissent.

Then pops up the Greek democracy. There had been some other forms of assemblies in India and Mesopotamia already, but the Greeks were great at documenting; perhaps this is also a reason why we acknowledge them as the first democracy. Perhaps it is the democratic regime that inspired people to write and gave them the freedom and free time to do so. Even if women were not included in the decision-making process, the system was by far the most ambitious democratic form of governance: Up to 40,000 citizens participated in legislative and judicial decisions, directly and physically, creating a phenomenal ideal: democracy seemed to provide many of the qualities of governance they missed, especially that of agency, in this new, large population and settled civilization format.

Over time, though, their institutions eroded. Increasing numbers of younger men were unable to attend the meetings due to military service and work, while the wealthier and often older ones were there dominating the democratic gatherings. Inequality undermined the democracy by reducing participation and also introducing divisions that eventually reduced their military strength. Demagogy by charismatic orators started appealing to emotions over rationalism, becoming populistic. Growing empire brought with it increasing need for expertise, which meant increased reliance on professionals, thus undermining democratic process.

Sounds familiar? It indeed is, with the strong influence of the rich and elderly who are reliant on experts cutting off the direct and transparent process, all packed into a populistic spin-doctored, inauthentic public appearance.

Thereafter, the history of modern, Western democracy is rather young. The United Kingdom started having elections and a parliament, though far from having power over the king, in the thirteenth century. It had the two-chambers representing the nobility and the commoners and took its shape of what it is today with larger adjustments in the nineteenth century reforms in expanding representation, and early twentieth century where women's representation was secured next to men. The US and French democracies were the other pioneers although they didn't have a smooth power transition from a monarch. Both established their frameworks for representative democracies in the late eighteenth century. The United States was inspired by the experiences in the United Kingdom, as well as enlightenment thinkers, and the French were inspired by the experience of the Americans. In a way, the enlightenment philosophy and a few successful experiments together with the United Kingdom's centuries' long transition of power while among the most powerful, was inspiring for the leading thinkers of the time. They could see the future was to be built on a new system of democracy. They dared to try something new, unseen, and unheard of except in the dusty pages of some books, and a few experiments that resonated with them.

We are in a similar situation today. We find ourselves at a moment in time when representative democracy has clearly shown us its limitations, and we have to leap forward. The US and French democratic revolutions made governance look very different over a short period of time. The kind of democracy we might find working best for us may look very different to what we have today.

The evolution of democracy from what the French and Americans had achieved in the late eighteenth century changed rather little, relatively speaking. The French have gone through five republics, with different constitutions, yet the essential design of democratic institutions and processes varied little. The United States has become more democratic, abolishing racial and gender discrimination over time, and its presidency became more powerful in the twentieth century with the increased executive orders and emergency powers. Other noteworthy changes to be mentioned are perhaps campaign finance, a critical topic on how money could trickle to support election process, which went through a period of limitations until recent *Citizens United v. FEC* in 2010.

In both of these democracies, much has stayed the same: you vote every few years to appoint (powerful) people to take charge; they are subject to support from interest groups before and after their election. In the meantime the ratio of citizens per representative has grown over time with increasing populations to the current levels, distancing politicians from their principles. While 40,000 citizens were represented by elected officials in France in the late 1800s, that is now at around double that population. The figures in the United States are more staggering: from the nineteenth century to now, the ratio of citizens per representative in the United States grew from 45,000 to around 500,000 – a more than 10-fold increase.

EXPERIMENTS WITH VOTING

The pursuit of fair and effective elections to determine who will represent the society has been one of the most debated topics in democratic understanding and reform. It's almost as if our imagination for democratic innovation stops at the boundaries of election methods.

Surely, whom we elect, and the incentives that we place on the candidates, have considerable impact on democracy's health. Also, campaign finance rules, if those with wealth and interest are allowed to influence election outcomes is an important consideration. Across the world, various voting methods have been tested, each offering unique approaches to representation, voter engagement, and political stability. Experimentation with different electoral systems reveals key insights into how these frameworks shape democratic health.

Voting methods influence not just the outcomes of elections but the impact of the conversation. In a **simple plurality system**, used in countries like the United States, the candidate with the most votes wins, even without a majority. While easy to understand and administer, plurality systems fall short in representing the full spectrum of public opinion. A simple plurality system leads to entrenchment of a two-party system, which researchers found (Foley, 2024) to contribute to polarization as candidates focus on making the other side look bad, with the logic of "a vote against them is a vote for us." While swing-voters' influence grows, minorities on either side can be disenfranchised.[1]

To address these shortcomings, many nations and cities have experimented with alternative systems that promise more equitable outcomes. **Ranked-choice voting (RCV)**, or **instant-runoff voting (IRV)**, is one such alternative. In this system, voters rank candidates in order of preference. If no candidate secures a majority, the least popular candidate is eliminated, and votes are redistributed based on second preferences. This process continues until one candidate achieves a majority. This encourages candidates to focus on what difference they will make, instead of fighting the others, reducing polarization. Experiments in New York City and Maine have shown that voters can switch and adapt to this system with some education and clear communication efforts.

Approval voting represents another approach. Voters can select as many candidates as they wish, and the candidate with the most approvals wins. This method, tested in places like Fargo, North Dakota, seeks to reduce strategic voting and give a fair chance to candidates with broad (but not necessarily passionate) support. Early results suggest that approval voting helps elect consensus candidates, but it can still disadvantage more polarizing figures. It shows promise in simplifying the voting process while delivering outcomes that reflect a wider base of public support.

While the systems so far create a single winner, the **proportional representation (PR)** systems have fundamentally changed the political landscapes of countries that employ them. Unlike majoritarian systems, PR allocates seats based on the proportion of votes each party receives. This model is used widely across Europe, including in Denmark, Sweden, and the Netherlands, and ensures that minority groups and smaller parties have a voice in parliament. Proportional systems have been praised for reducing wasted votes, promoting political diversity, and creating incentives for consensus-building and coalition governments. However, PR also comes with challenges, such as the potential for fragmented parliaments and the difficulty of forming stable governments.

Another variant of proportional representation, the **Mixed-Member Proportional (MMP)** system, has been a defining feature of democratic reforms in countries like Germany and New Zealand. In MMP, voters cast two votes: one for a local candidate and another for a political party. This system blends constituency representation with overall proportionality, seeking to balance local and national interests. In New Zealand, the adoption of MMP in the 1990s revitalized democracy by increasing representation for women and ethnic minorities and breaking the dominance of two-party politics (Simpson, 2022). The German experience could be argued to highlight MMP's success in encouraging political cooperation and stability.

The impact of voting systems on democratic health is substantial. Systems that encourage inclusivity and proportional representation tend to produce governments that are more reflective of the electorate's diverse views. Proportional representation methods, for instance, have proven effective in reducing the dominance of major parties and providing smaller or minority parties with a voice.

Nevertheless, while proportional representation fosters a sense of fairness and representation, the challenge with these systems is operating coalition governments. Many countries with proportional representation found it difficult to even form a government. Once formed, governments are less stable than single winner regimes.

Furthermore, even though many countries run different election regimes, as well as strict campaign finance rules, we see the general trends of citizen mistrust, populism, and decline of democracy across the spectrum of countries. France and Germany both have extreme political movements, coupled with low trust in politics, movements, although France runs a single winner system while Germany a proportional representative system.

My point is that election rules in a democracy are important but are far from fixing the deeper issues with our democracies, covered in Chapter 1. We shall see the voting rules and campaign finance rules as a relevant adjustments in our democracies, but even with these reforms we cannot achieving the kind of capacity, sophistication, and transparency we need. They are merely marginal changes, where we are in need of radical transformation.

PARTICIPATORY BUDGETING

One of the recent and radical democracy innovations is participatory budgeting (PB). Its name describes what it stands for: citizens have a platform for deciding collectively what they want to do with some of their collective budgets.

The concept of PB was first tried in Porto Alegre, which came about when the Workers Party in Brazil decided to run an experiment in the late 1980s. The party wanted to give citizens direct control over a portion of the city's budget, especially with regards to infrastructure and social services. Typically, 10–20% of the city's budget were spent through this process – though usually on highly visible projects, while some reports suggest about half the city's budget was impacted by the discussions.

All citizens were invited to take part in neighborhood assemblies, where they discussed their needs and could propose new initiatives. Citizen participation reached around 40,000 people (around 1% of city's population) in a given year, with a distribution of ages closely following the general population. Citizens also identified delegates to meet to discuss thematic topics regionally. Delegates or citizens participating in the process were not paid for their time or input. Online channels for engagement were introduced in the early 2010s, which cater for about 40% of participants.

The practice in Porto Alegre with PB is quite significant because it gave inspiration to other cities to try it out. Today, such PB processes are running in many major cities, including Paris, New York, Seoul, Madrid, and Chicago, though deploying a much smaller fraction of the cities' budgets for the PA. The impacts of Porto Alegre have also been studied throughout the years by many economists, including a thorough report by the World Bank, noting the following benefits (The World Bank, 2008):

- PB contributed to the election of the party whose agenda was inclusion of especially the poor. It is an important lesson to learn, that citizen participation is a winning political strategy, most likely the leading reason many other parties repeated similar processes in other cities, and it gained popularity especially among the lower class.
- PB created pro-poor distributional effects in Porto Alegre; the living conditions of the poor improved more significantly compared to other similar cities.
- The feeling of transparency and accountability improved, along with a feeling of reduced patronage and corruption. One study also found less corruption as an outcome due to more transparency.
- The process engaged different age groups and genders in a balanced manner reflecting the population, in contrast with the official office where older citizens are overrepresented by a large margin.
- More granular investments were undertaken with priority given to roads, sewage, water, and housing.

At the same time, the process has not been without problems:

- **Participation** remained at around 40,000 citizens in a population of 4 million, which is only about 1%. Besides being highly time-consuming one of the explanations for this is that the whole process is perceived by many as the political project of one party, thus people not affiliated with that party were not as present.
- PB seems to have been a tool for various groups to use budgets for their **own benefit**, rather than the overall benefit of everyone.

Crucially, citizens engaging had their main interest in ensuring their own local demands were prioritized over the city's overall goals.

- Interestingly, many **associations felt undermined,** as there was less of a need for them in order to influence the political process, as citizens could directly voice their needs in assemblies. Despite being seen as an important asset in democracies, can the civic sector undermine more effective and direct forms of governance to protect their interests?
- Overall fiscal discipline of the city did not improve in terms of delivering and executing on a balanced budget, again pointing that the process seems to struggle to focus on collective priorities over individual and local ones.

When I speak about the future of democracy with people closer to the field, participatory budgeting jumps in quickly as one of the possible ways forward. I believe PB experiments offer a lot of insights that allow us to go further, and by learning from their limitations in the current form, which are clearly seen.

The biggest handicap of participatory budgeting is the focus on one's own interest, which is justifying one's participation, and lack of incentives for broad participation. The way forward should consider rewarding participation based on the impact participants have on the whole group's needs. Currently, the answer to the natural question "what's in it for me?" is "a small share of the city's budget in exchange for a lot of time where you show up and speak up relentlessly." We need a system where citizens are incentivized to show up to solve problems for all of the city, nation, continent, and the globe, instead of just their own backyard.

PB risks serving as a "citizen engagement marketing tool," where politicians can promote that citizens have a voice to determine (some) of their budgets. In the meanwhile, the reality may be that the process is "informing" central decision-making instead of being binding or having a direct voice over a very small part of the budget (typically less than 1%).

CITIZEN ASSEMBLIES

Next to participatory budgeting, the other popular trend about the future of democracy are the citizen assemblies (CAs). The essence of the CA is a group of citizens that make recommendations (and rarely. but possibly, binding decisions) on a specific issue following a deliberative process. OECD records in their database 733 CAs from 1980 to 2023, globally, and the number of assemblies have increased in the past decade, averaging 40 per year globally. Most of them are run through in-person meetings, although online CAs were conducted during the COVID-19 epidemic, and some are continuing online or hybrid forms. The largest included thousands, while average size is around a hundred.

Practitioners working with CAs focus on three aspects in order to make them legitimate and valuable: (1) how were the participants chosen, (2) the inputs and process with which they arrive at their decisions and recommendations, and (3) what follows their recommendations and decisions in the real world.

CAs are in general used for bigger issues, such as rewriting of a constitution, ethical dilemmas such as abortion rights, and how to deal with climate change. So far, CAs have been used to provide recommendations, and not binding decisions with the exception of the case of Gdansk in Poland with a CA on climate effects mitigation policies: the mayor committed to use her office to implement any recommendations that achieved minimum 80% of the city assembly votes.

The CAs are intended to be composed of ordinary people. To do this, typically a two-stage sortition is used, where a large number of citizens, picked randomly, receive an invitation that they respond to. Out of those responding positively, subgroups are created based on demographic characteristics, and then a lottery process is run to select final group members. This way the members are both selected randomly, but also reflect demographic indicators such as age, gender, ethnicity, area of residency, income, and wealth. Unlike PB participants, the CA participants typically earn a significant stipend for participation.

Then, the CA typically runs a three-stage process to come up with their recommendations. The first step is learning. The CA members are exposed to experts and background material that informs them about the issue and perspectives at hand. Second step is a consultation phase, where people with different views on the topic of interest from outside present their viewpoints. One could argue at this stage the platform is open to biased stance points, whereas the first step is more seen as an objective view and formation step. The final step, deliberation and discussion, is where the members discuss the subjects, arriving at a set of recommendations. Facilitators are not to express personal opinions on the subject while also ensuring sufficient balance of views are brought up.

Some of the famous CAs include the Irish one on abortion rights, where the CA recommendation was put to referendum and was finally voted in. Both France and the United Kingdom have used CAs in order to identify the country's way forward with reduction of their greenhouse gasses. The French group of 150 members had suggested 149 proposals in total, of which only 40% were then included in country's policies, disappointing many (Girard, 2021). Similarly, the Dutch had convened a CA in order to discuss reforms to the country's electoral system – obviously a highly political subject. The 140 person assembly met over several months in 2006, producing a recommendation that was rejected by then Dutch government that had set up the CA in the first place.

While CAs are an interesting construct, I see some critiques of their ability to produce high-quality decisions:

- The selection of the experts and background information is undeniably biased, based on who provides and presents the information to the group. Similarly, facilitators who are to give "balanced" room for expression of "different sides" are using a lot of subjective opinions in their work.

- Citizens are socializing throughout the process, and their individual connections with the experts, facilitators, and one another are an important part of forming their opinions, which has nothing to do with subject matter.
- Perhaps most importantly, the CAs are meeting to focus on one problem. However, the issues we deal with are interconnected, and cannot be dealt with one at a time. Our society is complex, just like the human body. We both want to reduce our environmental footprint and at the same time enjoy energy intensive lifestyle and have to compete with other nations in terms of exports as well as race toward critical technologies shaping the future. You cannot make energy more expensive by simply placing high CO_2 tax, if at the same time your goal is to make your industries competitive with low cost of energy. We might recommend people to stay home during the epidemic, but that also creates mental health problems if we don't have the opportunity to be a part of our communities. Whether an individual or society, we cannot reduce complex issues into verticals to attack them. We must maintain a holistic picture.

The application of citizen assemblies carries some degree of political marketing and storytelling, due to the absence of binding decision power and politicians cherry picking recommendations they perhaps anyway would have gone forward with.

Yet, despite their shortcomings, CAs are an important effort in overcoming the political interests. Opening up citizen participation needs further studying and understanding.

DIGITAL CHANGEMAKERS FROM WIKILEAKS TO LIQUID DEMOCRACY

As the internet became the normal way to share information in the early 2000s, there was an expectation by early internet adopters that the future will be more idealistic, shaped by the free sharing of the internet. In 2004, a new conference was created in New York, called Personal Democracy Forum that brought together politicians, civic sector, and activists to explore how democracy was to be redefined in the age of the internet.

The conferences were idealistic, exciting, and hopeful. I've attended two of them, in Barcelona in 2009 and 2011. The discussions evolved around three tracks of digital governance innovations: transparency, execution, and legislation. Transparency came from innovations such as WikiLeaks, that would help increase transparency of the state. The execution track was about innovations like the Fix My Street platform, which would help governments get things prioritized and done. The last one about legislation, which I felt most drawn to, handled around making new legislation.

The early 2010s saw a number of digital initiatives starting to make dents into governance. These were special times: the financial crisis of 2008 was still deeply felt in European capitals, making people question their governments. Notably, WikiLeaks has released secret government documents that revealed not only the brutal truths about warfare, but also how apparatus of state acted in ways that most people could not see aligned with their values. A sense of transparency and change through the opportunities of the internet emerged.

On the legislation track of democratic innovations one of the initiatives that received global attention was the concept of Liquid Feedback. This was a software to facilitate the idea of Liquid Democracy. It combines the delegative and direct form of democracy, where one could vote themselves, and if they didn't, their vote would be represented by a pre-identified delegate. Liquid Feedback not only facilitated voting on proposals, but also the development of them. Anyone could start a proposal. All proposals could be voted on and could also be changed through change requests. Change requests also needed a majority to be accepted.

In Germany, in 2011 and 2012, PiratenPartei, who used Liquid Feedback for direct and binding party decisions received above 10% of the vote in the Berlin region, and also a high enough a share of votes in three other regions to place a representative in the regional parliaments. The party caught a lot of attention not only for the actual votes they received, but also for not having any other agenda besides being governed directly by its members and seeing itself as the pioneer for transitioning democracy into a digital form. It especially caught the attention of the younger generation, and in 2011 elections, it was reported that up to 30% of voters considered voting for the party. The promise of giving more direct power to citizens worked as an election strategy.

WikiLeaks and PiratenPartei coincided with the Occupy Movement. Starting in September 2011, there were Occupy protests going on in almost a thousand cities globally in more than 80 countries. Their prime concern? Disproportionate power of large corporations and global financial system controlling the financial benefits of capitalism. The origins of the Occupy Movement go back to UC Berkeley and other campuses in the University of California system. Students protested in 2009 through 2019 against tuition increase due to cutbacks, and the protests were joined by many of the faculty. Later, the movement took foothold in its known form in New York.

I found myself linked to these exciting developments. My professor, Robert Reich, secretary of labor under Clinton, a prominent economist and author of many books criticizing the neoliberal capital system has been a vocal supporter of the Occupy movement at UC Berkeley. Also, in that period I became friends with Julian Assange through the meetings at the Personal Democracy Forum, then later during his visits to Copenhagen during COP15. He was a well-praised figure for his work with WikiLeaks at this point, revealing tax avoiding Americans, and election fraud in Kenya, speaking at conferences around the globe about the importance of government transparency.

Finally, I visited the people behind Liquid Feedback and PiratenPartei in Berlin over a hackathon where we debated the features of the platform to make engagement even easier and more effective. I recall one day in 2011, on my way home to Copenhagen after a workshop, listening to Joshka Fischer, the cofounder of the German Green Party. In the interview following regional elections and success of the PiratenPartei, he said they were trying to do what he and his fellows tried 40 years before, reforming politics. Despite many of his party's voters considering a shift toward the pirates, he was in clear support of the movement, naming the digital era for democracy as the future. I found Mr. Fischer highly inspiring since I had met him in 2006 – an activist, taxi driver, and librarian turned into Europe's most popular politician ever, with above 90% approval ratings as Germany's minister of foreign affairs who had blocked the support of NATO for US wars in Iraq and Afghanistan.

This was clearly a special time, and a time for change. The events of early 2010s marked a time when social media was young, and digital tools were used for organizing the Arab Spring, the Gezi Movement in Turkey, Euromaidan in Ukraine, 15-M in Spain, Five Star in Italy, June Journeys in Brazil, and Clean Movement in Malaysia.

Unfortunately, looking back to this moment in history from where we are in 2024, the opening of that time seems to be lost without turning the momentum into real change. They did lead to real change in a few, such as Ukraine and Tunisia. Others were more disappointing, especially Syria's long civil war, and crackdown on freedoms in Hong Kong. In others the movements became a part of the political system and lost their radical edge to change the system.

A few other movements are worth mentioning, that were in the circles of the new democracy fueled by digital revolution.

In Spain, the protests under "Democracia Real YA!" (Real Democracy Now!) campaign turned into the 15-M Movement, as large groups took to streets on 15th of May in 2011. They were frustrated by the austerity measures, asked for more social justice and democratic participation. They were inspired by the similar campaigns around the world, and enabled by social media. The movement gave rise to a political party, Podemos, that promotes direct democracy, along with many other, far-left agenda points. Upon winning 15% of parliamentary seats in 2015, Podemos faced the reality of politics, and took a pragmatic approach and blended in. It took 1.5% of seats in 2023.

Podemos's story is not alone. Five Star in Italy and Alternatives in Denmark had similar aims and followed a similar path. In the case of the Piraten-Partei in Germany, they did not adapt to the system, but they also found it difficult to function with a direct decision model in the existing structure.

It seems difficult for political movements to join the system and change the way we govern. The system resists change.

Nevertheless, what came out of the movements in 2010s are some small steps that show recognition for better participation of citizens in legislation. Obama launched We The People platform, where he enabled more active listening to citizens, though its impact to actual policy is highly doubtful. The EU and countries like Denmark and Finland have created mechanisms for citizens to petition new laws, and to give feedback to the laws under legislative review. However, the impacts of these initiatives have been very limited as the political system did not see value in responding.

One story remains truly an inspiration for the future of direct democracy today, and that is Taiwan. Audrey Tang, who is considered a genius who started programming before she was eight years old, entered politics through Sunflower Student Movement in 2014. In 2016, she joined the cabinet as a minister for digital affairs and served again as Minister of Digital Affairs between 2022 and 2024. Her wish is to eventually see abolition of all states, and that technological advances are adopted for the benefit of humanity, somehow overcoming hierarchy.

She led popular projects such as "g0v," that created more accessible viewing of government websites, and the "vTaiwan," which is a petitioning platform. In contrast to Finland and Denmark where 50,000 citizens (about 1% of the population) has to digitally sign a petition for politicians to review their proposal, in vTaiwan, it took less than 5,000 citizens (0.03% of the population). Between 2015 and 2018, vTaiwan gained a lot of traction, and used it for developing legislation for 26 issue areas. In 80% of these, the platform resulted in "decisive government action." More than 200,000 citizens took part in vTaiwan over time (Horton, 2018).

Nevertheless, after the change of government in 2016, the political support for the platform declined. According to co-creator Jason Hsu, the platform did not contribute to major decisions beyond 2018. He believes lack of political support and binding decision power are to blame.

vTaiwan handled some pretty serious debates and had success in pushing through regulations for ride-sharing as well as for fintech companies. It has attracted a strong digitally savvy user base, and leverages Liquid Feedback principles. Over time, it opened for real life meetings in combination with those held online.

vTaiwan is a source of inspiration, although it did not have binding decision power. It showed inclusive and transparent decision-making can happen. Its main weaknesses have been ability to engage experts in ensuring the proposals live up to necessary standards. Further, its participation fluctuated a lot depending on the issues at hand, noting participation was not remunerated or financially incentivized in any way.

DAOs – DECENTRALIZED AUTONOMOUS ORGANIZATIONS

The internet revolution in the 1990s not only gave rise to tech companies. There was also another breed of tech enthusiasts who identified as activists and change makers who were highly idealistic and also highly capable.

Julian Assange, founder of WikiLeaks, Aaron Schwartz, cofounder of Reddit, CreativeCommons and OpenLibrary, and Peter Sunde, founder of Pirate Bay and Flattr, are examples of such people.

The digital native community with their idealistic leaders, open-source, and transparency ideals wanted to give rise to another system. With the rise of blockchain technology and Bitcoin, some of this community saw opportunities to build brand new institutions in the back of this technology.

Besides making a new breed of tech enthusiasts rich, Bitcoin also gave way to something else quite special: it created an institution without people to safeguard value. Unlike central banks, who decide when and how much to print money, Bitcoin has hard-coded, human and interpretation independent rules that create its internal economy. Further, it operates in full transparency as transactions can be traced on the blockchain. Bitcoin started to gain value as more people globally saw its promise. People trusted the institution based on a code, a system not bound by any individual judgements or bias, but fully transparent by design.

Bitcoin created unforeseen wealth for its holders; the currency is valued at a total of $1.4 trillion. Such value created a new breed of young technologists, who also see the boundaries for what is possible are far and wide and dream big. While many of them went on to create companies using blockchain technology, where governance is not a focal point and handled in a traditional way as a company does, some of them took interest especially on the governance aspect of their initiatives, embedding governance as a part of their digital platform.

They coined the term DAO, decentralized autonomous organization, which symbolizes that its members govern the organization through decentralized voting and automated smart contracts, eliminating any central authority. They want to see code, and not individuals that safeguard the rules and procedures of governance. Votes are "on-chain," indicating that they are not only digital, but also traceable, and unfalsifiable. They don't give much credit to in-person meetings, facilitated by other persons – all that we see with participatory budgeting and with citizen assemblies. In fact, there are people who work for DAOs without necessarily having met others they work with in real life or on camera.

DAOs aim to capture areas of the traditional economy with a decentralized institutional setup: GitcoinDAO enables funding of open-source software, AaveDAO provides a platform for lending and borrowing, DeSo (DecentralizedSocial) empowers a social media platform. By doing so, they would create more flat organizations and create public infrastructures that are natural monopolies, and work for public interest. Each DAO has a currency, similar to Bitcoin, which increases with the value they generate. For example, coins are issued with each content shared and commented on the DeSo platform, which in return approximates the value of the platform.

One of the key challenges in the communities is of course decision-making. Whether they are in the process of building the world's next banking infrastructure or the social media platform, a scalable governance model without central powers is essential to these organizations. As they build their platforms, they need to make many decisions to find out how they create value and develop their products. Currently, many of them rely on a small group of leadership in developing the concepts forward, along with large non-executive holders of their coins.

Governance of DAOs has revolved around the following strategies:

- Voting: community votes on proposals made based on coin holding. Typically, there is a deadline for such voting. Large coin holders (whales) define the direction of decisions, as small holders have not much staked and do not engage.
- Liquid voting: delegations are made possible and increases the overall representation of the community during the votes.
- Quadratic voting: aims to reduce the gap between large coin holders and smaller ones, where one's voting power is equal to the square

root of their coins. If A holds 1 coin, and B holds 4 coins, B will have twice the voting power.

- Holographic consensus: in order to prequalify which of the proposals are more important to vote on, there is a prediction market where people can predict likelihood of a positive vote. The job of predicting correctly is rewarded so engagement is financially incentivized. Research shows this method offers promising results (Faqir-Rhazoui et al., 2021).

DAOs struggle with creating platforms that would eventually become public infrastructure. Yet they need to use funding to develop these platforms, and people who initiate them expect to at least recover their investments, and thereby have a high stake in the decision-making process. Thus, instead of one-man one-vote principle, DAOs dedicate votes to the coin holding in some shape or form.

One of the well known figures in the community of DAOs, Vitalik Buterin, whose Etherium empowers many platforms, is highly active in the debate of DAO governance.

Coin voting governance empowers coin holders and coin holder interests at the expense of other parts of the community: protocol communities are made up of diverse constituencies that have many different values, visions and goals. Coin voting, however, only gives power to one constituency (coin holders, and especially wealthy ones), and leads to over-valuing the goal of making the coin price go up even if that involves harmful rent extraction. (vitalik.eth.limo, 2021)

Vitalik points out that future public infrastructure platforms cannot act like corporations as these organizations do not consider the interest of non-members, which is the large majority of users who the platform is eventually to serve.

In the meantime, DAOs remain an interesting space for learning for the evolution of governance and decision-making.

* * *

To sum up, we have had a lot of experiments in the space of public deci-sion-making in the past couple of decades. Each category has its unique culture and pitfalls:

- PB is heavy on time, mostly in real person, F2F, somewhat binding, but with small budgets.
- CA is non-binding, heavy on time, and skewed based on many opinions.
- Direct democracy parties had difficulties working with establishment, became either marginalized, or became mainstream like others.
- DAOs have ambitions to govern democratically, and struggle between running corporate style governance focusing on ownership versus inclusion of broader communities. They are nevertheless creating important learnings and data about direct and transparent governance.

Common pitfalls are that:

- Engagement is limited by simply offering people access to a decision-making platform. They do so for their personal gain.
- Requiring people to spend substantial time to engage leaves out many groups that simply do not have such time available, even if (somewhat) remunerated.
- Not having a binding decision process demotivates groups and initiatives.
- Politicians and people in power positions are usually not interested in letting go of power, by committing to making decisions binding. PB, where budgets are binding, tend to be a very small part of the total (<1%).

And in contrast, the following are the reasons to remain hopeful about a democracy revolution in the making:

- Large groups of voters from all social classes respond positively to the opportunity of having more influence over their governance and vote for parties that carry this promise.

- End-to-end processes can be established and carried out using modern digital technologies, bringing transparency that motivates stakeholders.
- People are motivated to engage with the ideal of creating something of public value and also something that provides them personally with individual benefits, and the combination of these two, whether the case with web3 companies or other impact companies, attracts top talent. Either one alone, creating only public value, or focusing only on filling your pockets, seems to lack sustained followership.

CHAPTER FOUR

THE STRUGGLE TO DELIVER PUBLIC GOODS

t is early 2017; Donkey Republic had around 1,000 bikes in Copenhagen for rental, and tourists seem to love them. My cofounder and I sat at a café with Niels, a local politician. He had led the city's procurement of a bike share service a few years earlier. That system was not doing well despite large public spending on it. And despite him being known for supporting cycling, Niels was not happy about the presence of our company.

Earlier in 2015, when we were experimenting with different business models with 100 bikes, we informed the city about our initiative and they told us informally we were fine, we could continue. We were world's first bike share to place bikes in public spaces that were rentable on a mobile app, and where a city was not paying to provide such service. No city before had to think about regulating a bike share service at this point. Over a meeting, some officials in Copenhagen city unofficially said we were fine.

But now, with a few more bikes and our innovative service turning out to be quite popular, we started to realize creating a positive impact and innovating for public benefit did not mean we could expect support. The café is inside the city's new theater, overseeing the beautiful canal. We are rather informally dressed, whereas Niels is in his white-collared shirt, looking smart. Besides being the chairman of the official city bike-share, he held another politically appointed position at the theater. He tells us briefly the intentions behind Bycyklen, and we all agree that the idea of having a bike share made affordable through public funding is a great idea given it would move people away from cars and to using public transport and bikes for the last mile. We agree that bike sharing should be considered public transport. I compliment Niels for his time at UC Berkeley, where he did a semester of exchange in the business school. I told him I did my masters there, in the policy school. Now he's holding the public office, and I am the entrepreneur.

Niels tells us that he doesn't think we should be allowed to run a private bike share service in Copenhagen. I ask for the reason. He says companies are profit seeking, and hence they will never make as good a service as the publicly owned alternatives, who are, instead, seeking the public benefit.

This conversation remains with me as one of the great ideological barriers in front of reforming government. As I will also point out later with a critique of our approach to assessing companies' impacts, governments tend to see profit seeking and market dynamics mainly as agents of *only* potential negative impact instead of enablers of experimentation and innovation and partners in delivering public services. The result is that our public services are organized top-down, centrally, not utilizing the dynamism of markets.

The review of democratic process so far focused on the legislative process, including budgetary decisions. What we also expect from our democracies is to somehow create public goods, executing their budgets, from collecting our trash, to taking care of us at the hospital.

How are governments doing on the execution front? Can we come up with more exciting visions of how we can reform delivery of public goods using markets and data? I believe so.

It seems that top-down decision-making in the public sphere, even with lots of money behind it, cannot match the iterative, data-driven learning process of companies when it comes to providing effective services. And this is a problem for our societies as we need to find effective ways to deliver public goods if we view companies only as trouble makers.

Public authorities have made allocation of responsibilities in terms of which level of activity is carried at which level of government: in Europe, schools are a part of city governments, so are social services, including unemployment support. Regional governments are often responsible for hospitals, and the central government for the police force and judicial system. The EU has taken on some federal responsibilities as well in the past few decades, such as funding for research and development.

In the United States, the allocation of resources to public goods is somewhat different with the states taking on important functions. The education system with primary and secondary education (elementary, middle, and high school) as well as public and community colleges are financed mostly by the state governments. States are responsible for the road, water, and sewage infrastructure. Both cities and states have their police force, cities also run public transit, parks, and social services. The federal government provides social security and Medicare and runs the military.

In order to provide public goods, we have a few options: we employ people at public institutions, and we also contract out work to private companies as contractors, and, we create price mechanisms to change incentives in the market, where certain products and services are subsidized.

Delivering public services through public institutions is the most classic way we create public goods. Many teachers, doctors, nurses, and social workers are hired directly by state authorities in many countries in Europe and the United Kingdom. They used to be the only alternative until we started providing private sector alternatives to them in the 1980s. Others are hired by publicly owned companies, many of them delivering services for public authorities from public transport to water management, and trash collection.

Public procurement accounts for about 13% of GDP, and about one-third of our public budgets including transfers. Examples of public procurement include NASA's contract with SpaceX for putting shuttles into space, the National Security Agency purchasing of Palantir's intelligence (spying) software, and New York City's shared bike service.

Besides contracting out a specific good or service, public authorities can "subsidize," a.k.a. provide public financing for a good or service, such as rebates on ebikes to make them more attractive over cars, and subsidies going into fossil fuel. Theoretically, such subsidies are in place as a result of government assessment that the good or service is contributing to desirable public goods.

HOW DID WE GET HERE?

Until the nineteenth century, many of the functions of state such as education and healthcare were in the control of charitable institutions such as monasteries. They had taken on the role of education in especially Catholic Europe, and also in the United States. Medieval hospitals in Europe had a broad social function providing refuge for all who needed it, be it the sick, the poor, or pilgrims. Care for elderly was also provided in the form of very basic collective housing with elderly men and women based on charity of the rich facilitated by the church. The church also facilitated care for orphaned children. The church dependence on (voluntary) charities from the rich was a major limitation, as well as social stigma of being in need of such care institutions.

The main function of the state was really to maintain law and order, and to protect all against external threats. It also provided for roads and infrastructure. However, the role of the state in social affairs was highly limited, and its relation with the church evolved over time, eventually gaining more control over the church.

By the start of the nineteenth century, with the start of the Industrial Revolution and growing cities, functions of the church started to turn into the state. Both in Europe and the US schools started to being funded publicly and not bound the religious curriculum. Public health also started to become a domain of the state in nineteenth century, also fueled by the scientific progress and development of medicinal fields.

Yet it wasn't until the end of the First World War that the state functions became formalized to cover much of what we know today. In fact, it was the time between the end of the First World War and the early 1970s that saw much of the development of the state's ability to regulate and execute on public goods. In the pocket of this half century, the state has taken the shape it has now in terms of its regulatory and delivery capacities that make up the executive function.

The New Deal Era following the Great Depression in 1930s introduced a number of public programs and expansion of the state role, known as the New Deal. It established social security for the elderly and unemployed, subsidies for farm products and industry, and regulation of the banking system. An important focus of the New Deal was to avoid concentrations of power. According to Matt Stoller, an author with a focus on monopolies in the United States, the democrats in the New Deal Era through 1972 made a great push to build public institutions to keep checks and balances over corporate power. In that era, the inequality in the United States saw significant lows, below a Gini of 35%, which is now above 45%, and the top 1% was taking home 10% of the nation's income; this now stands at above 20%. Annual income beyond $200k – which corresponds to around $1.8m adjusted for inflation today – in early 1960s was taxed at the rate of whopping 91% (Tax Policy Center, 2023).

Not only was the government providing service for the poor and the needy, but the New Deal Era also made a great deal of investments in science and technology. These investments not only helped grow the economy, but also to win the Second World War, and to win the Cold War. They are very important because they prove that the government (perhaps together with the private sector) can be a leading force in growing the economy through fueling technological advancements – a concept we seem to expect only from the private sector today.

Some of the noteworthy government-led technological advancements in the 40 years ending in the 1970s varied from the Tennessee Valley Authority (TVA) that invested in modern agriculture and energy, to the Manhattan Project, that brought top minds to push through cutting edge scientific research in nuclear technology. Such projects showcased a model that brought together government, academia, and the private sector.

Investments into science research and R&D by US federal government agencies took off in the 1960s and continue today. The agencies contracting research projects include the National Science Foundation (NSF) and the Defense Advanced Research Projects Agency (DARPA) and NASA. At their peak, the investments made into R&D totaled about 2% of US GDP, and total about $1tn in today's dollars.

This ambitious state building came to an end in 1970s. The strong development of state functions from environmental to banking regulations, and services covering healthcare and elderly care have come to a halt, and have been at a standstill in the 1980s until the present day. The institutions around such state functions have been stigmatized as old fashioned, anti-growth, and a resort of the poor. Working for the government functions has lost its appeal.

Instead, the past 40 years, state functions can be best described as "stable" and in many ways, have lost their influence on the economy. Instead, the past 40 years have seen a new ideology play out, compared to the 40 years prior, the 1930s through to the 1970s: the Keynesian economics was the guide that gave an important role to the state in leading the economy with its decisions and spending as and when needed. In the 1970s, the Chicago school asserted its influence with neo-liberal capitalist ideas, where "free markets" were introduced as the way to achieve growth and prosperity. The trickle-down economics that had gone out of fashion following the Big Depression made a comeback with Reagan. According to this idea, lower taxes on wealthy and business would stimulate investment and growth, and ultimately benefit everyone. This idea has been long contested (Longley, 2021).

Matt Stoller gives a short yet crucial insight into how power shifted toward big business in the 1970s (Stoller, 2016). It was the baby boomers with a focus on social liberties on gender and racial equality who did not perceive the big business as a threat. This young generation of democrats such as Bill Clinton were a breakaway from the older ones such as Wright Patman, whose political career was successfully spent making sure the wealthiest and the big businesses were kept on a leash. The young democrats became best friends with corporate America and stopped worrying about regulation unless the business wanted it.

In Europe, for the most part, state building and free-market ideologies followed their American counterparts. Europeans maintained a higher level of welfare services and a higher level of taxes but adopted the American free-market principles and also reduced taxes on business and the wealthy. Nevertheless, Europeans did not let go of the state's role as the one setting the agenda for the markets until much later, and they still have a more assertive attitude. But its regulatory efforts to shape markets have also been correctly challenged for making life for businesses unnecessarily difficult. In an increasingly complex world, Europeans struggle to regulate markets effectively for the benefit of society while maintaining a dynamic and innovative economy.

FROM LEADING TO FIRE-FIGHTING

The past 40 years have largely made the government a reactionary force to put out fires instead of defining the future for the markets and economy. In this sense, Joe Biden's Inflation Reduction Act and its incentives for green transition marks a change with recent history but remains too small to change the trend.

In these decades, corporate power and growth and technology reshaped our world: everyone had a car, we invented the internet, and smartphones, and capabilities of companies appealing to consumers have sharply increased. Companies received access to unseen amounts of information and innovated ahead, and became highly influential in defining the way we live, and our values through their products, media and lobbying.

To get out of the way of business, governments have taken the strategy to reduce taxes overall. That meant in return an increase in government borrowing, a part of the budget going after debt repayments. In Europe, the United Kingdom, under Margaret Thatcher, became the champion of austerity. She led cuts in welfare and social spending in the 1980s and deregulated the financial sector in order to seek more friendly market conditions for companies. It also meant a strong rise in unemployment, and increase in inequality (Johnson and Stark, 1989; Ebrary.net, n.d.).

The race for attracting corporations is also a trend that continued. The recent examples of Amazon and Tesla moving their HQs to states and cities offering them more favorable conditions, and the preceding negotiations, are signs of how big business goes around catering deals for themselves. In Europe, Dublin is known for its corporate-friendly policies attracting tech companies to establish campuses to cater for services for the European market, whereas Portugal established super friendly income taxes to attract expat workers. The success of the latter came at the expense of the locals with a high cost of living.

Reducing government spending and austerity has the upside of generating business in the short term. In the long term, it may create a deficit in investment in welfare. Studies show investing in early childcare, for example, has very significant lifetime earnings at around 7–13% per annum (Heckmanequation.org, n.d) where the social return includes increased lifetime earnings, reduced cost of public services, and improved health outcomes. But not offering it may mean more friendly conditions for business, and seem beneficial in the short term. Ironically, the return on social investments compares favorably to many projects that the private sector could invest into, and higher than the average earnings on the stock market, yet the Americans and many other democracies are unable to make such favorable investments into their societies. That is a bug, not a feature of our democracies.

Getting fully out of the way has not been possible for governments. The stock market crash of 2008 and COVID-19 health pandemic were major events that made governments lead society. However, these events did not change the consensus view of the government, which is to ensure the status quo. Despite strong pressure for interventions to deal with climate change, we see governments struggle to make any significant promises and fail to act quickly to obtain public goals. They look at the business world to seek their lead and their job to fight fires.

THE MOVE TOWARD PRIVATIZATION

During the 1980s, under the rule of Margaret Thatcher, the United Kingdom led a series of government reforms under the name New Public Management (NPM). It was a project of the Conservative Party who promoted the idea of a small government. Before long, the ideas of NPM spread to become the mainstream tool for many Western governments, thanks to the political sentiment of the decade. NPM became incorporated into a US reform called the Government Performance and Results Act in 1993 during the Clinton presidency. Al Gore led the initiative National Partnership for Reinventing Government, to make it work better and cost less with emphasis on reducing bureaucracy, improving accountability and service quality. It implemented strategies to measure output to improve government efficiency.

Some of the key ideas behind NPM were to bring competition to the delivery of public services. Instead of treating the delivery of education and health services as the sole job of government, the approach was to open up opportunities for the private sector to provide the services, and get paid for it. This meant they have the choice of pursuing the public or the private service providers, hence the idea of competition. The contractual relationship between public authorities and delivering companies was then identified through some metrics.

The reason behind such public reform in the United Kingdom and the United States was, to a large extent, to cut costs. While introducing efficiency, critiques also bring up issues around accessibility and equity. That is, post-privatization of public services, companies delivering the service with the least cost, and this led to often reduced affordability or quality on the end of receivers.

However, absent the agenda for new public management, the public sector was perceived as rigid, and lacking innovation. There was little accountability and performance measurement, and little room to change anything. If the government was a company that had to compete, it probably would lose customers, but it was a monopoly. And the same thing happened to government that happens to monopolies: they tend to exploit their position over the rest, to their own benefit.

The benefits of privatization, introducing competition and linking metrics to public–private collaboration, has introduced efficiency and brought accountability. Especially in Scandinavian countries, the Netherlands and Germany, the principles were implemented not with the emphasis on austerity but on improving public services. They maintained relatively high quality standards and access, while introducing privatization and competition, and results of privatization are more favorable compared to those in the United Kingdom and United States.

I had the chance to observe how governments and companies collaborate, especially in the area of public transport. Governments buy from private sector companies the service of buses and trains servicing certain routes. The metrics in this kind of service agreement are established based on the availability of the transport: namely the routes to be covered, and timeline to be met. There are quality measures that ensure that the buses should be cleaned frequently. Nevertheless, fewer and fewer people are using public transport in Denmark. This is also the case for other cities in Europe and the United States.

Could the reason also have to do with the fact that the way we reward public transport contracts to authorities doesn't target the companies chasing the innovations that make more people want to ride them?

Jarrett Walker, a public transit consultant and author of several books, including *Human Transit*, thinks so. He believes public transport incentives put forward by cities focus on operational convenience and cost reduction, pretty much defining how the service is to be delivered, rather than focusing on outcomes such as rider satisfaction and ridership levels. Paul Barter is a researcher specializing in public transport systems, who also believes the focus on service coverage and frequency over rewarding for the ridership increase is a problem. It is a problem because once the operator wins the public contract, it doesn't have the incentive to really make riders happy. Is the bus too noisy? Or a bit too warm? Too bad – it's not a part of the contract.

RETHINKING PUBLIC PROCUREMENT

Much of our public funding is linked to contracts delivered to us through companies. This is increasingly the trend, as it brings scalability. When the public sector engages companies, it uses traditional procurement models that focus heavily on inputs rather than outcomes. That is, when governments buy services from companies to address social goals, contracts often specify the goods to be provided, and activities to be delivered, but not the actual results or impacts these services should achieve.

This emphasis on inputs – such as the number of hours worked, or the quantity of resources provided – ensures that companies meet the minimum requirements but often stifles innovation and creativity in finding more effective solutions.

One could say this is fine, as measuring outcomes is too hard anyway. Even so, we shall try: contracts focusing on inputs and not outcomes incentivize companies to find ways to deliver the contracts with minimum possible cost and disregard the social outcomes. This often means making their service less interesting from the perspective of its users.

To demonstrate what this means, imagine what an Uber ride would be like if it was a hypothetical publicly sponsored service. In this service, the drivers are now paid based on how many hours they were on the streets, with or without carrying passengers, and riders are not delivering any feedback.

In this service, drivers would not be incentivized to pick you up quickly or make your journey pleasant. When keeping a good score doesn't matter, rider experience will likely suffer, and with that, also the overall business.

When public money is spent on creating public goods, we place it based on applications for a call, and our forecasting for what good the project application will bring. This is the case for both tenders and for grants. In the case of grants, we tend to not define the service, and we try to estimate the goods we get from providing public money to the project. In the case of tenders, we do specify a service, and we also have an end to end idea how that service will create results.

Such focus on applications instead of results is problematic. Our models and view of the world are too simplistic compared to its complexity. If we instead rewarded companies by results we would delegate the problem of dealing with complexity to them. And this is where they can use data-driven iterations to achieve the innovations we need.

Another problem is that institutions favor applicants they like and trust. This doesn't necessarily equate to corruption but reflects biases that often lead to poor judgment in determining what truly matters. A company you've worked with as a partner for over a decade is preferable to a new one from a risk perspective, one could say. When we focus on buying inputs, our focus on the procurement side is to ensure the risk of not getting those inputs is minimized. This favors the old and large companies who have a reputation and are experts in the application process.

Adding to this, in an environment where we pick services based on whom we like, we might lose support for services that keep questioning those in power and hold them accountable. In Denmark, where public funding for media, especially radio, is crucial one radio channel that was popular was shut down because their application for a grant did not score very highly. Not surprisingly, they were highly critical of the government and exposed some of their mishandlings.

Contrast the focus on inputs with the approach seen in many successful private-sector contracts, where companies are rewarded based on the value they deliver. For instance, in the technology sector, businesses are increasingly paid for the results they generate measured in clear metrics, such as user conversions in marketing or product performance. This outcome-based approach aligns incentives, focusing on results rather than process, and it allows for continuous improvement and innovation as companies strive to achieve better outcomes.

This shift to outcome-oriented contracts is beginning to take hold in the public sector, but at a very slow pace, as I will cover in the next section.

Ultimately, the future of public service contracts should prioritize outcomes over inputs, enabling a more dynamic and innovative approach to solving societal challenges. Governments need to rethink how they engage with the private sector, moving away from rigid specifications and toward frameworks that reward the achievement of social goals.

EFFICIENT BUT NOT EFFECTIVE

There is something about capitalism, the decentralized market structure, that the efficient public sector lacks: effectiveness.

Efficiency is trying to do something with fewer resources by producing less waste, eliminating all non-required elements. For instance, if you want to make a supermarket increasingly efficient, you will pack the shelves more carefully, make sure the cashier is kept busy, and so on.

Effectiveness is different. Being effective can involve doing things in a completely different way to get to the outcome, and in the meantime, involves wasting resources in experimenting with methods that won't work in the end. Markets are effective, and not necessarily efficient. The way innovation happens usually involves many companies trying to find the best way to achieve certain outcomes, be it delivery of a search engine, a bike share, or groceries. Often companies that try something radically new do not achieve success. A general rule of thumb says about one out of 10 startups succeed.

In the meantime, the few businesses that combine the learnings in the best way will pave the path forward with a better business than before. In the case of supermarkets, the bigger innovations that change the landscape have been online orders, home deliveries, and cashierless checkout. These are strategies to be more effective.

As with legislation, also with service delivery, our governments are not designed to be effective. That would require willingness to take risks, and to experiment. It also requires rewards for entrepreneurial enterprise.

I find that people working in the public sector do not appreciate companies as they see them as profit seeking agents, which they are, who will do anything to make money, which they do. But looking at it from another perspective, companies are good at inventing ways to do things very differently to get to their goals. Markets are effective, bring creativity and competition to play that we simply cannot in a top-down hierarchy, nor ask some expensive management consultants to tell them how to do things. And if we figure out how we use the markets to the benefit of society, I believe we can have the best of both worlds, where the public sector defines the problems and creates proper incentives, and the private sector works on solving them.

In summary,

- Delivery of public service in past 40 years has undergone some changes.
- We moved away from top-down managed, politicized, and highly inefficient structures into delivery structures that are more decentralized, and organized around metrics that measure the inputs that go into public service delivery.
- Additionally, we made contracts with the private sector, to outsource the services to them.
- When doing so, we decided to pay them based on the activities they provide, essentially seeing the public services as "commodities," standard bits of services that are well-defined.
- This approach has the mindset of cost-minimizing and focuses on keeping the private sector margins rather tight while delivering highly defined public services.
- However, we also clogged any incentives and innovation on the side of companies delivering public goods by asking them to focus on the defined activity instead of the outcome.

BUYING GOODS FROM COMPANIES BASED ON OUTCOMES

By the 2000s, the UK government understood that the private sector can innovate fast and decided to let it help with social innovation. Seasoned investor, seen as father of venture capital in the United Kingdom, Sir Ronald Cohen, was then also wondering how companies could include social goals in their mission, while seeking to make a profit. Could there be a case where the private sector gets paid for fixing a social problem? And they get paid only when the problem is fixed?

Indeed, until now, the private sector has been paid for delivering specific services, but not to solve problems. Much of government-led innovation has been in the form of grants, focusing on the research, and not on the delivery of products and services that fix a problem. If the basis of a contract is a social outcome, we no longer need to define the solution, which has been the basis of public contracts. And we leave it up to companies to figure out those solutions. They can then be paid in the future, once they show delivery of the results.

This was the premise of the concept of a *social impact bond (SIB)* (Figure 4.1). The concept was invented in 2009 by the company Ronald Cohen created, and Toby Eccles led, with the name Social Finance, based

Figure 4.1   Visualization of a Social Impact Bond.

Source: Rania et al., 2020 / MDPI / https://www.mdpi.com/2071-1050/12/9/3854, last accessed on 14 December 2024/CC BY 4.0.

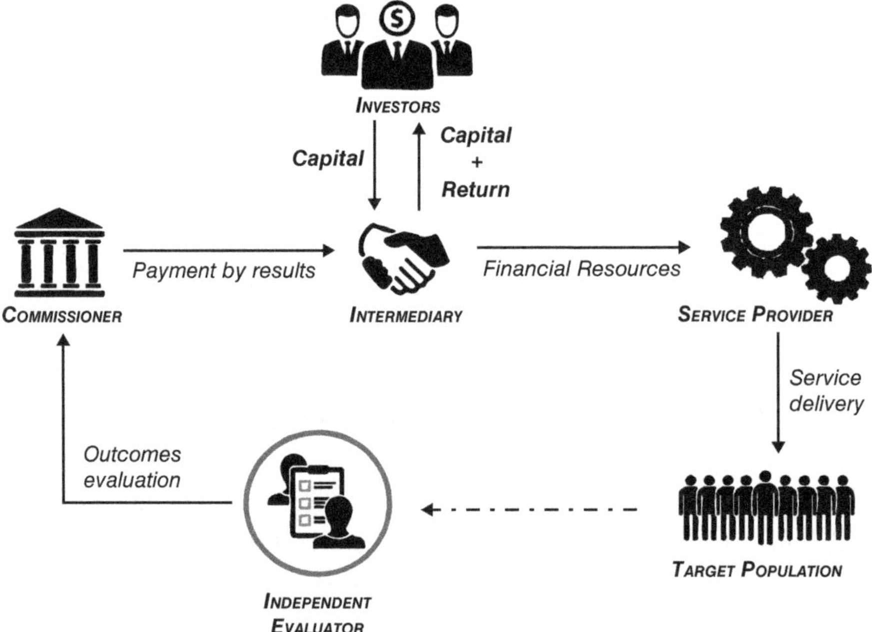

in London. Since a SIB needed to fund activities to deliver services before the service delivery organizations get paid for their outcomes, it needed to have external financing to enable the projects. The name of the "bond" of this construct is derived from payout to investors conditional on the success of the project.

After many months of discussions and negotiations, the first SIB was established in Peterborough, United Kingdom, in order to reduce the re-offending rate of ex-prisoners. At that time approximately 60% of the short-term prisoners were re-offending within a year after release (Social Finance UK, n.d.), and, the social cost of ex-offenders re-offending is very large, especially when considering the scenario where they instead would be productive members of society. Toby's team led an effort to calculate the financial impact on the government to understand if one fewer prisoner were to go back to prison. That amount then establishes a basis for the government's potential payment to Social Finance.

Social Finance also met with cutting edge social service providers, to discuss options, and they set out a plan to engage the prisoners through a set of tailored programs that would increase the chances that they would integrate back into life outside successfully. The set of initiatives that were planned were at first adjusted every few months based on how the services fared. Remember the data-drive that enabled Donkey Republic with company decisions? That is simply the same logic at play here. Social Finance engaged each prisoner in a program and kept adjusting the programs to find out how each individual responded to each initiative. They measured metrics such as self-reported well-being and attendance to various programs. They updated the initiatives and service providers to try out what may perform better. As a result, the project has reduced reoffending by 9% compared to other similar ex-prisoners (Social Finance UK, n.d.).

Note again the contrast between this approach and how public procurement works. Normally, a service provider would be paid to carry out certain specific tasks, such as training programs, and are paid for doing so independent of final outcomes. The service providers are competing with one another to give the lowest bid, and in turn, to remain profitable, they cut costs with everything they can. The result is often a supplier that is receiving government pay and delivers suboptimal outcomes, because what we ask them to do is to focus on fulfilling the defined input with least possible cost, and not to focus on the outcomes.

Companies are reliably logical. They focus on financial performance. They have to. If they don't, another company can do that and replace them. With this lens in mind, we need to understand companies can innovate but they need to remain focused on their bottom line. With that, it becomes clear that it is the job of the government to incentivize companies sufficiently to focus on creating desirable social outcomes.

The SIB concept got a lot of attention, and many SIBs have been created since. Up to the end of 2023, around 230 SIBs have been launched. Project sizes vary a lot, from a few hundred thousand USD to the largest ones worth $10 million. The total amount for SIBs is estimated at $0.5 billion. Table 4.1 shows the largest 10 SIBs, and their success rate.

Despite their general success, SIBs have not scaled much in the past decade. They make up only a tiny fraction of overall governmental

Table 4.1   Largest 10 social impact bonds.
Note that typical success threshold for a social impact bonds to recover its cost of activities is around 75%. All in the list except the one in New York City have recovered their costs, in other words, met the minimum success threshold.

Start Year	City	Focused Social Area	Duration	Budget ($)	Success	Source
2010	Peterborough	Reducing reoffending	6 years	$8 million	100%	UK Government
2017	Massachusetts	Youth recidivism reduction	5 years	$12 million	99%	Massachusetts State
2015	London	Homelessness prevention	3 years	$7 million	90%	UK Government
2012	New York City	Reducing recidivism	4 years	$9.6 million	47%	Harvard Kennedy School
2013	Utah	Early childhood education	5 years	$7 million	95%	Gates Foundation
2018	Adelaide	Homelessness prevention	3 years	$7.3 million	86%	South Australian Government
2016	Toronto	Employment for marginalized youth	4 years	$2.6 million	85%	SocialFinance
2020	Tokyo	Employment for the disabled	4 years	$3.2 million	80%	Japan Times
2017	Chicago	Early childhood education	5 years	$16.9 million	76%	Chicago Public Schools
2015	Sydney	Child protection and family support	5 years	$30 million	85%	NSW Government

contracting. Some of the key challenges of the SIB approach have been longevity of outcomes versus cost of funding and complexity of making the deal.

Many social issues have large, but long-term outcomes. While prevention is by far the most cost-efficient way to handle the issues, if one needs to deploy private capital to finance the projects, then investors expect market returns, and over a long period of time cost of capital makes projects less attractive for investors. This creates a dilemma as the future costs of not acting will be even higher.

Also, the way SIBs are structured calls for a data collection and analysis framework to be established for each project. Such administration costs easily create too much overhead for projects to be financially viable.

PRICING WHAT MATTERS

The idea that governments use pricing to reach goals is not new. In the world of policy making we have a wealth of experiences with how prices can change behavior. That is true for individuals, and even more so, for companies. Individuals are not as rational as companies, but still they respond to prices quite strongly, except for some edge cases.[1]

Extra taxes are placed on things we want less of collectively, and tax-rebates, and even subsidies, are placed on things we want more of. Alcohol is taxed heavily in many countries, and so are cigarettes. Government subsidies are commonplace for public transport, various agriculture products, for oil and gas extraction, and more recently for electric vehicles, heat pumps and solar cells.

In a way, a tax rebate or a subsidy for a product is similar to public buying of goods and services. At the end it is the government paying for things in order to achieve more public goods. The government's role as market maker – managing the levels of supply and demand by intervening with the prices – is very similar to government's role as the provider of public goods. And it turns out to be a very effective way of adjusting and aligning markets to act in the direction of public benefit (Tables 4.2 and 4.3).

We know price mechanisms are quite powerful in changing behavior and making transformations happen. The WHO reports that for every 10% increase of tobacco prices, the consumption drops by about 5% (WHO, 2023b). Large protests are held if subsidies for gas or agricultural products are removed, because everyone knows it's a hit to their industry.

Essentially, the reason for taxes and subsidies is to indicate the price of the externalities (Figure 4.2). If you take a ride-hail, you get a service of moving from A to B, and thus you pay for the value to the driver and car owner, and Uber. But actually, you are also stealing value from society. The steal is in the form of space the car takes away from everyone else (untaxed unless there are congestion charges), additional waiting time added for others in cars in congestion, health-related costs (accidents, particle emission related health issues – and yes, EVs also emit a large amount

Table 4.2   Examples of goods and services with extra taxes in various countries.

Country	Cars (% of sales price)	Alcohol (% of sales price)	Gasoline (% of sales price)	Tobacco (% of sales price)	Sugar (% of sales price)
USA	Varies by state (up to 10%)	40% (spirits)	13-22% (fuel excise + state taxes)	Federal + state: 25-35%	Up to 15% in cities with sugar taxes
UK	10-15% depending on emissions	57% (spirits)	33% (fuel duty + VAT)	46%	12-16% (soft drinks levy)
Denmark	Up to 150% based on emissions	75%	42%	65%	20%
Germany	15-20% based on emissions	65%	36% (excise + VAT)	47%	No tax
Holland	20-25% based on emissions	81%	45% (excise + VAT)	64%	12%
France	Up to 50% for high emissions	45%	37%	70%	12%

Table 4.3 Examples of goods and services that are being supported by the government.

Country	Public Transport (% of Value)	Wheat (% of Value)	Oil & Gas Extraction (% of Value)	Electric Vehicles (% of Value)	Heat Pumps (% of Value)	Solar Cells (% of Value)
USA	Tax breaks at state/local levels (10-15%)	Varies by state, typically 10-15% of production value	5-10% in the form of tax breaks and incentives	Up to 15% federal tax credit + state-level rebates (10-25%)	Federal tax credits up to 30%	Federal tax credits up to 30%
UK	0% VAT on public transport (full rebate)	~15% of production value	10-15% through tax relief and investment incentives	Grants up to 35% of EV value (max £2,500)	Grants up to 30-35%	Up to 25-30% of system cost (via grants)
Denmark	25% VAT on public transport, no rebate	~10% of production value	5-8% in indirect tax relief	Registration tax rebate of up to 20-25% on EVs	Subsidies up to 25%	Subsidies up to 25-30%
Germany	7% reduced VAT on public transport (~13% rebate)	~12% of production value	8-10% through tax incentives	Subsidies up to 30-35% of EV cost	Grants and rebates up to 25-30%	Grants up to 30% for residential and commercial systems
Holland	9% reduced VAT on public transport (~16% rebate)	~12% of production value	8-10% through tax incentives	Subsidies up to 25-30% for EVs	Up to 20-25% rebate on heat pumps	Up to 30% subsidy on solar cells
France	10% reduced VAT on public transport (~14% rebate)	10-12% of production value	8-10% through various tax breaks	Up to 30% subsidy on EV purchases	Subsidies up to 35%	Up to 25-30% of system cost (grants and incentives)

Figure 4.2 A transaction between a business and a consumer almost always has forms of side-effects that improve or worsen the state of public goods.

These side-effects are called "externalities" as they are not accounted for in the transaction.

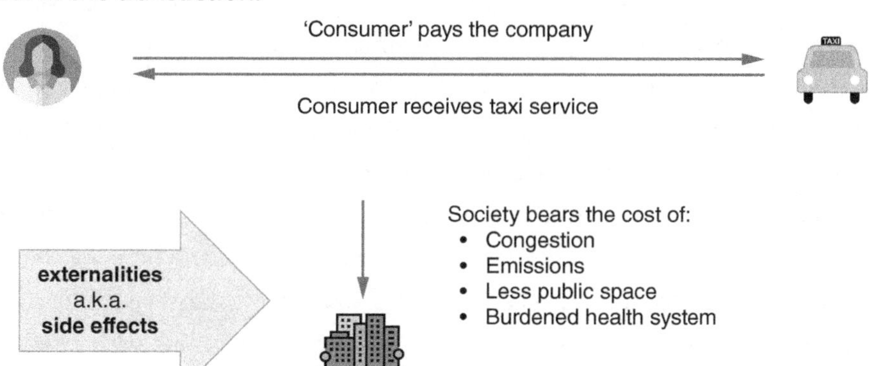

of particles), and cost in global warming even if the grid is green, there are still a lot of emissions involved in producing the electric vehicle, and maintaining the roads.

If you bike instead of using the car, research shows that increased physical activity will bring around $3 of health benefits to society per trip (Garrett, 2018). The health benefits stem from the decreased chance of developing chronic diseases (including cancer) due to moderate activity. No one pays you to bike the 3 km, yet, if you do that instead of taking the metro or car, you are creating a social benefit. You are offering a gift to others. That is a positive externality and governments are aware that physical inactivity is costly in the long term.

Importantly, price interventions do not limit our freedoms in an absolute sense. Instead, they align our individual preferences with those of our collective. If the utility of the tobacco consumer is so high that they are willing to pay for the negative impacts on society, they can do so by paying a high price for the product.

Even though we know the impacts of many goods and services on our collective properties, we are not using taxes and subsidies in modern ways, leveraging data. It seems we have abandoned applying those mechanisms as historic market interventions that are no longer needed.

I believe the future of public service delivery is at the cross-section of using price incentives and using the learnings from outcome-based procurement. Merging these two, we can essentially create markets for public goods, defined by various metrics, be it physical activity, or accuracy of facts, and reward goods and services that improve them, and penalize goods and services that go against them. Using these principles, we can create everything from the future for transportation to the future of media and housing.

We often have public discussions about small versus large governments. Solving the issues by simply increasing government spending with existing methods won't work. If governments keep repeating ineffective methods to put out the fires, while markets continue exploiting public goods with their vast externalities from chemicals in the land to mental harm caused by digital platforms, we will not be able to keep up. Our quality of life will struggle, affected by environmental and social pressures.

Now is a good time to awaken the citizen and see how we can adopt modern governance methods for a better future.

BEYOND ESG AND CSRD

ESG is a financial framework that stands for Environmental, Social, and Governance. It refers to a set of criteria used to evaluate a company's impact on the environment, its social responsibility, and the quality of its governance. These factors are used by investors to assess the sustainability and ethical impact of an investment in a company or business. One might argue that companies with positive externalities will have a high ESG score, and therefore will receive a significant bonus from conducting such impactful business. Despite its good intentions, the mechanism is far from being effective. Let me explain.

At Donkey Republic bike share, we have strong evidence for how much we have moved car trips and trips in buses toward bikes. Each of those trips has substantial social gains, mainly driven by increase in physical activity, then also reduction in congestion and taking up less public space by cars. Research suggests that the impact of an otherwise physically inactive trip, taken on a Donkey bike (not electrified) would gain society to the tune of $3 per trip for reducing development of chronic diseases and related health and care costs as well as preventing loss of future earnings. This figure is about double the amount that the company charges for an average trip.

Yet, Donkey Republic does not get any of that (social and environmental) value created. And even though the company is seen as a strong ESG case this does not turn into any substantial financial value. Studies show that ESG companies can expect 1% lower cost in debt financing, which is the main financial impact on the business. That is equivalent to less than 1% impact on the company's revenues. Thus, in summary, a company like Donkey Republic, whose rider revenues have an external value of 200% to society, receives less than 1% upside from being an ESG case.

ESG ratings in essence are about "reducing risks" in production, and not about measuring a product or services' overall impact out in the world (Bartels, 2022). Further, as S&P analysts argue, companies with little in the way of operations (such as software companies, or consultancy services) can obtain ESG certifications rather easily, while such certification does not assess the impact that these services have (Marsh and Robinson, 2021). A software company can run on green energy, pay handsome salaries to its staff, yet it might be a game-fueling addiction, or a media outlet creating misinformation. With ESG, the impact assessments are shallow, and rewards limited, creating little reason for companies to rethink their business models.

CSRD, Corporate Social Responsibility Directive, which entered law in the European Union in 2023 is not very far from the ESG scoring, while promising to be more impactful in terms of financial impacts. Defining broad scopes, CSRD aims to bring reporting requirements for an estimated 50,000 companies across Europe. Companies will need to disclose their impacts not only on carbon emissions, but also other environmental impacts (i.e. biodiversity) and social factors such as employee rights. It introduces a new requirement for companies to report not only financial risks, but also risks on how the business activities may negatively impact people and environment.

I find CSRD an attempt to internalize externalities, and that it is created with great intentions. While trying to deal with this very necessary problem, I think it is missing out on some really important points.

Need for focus on rewards, beyond risks and harm: In its essence, CSRD is a risk-based analysis similar to ESG reporting, instead of a holistic impact assessment. CSRD is creating potential fines for businesses due to their harm to society and environment, but it is falling short of giving weight to their positive impacts. Therefore, CSRD makes businesses "apologetic" by only using a language of risks to society and environment, positioning them as the enemy of both. This is dangerous as businesses can and must become partners in creating public goods. Instead of only threatening companies with sticks, we should offer them carrots for the positive impacts they achieve.

Lack of financial consequences: it assumes businesses would make serious efforts in changing core business practices due to disclosures without any prices attached to such practices. Currently, there are no financial consequences of reporting impacts that are harmful, and it is unclear if and how they will carry any financial value.

Impact assessment is not the job of businesses or accounting firms: businesses are required to make their own impact reporting, together with accounting firms who will approve their reports. Though there are some standards emerging, much of the impact attribution of CSRD is too simplistic, and the evaluation of CSRD does not have access to the kind of social and environmental data to even attempt to make a proper impact evaluation, considering not only first but nth order effects. The practice also puts unrealistic pressure on accounting firms, who are supposed to take an objective view when guiding businesses in a highly subjective assessment. It is public authorities who have the social and environmental data to make impact analysis. Such data are key to utilize in mapping products' and services' impacts on us. Therefore, we shall see the job of impact assessment belongs to public authorities, not to companies.

Limitations of factors to be reported: many key social and environmental factors are not part of CSRD reporting, from physical health, mental health, or loneliness to media misinformation, growing wealth inequality, or making a nation economically more competitive as mentioned in Draghi's recent report to the EU. Factors included in CSRD are static, and to a large extent de-linked from what people care about in a specific jurisdiction. People have no say on what these factors should be, or the financial pricing of these factors.

ESG and CSRD are frameworks primarily interested in the supply and operations of how products and services are created. They are not appropriate designs for accounting for the impacts of those goods and services on society and environment. "Do no (or less) harm" in production is a good principle. But it is a far from a holistic approach that turns also rewards businesses for creating positive outcomes, and hence truly creates a pull for businesses to change course.

Instead, what we need is a dynamic, iterative price setting of externalities, and linking them to companies' products and services. The attribution job requires a great deal of data analysis, including social data only available to our states. We should put resources behind such data exercises as we do with national security, where complex data reporting tools like Palantir provide services for security agencies. I fear ESG and CSRD risk creating backlash for the administrative burdens in exchange for little financial or social impact.

CHAPTER FIVE

MERIT DEMOCRACY: THE WAY FORWARD

I was having a jog in Washington DC, in the golden triangle. It was summer of 2007, a hot day. One could run past many jazz bands from New Orleans that made DC their new, perhaps temporary, home, due to Katrina hurricane. It was my first month living there, and I was crashing at my friend's place, who was a consultant at TechnoServe, a not-for-profit organization supporting international development, where I had also worked on a couple of projects overseas.

I was working for the World Bank's microfinance initiative and had just finished my degree in public policy. I was dropping in at various talks at Brookings Institute and Johns Hopkins University, experiencing some of the most influential discussions from the upcoming financial crisis and US economy, to international development, and the rise of China to power. Feeling the power of the city, I was inspired not only by what these discussions meant for the United States, but for humanity.

What I had been studying and learning at Berkeley was resonating in my head. And looking around on my jog, I could once again see the contrast of what we knew and what we were able to implement as public policy. The reality of the streets struck me with homelessness, obesity, aggression and congestion. The dream society I imagined involved many different policies than the reality.

And then it happened, the heat of the moment could not make my clarity go away. I saw the contrast between what was studied and known to be beneficial to the public versus what was the outcome of the political process between those glorious buildings surrounding the golden triangle. Despite their glory, I realized they were not delivering what was needed and change to governance had to happen.

Having seen glimpses of the tech hype in the West Coast Bay Area, I sensed the two coasts will need to collaborate: we must innovate how we govern, using data and markets. In order to look at the possibilities for a new democracy, we need new lenses. Time has since confirmed my hunch that day and added perspectives to it. I tried running a direct democracy platform as a startup, and worked on structuring social impact bonds, later trying to run an impact business, Donkey Republic bike share.

At the end of 2018, I wrote the first draft of this book. Only six years later I thankfully could focus my time and energy on finishing it. In those six years, the vision for what could be a new government only became clearer. That is thanks to the events that took place in the world, the thinkers I had access to, and my own experiences especially interacting with public institutions.

I call this vision for a future governance model Merit Democracy. It is a vision for a strong democracy taking care of our collective. It is built on data and markets, thus decentralized and transparent. It aims to quantify and value everything we care about in our collective sphere and links our decisions and economy to see how we improve or worsen those things we care about.

* * *

Yet, my main message in this book is not that we shall implement Merit Democracy. It is that we must innovate governance technology and we need new visions. We must not be constrained by ideological thinking, or dogma and explore new, inspiring territory. In that sense, Merit Democracy is laid out to inspire.

Inspiration and aspiration are incredibly important in order to unite us and create hope over fear to bring us together in a conversation. The conversation needs to start with the understanding that our tools are out of date, and doing so without pointing fingers. Sure, various people have tried to take advantage of their status and position, exploiting the old tools, the system they found themselves in.

I can feel the anger when I think of numerous instances of interactions with political figures and public officials as well as impact-promoting investment managers, and greenwashing companies. The anger is highly valuable, it gives us the fuel to deal with difficulties. It tells us some things are worth fighting for. When we translate our anger to bring about change, we have two options: We can dig deeper into a blame game where we focus on the individuals, or we can stay at the systems level thinking, and look ahead for what is possible, new and desirable.

In Chapter 1, I argued for the four metrics that would measure the quality of a democracy: quality of policies, pace of decision-making, transparency, and agency. My hypothesis is that the system I will describe as Merit Democracy would improve democracy in those dimensions.

The actual performance of any proposed democratic process will be subject to experimentation and learnings, and we will always need to align and improve what we thought was true based on what we learned. This is true for any constitution, no matter what the authors imagined, as it is for me promoting a new system.

The future will not be one where an old idea wins against another old idea. It is not about socialism against capitalism or left versus right. Defining the future requires leaving behind such labels and reconstructing a language and approach that defines what is of value. The future also belongs to those that respect the superiority of scientific, experimental knowledge over information that is personal, subjective, or dogmatic and hence unquestionable.

With this in mind, I will now move onto listing principles of Merit Democracy in the rest of this chapter. My aim is to give you a good sense of the ideas that shape the design I suggest. Thereafter, I will continue with the mechanics of Merit Democracy.

HOLDING OURSELVES ACCOUNTABLE

"The price of greatness is responsibility."
—Winston Churchill

Our future democracy must be based on **merit** and **accountability**. This is perhaps the most important point: creating value for society needs to have implications for the individual, aligning the interest of the collective and the person. Our current democracy has too vague a link between creating public value with individual value. Our politicians have a lot of power in their hands, but little accountability. That is, we don't have proper mechanisms for either measuring, or rewarding or punishing people who are adding or removing value from public space.

We need a system where everyone can easily participate in the legislative process and get rewards for participation that creates value. It means if you are able to engage in policy making and contribute to making society better off in its declared metrics, then you shall gain from it, just like someone investing in a company from the convenience of their home after work.

Similarly, we need a system where all companies are easily evaluated with regards to their ability to deliver public goods. Any company shall be able to join creation of public value – that is execution – and obtain rewards for how they created a better society.

The idea of merit readily captures in itself the ideas of measuring and acknowledging value and rewarding thereof.

Accountability means the obligation of individuals and organizations to account for their activities and accept responsibility for them. While merit implies a positive feedback loop, accountability is often used in the sense of a negative loop. Where there is proper accountability, taking decisions that negatively impact public life would need to have negative consequences. The minimum should be reducing the person's influence in future public decisions. The damage signals what is to come.

Similarly, in a society with proper accountability, a company that creates negative public outcomes would be instructed to deal with the burden. That only makes sense, as such accountability would shift the company to revise its business model in order to create fewer negative outcomes, and more positive ones.

Reflect on the fact that Meta platforms understood well their impact on youth mental health, as Frances Haugen has disclosed, widely known as "Facebook papers" (Socialmediavictims.org, 2024) These papers showed that the company knew that it had negatively impacted the mental state of their users, including creating anxiety and depression, body damage, sleep disruption, and cyberbullying. In a world where the companies' impact on things such as healthy social interactions is not measured and turned into appropriate costs to the business we cannot say accountability exists. Meta continues to sell our attention time without focus on our mental health. It is not their fault, it is our fault for not governing it correctly.

The point here is not to blame Meta at all. The point is that all companies operate in similar conditions and environments. They need to maximize profits and they will do so within the framework they operate. Want them to act differently? Change the framework they operate in and reward them differently.

On the point of accountability, similarly consider the accountability of politicians. Consider the gap between promises and reality, and the impact of that reality on the politicians' credibility. The link between promises and reality simply does not exist. Imagine the promise of Brexit and the reality of it. Brexit had promised the Englishmen great economic impacts, and trade deals. The economic impacts have not materialized; the country now deals with a lot of additional bureaucracy to trade with the European Union. It also failed to create more advantageous trade deals with other countries. But how has that affected the decision-makers behind Brexit? What have they suffered as a consequence?

Not much. In fact, despite the large gain in seats for the Labour Party in the UK parliament, the elections in 2024 showed strong gains for the far-right, who have been adamant in supporting the Brexit. Imagine if a company collected a large amount of capital with a promise of pursuing a business, and then completely fails. Would it be able to raise more money from those investors? No it couldn't. The reason we don't have this mechanism working in politics is because we don't have the "accounting system" in public KPIs that link public decisions to such metrics. Had we done so, we would be much clearer in knowing which policy-makers know what they are talking about, versus those spreading harmful beliefs.

EXPERIMENTING OVER FORECASTING

Dave Snowden, a Welsh researcher renowned for his work in decision-making processes and frameworks, created the Cynefin framework of decision-making model. This model, praised by Harvard Business School, differentiates between four kinds of environments for decisions: obvious, complicated, complex and chaotic (Figure 5.1).

According to this framework, clear environments offer obvious relationships between causes and outcomes, such as your pen falling due to

Figure 5.1 Cynefin framework provides orientation for the kind of decision mechanisms to use, depending on the context.
Treating a complex situation like a complicated one could result in failure despite much well-intended analysis effort, instead of experimentation, which is what a complex situation requires.
Source: Cynefin framework. Visualization by AGILE COFFEE / https://agilecoffee.com/toolkit/cynefin/, last accessed on 14 December 2024.

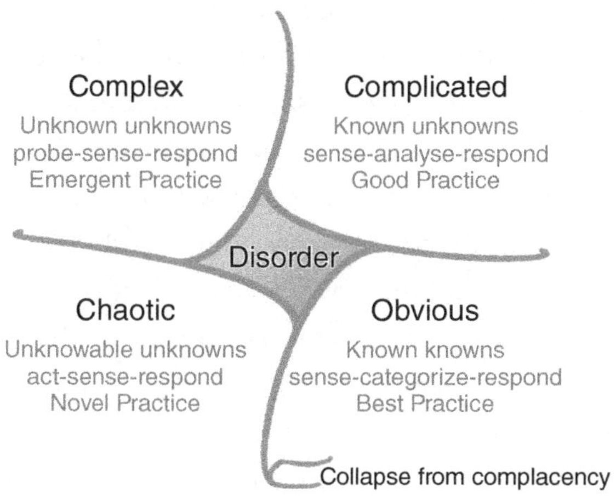

gravity, while complicated environments require modeling and expertise. Yet, increasingly, today's decisions involve complex systems, according to Dave and Harvard Business, where the remedy is not using models or experts that can predict what will happen.

Complex environments call for experimentation. Dave calls out the actions necessary to explore the relations between the causes and outcomes with three words: probe – sense – respond. This is very much in line with the lean startup innovation model I've discussed in Chapter 2.

Dave states that our bureaucracies typically treat situations as obvious or complicated, where they try to govern the complicated category by implementing solutions based on expert opinions, or as a result of some simulation models. In Denmark too much attention and influence in policy-making circles is paid to ADAM, short for "Annual Danish Aggregate Model." It is a macroeconomic model that provides a simplified mathematical description of the interactions within the Danish economy (Statistics Denmark, n.d.). Many government policies are simulated through ADAM and similar models in order to find their impact. But they are often incorrect in estimating those. As an example, tighter lending regulations of 2015 with the intention of reducing average housing indebtedness in Denmark did not work as they continued to rise (Danmarks Nationalbank, 2022).

Similarly, I've heard transport ministries and cities taking decisions on new road infrastructure based on simulation models for traffic. Transport behavior is a complex matter. Based on models, Denmark invested in public transport with a transport strategy initiative in 2018 with the expectation of curbing car traffic, which did not work. On the other hand, models predict building specific new roads to reduce congestion, yet often that is not the result in medium term: people change behavior, possibly obtain more cars, move, change jobs and routes, or their own routines, and congestion pops up again. Neither is the situation any different for other countries: they rely on models to simulate the future and solve challenges. They assume certain behaviors, and leave out many second, third, and fourth order factors that influence behaviors. Their models are not iterative learning loops, they are not getting smarter by interpreting reality to form a new policy.

Let us take inspiration from the advertising industry: Focusing on outputs and rewarding outputs over inputs was a transformational change (Figure 5.2). It used to be that companies hired experts to make cool ads, which they ran with big budgets. They did not know what the impact of these ads was, nor did they have good ways of assessing which ads would succeed over others. That is similar to our state of public decisions and spending.

Digital marketing changed the industry for bringing measurability into the picture and allowing focus on the outputs. This way, new ideas could be tried out at a low cost and quickly. Instead of the ads that experts deemed good, the ads people actually reacted to won. This is how the advertising

Figure 5.2   The advertising industry changed radically with digitalization.

It used to be that advertisers had to approve a large budget, trust expert opinions that they work well, as they spent their money on the TV ads. Now, using digital platforms, advertisers test marketing ideas (a.k.a. variations) in a market setting. Companies bid on conversions (output instead of input), while different ads can be served and scaled for various audiences.

Source: Kaspars Grinvalds/Adobe Stock; Rawpixel.com/Adobe Stock Photos; Scopio/Adobe Stock Photos

Expert led decisions: **TV ads**
- One ad
- Large & long commitment
- Outcomes unknown

Experimentation led decisions: **Digital ads**
- Test all ads & scale
- Many smaller commitments
- Measure outcomes

industry has shown us that we can move our focus on results rather than on inputs. It calls for a data infrastructure, speedy iterations, and accepting loss of control on the inputs – welcoming new ones.

Currently, we struggle with both our legislative process and public service delivery. Just like the old way of placing TV ads, we seem stuck in the paradigm of focusing on forecasting the future with expert inputs and simulations. Then we commit ourselves to buying services or new legislations, which fall short of creating the outcomes we had imagined.

Unfortunately, such model simulations or expert opinions are not going to provide effective solutions in solving challenges in complex settings. We put almost all of our analytical resources into forecasting and almost none in actually tracking and adjusting. It should be the other way around.

We need the build–test–learn kind of experiential learning loops, where we can learn from real life experiments. In the meantime, those who are shaping the world are those who learn fast, and tech companies have shown us the way. We must apply this in the way we deliver public services, in the way we do public procurement, as well as in the way we make laws.

Thus, one of the key pillars of Merit Democracy must be to facilitate data-driven learnings that shape both our legislation and delivery of public goods. Our governance needs to get comfortable with forming hypotheses, creating (small scale) interventions, observing results, concluding learnings, and updating hypotheses. Big data capabilities need to support the processes. Experimentation needs to take place within regular intervals as a practice instead of ad hoc and subjective agenda setting. In other words, our governance process should be constantly seeking to make changes to laws in order to find out how our legislation can work even better for our society and environment.

This means a call for fundamental changes to how we govern ourselves in order to function in complex environments. Currently, we do not define the success metrics when we legislate. We do not measure the impact of laws on metrics they were intended to improve. As a result, we do not learn about the impacts of a specific legislation on narrow metrics observed, or broadly on all metrics of social interest. At best, we make ad hoc research into some policies and social phenomena. Instead, we make models for how legislation would impact the world, *before* they are implemented. And we celebrate a new legislation when the law is passed, not when we find out it actually worked.

The Finnish government is likely one that is most aware of the issue and is working on experimental legislation. They have also concluded that legislation can have unpredicted outcomes, and that they need to run experiments in order to find out the impact of various legislation. In 2015, the Finnish government launched "Strategic Research Council," which aimed at guiding policy research through experiments. They explain that a policy that worked in one jurisdiction at a given time cannot be assumed to work in another one. Instead of an expert-led approach, they recommend agile piloting. One of the examples they provide in the area of agile learning is in the area of student housing. The Ministry of Finance tested a new housing policy for students in 2016 with the aim of improving housing conditions for 16–29 year olds. The experiment showed that the policy that models and experts deemed to solve problems did not perform in reality and was iterated upon to find a better design to work (Kainulainen and Juutinen, 2017).

Sitra, a Finnish national innovation institution, has been promoting learning from experimentation. They write:

It is considerably easier to study the effects of past reforms than it is to predict future outcomes. For that reason, systematic effort in the post-monitoring of law reforms is needed.

An experimental society promises a shift away from a top-down expert-led approach. The old, rigid institutions are not able to respond to new challenges, and the current debate on the culture of experimentation is likely to attract mainly those who already have an interest in these subjects.

Change happens by getting people involved in the experiments. This also increases the legitimacy of institutions. Better legitimacy is also supported by low-level experiments such as Nopeat Kokeilut ("Agile Piloting") in Helsinki. They can be used to test less extensive interventions for which in-depth scientific evidence is not needed. Sitra report; evidence based approaches to policy.

(Hokkanen and Seppänen, 2017)

While still a tiny voice in the debate of better governance, the idea of experiential learning is spreading. Following a ministers council meeting in 2021, the OECD (Organisation for Economic Co-operation and Development) published a memorandum promoting the idea of agile regulatory governance (OECD, 2021). This memorandum is special as its recommendations go to the root of some of the challenges we face in our democracies, and it backs many of the key arguments in this book such as the need for data-driven experimentation, randomized (control group) experiment, non-control and quasi experiment, and pre-post experiments. It is noteworthy to mention that the big data capabilities make causational analyses increasingly affordable and reliable without costly control groups.

These methods are used commonly in all scientific research, as well as in data-driven companies. It is time we used them in the service of public policy. They point out the need for a change of culture in the public sector where the main goal is to avoid making any mistakes. An experiment generating negative results is seen as a mistake. A mistake can create unwanted public attention and reduce popularity. The mistake-aversion in the public sector is so widespread that we often do not want to measure the impact of the work, and if we do, it is often not shared with the public. The excerpt below is from OECD's report on agile governance from April 2024 (OECD, 2024):

> *While the notion of successful outcome has traditionally been associated with laws, regulations or processes "that work," effective regulatory experimentation involves recognising failure as an ally: "When taking an experimental approach, good failure is an unavoidable part of the learning process, and bad failure is a preventable failure that doesn't result in new learning"*

The future of legislation can make use of the lean learning loop, or in Dave's words, the probe–sense–respond loop. The concept of agile learning is well established in the business – especially tech – world, but has not yet become a practice in our law making. We shall bring this powerful practice into public life where it can create social value. We start by defining what the goals we want to achieve are. We then make hypotheses of which regulations can achieve them. By running the experimentation loop, at each step we get closer to the solution.

To make this work well for us, our aim will need to be to make our data platforms ever more accurate and robust, to make our experimentation fast and affordable, and to guide the experimentation with the overall goals we want to achieve. Thankfully, the technologies are there offering increasingly fast and robust solutions to the data problems.

From obesity to social trust and affordability, we see trends evolving in a negative direction for too long before we take action, often in the fire-fighting mode. We shall see legislation as a muscle we use proactively, where we shape markets iteratively until we see our problems solved.

EMBRACING MARKETS FOR PUBLIC GOODS

As discussed in Chapter 1, even very well functioning consumer markets cannot provide us with essential goods such as minimal congestion and social trust that are simply not available privately. These are the public goods and their availability currently depends on the centralized, top-down efforts of our governance system. For everything we cannot buy from consumer markets we rely on our governments to provide.

One of the key problems for how governments fail to provide us with public goods is the delivery mechanism, its reliance on controlling the inputs and treating complex social behavior problems as if they are simple or complicated but foreseeable. We deploy expert analysis and forecasting models to better understand what services we should deploy and expect the new service we funded to work well because some smart people worked on estimating its impacts for some years and used modern estimating tools.

However, as I mentioned in the previous section, approaching complex problems with more resources on expertise and forecasting doesn't work. What is needed is experimentation, and different approaches to be allowed in a market setting, to reach the impact we want. That is how companies solve complex consumer needs. Without seemingly wild ideas being tried, we struggle to bring about change, as change is not embedded in an expert opinion, or not an extension of the past that forecasting tools can provide.

We seem to have a few problems in making the leap. One is that we don't trust that we can measure and attribute impacts to companies' products and services. We are missing the general understanding of how data can be used to make such connections in general public goods and people working in government as well as politicians. This is a way of thinking and capability we really only have in tech companies.

The other problem is more of a moral question. As discussed in the previous chapter with ESG and CSRD, our system tends to view companies as agents that can harm public goods with a "risk minimization" approach. That thinking leaves out rewarding companies for improving our public goods.

Many politicians and civil servants feel they need to control and be in charge of the inputs. Paying companies for the public goods they create is a no-go for many politicians who have a view that public goods can only be created by public entities or not-for profits. What they say is that you cannot create public value if you are seeking profits. In her speech in January 2023, Danish Prime Minister Mette Frederiksen spoke against for-profit companies providing services such as childcare. She said she wanted those institutions to allocate funding for the welfare and development of the children and not to make profits for shareholders.

The view that all public services need to be delivered by either public entities themselves, or through the specific services they contract out based on specific activities (inputs) is problematic. It leaves no room for innovation, or thinking out of the box, and often we forget what goods we aimed at creating or measuring the efficacy of the service all together. Yet, this is how we currently run delivery of public services (Figure 5.3). Public sector organizations struggle to innovate. They lack the incentives

Figure 5.3   Can we use markets to incentivize public goods instead of traditional procurement?

Traditional procurement in the public sector involves a centralized (and top-down controlled) decision around which products or services should be bought. Only one company wins to deliver the service, creating a 1-1 relation to create value. This decision is based on various assumptions about the outcomes, and the assumption drives the case for procurement. Due to the high cost in running the process with dialogue and forecasting, contracts have long durations. In a market-based approach, multiple companies can compete in execution to deliver the goods. There is no longer a centralized need for decision around the inputs, taking out the need for forecasting and dialogue. Instead, the market-based approach has a pricing of the outputs, and strong data foundation to measure and attribute outputs to the companies involved. Notably, this process can be iterative, allowing output prices to be updated on an ongoing basis.

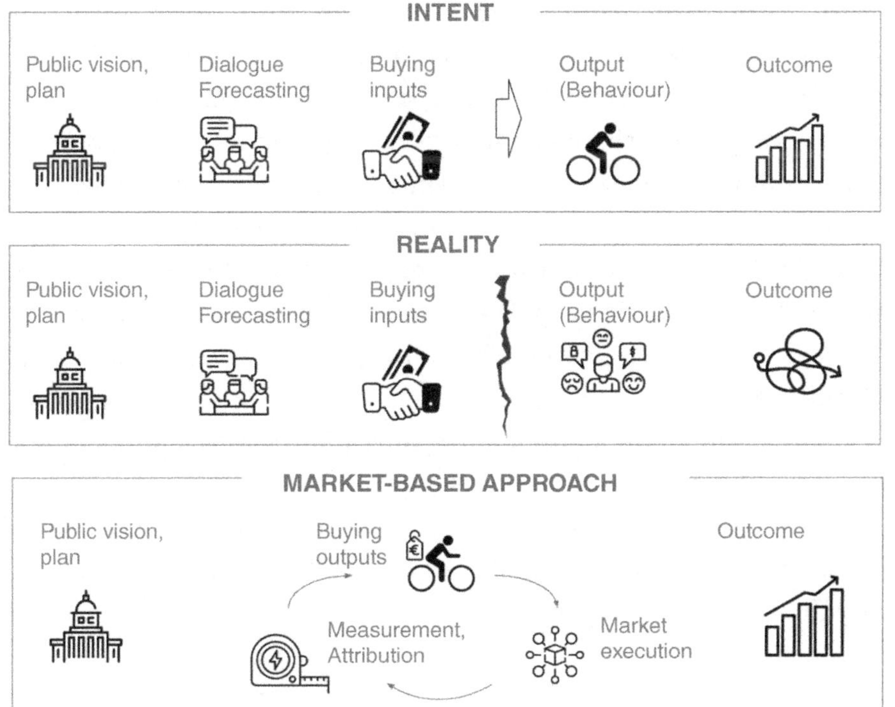

toward taking risks and generating learnings, and scaling their services across other areas.

The way forward is to create marketplaces where companies not only engage themselves in providing public goods for a short contract period, but are at all times considered a part of it. The role of government becomes management of the market, where they identify public goods in measurable metrics, and price them. They also need to ensure that attribution of impacts is done properly.

One of the key tenets of Merit Democracy is therefore to appropriately value what matters to us collectively and creating marketplaces to deliver them effectively. As a result, whatever social or environmental goods we value publicly will make their way into how companies' goods and services are priced. In such a marketplace, companies can compete to create the public goods for us.

We are not completely strangers to this concept: we already opened up the improvement of public goods to companies with CO_2 markets. The CO_2 cap and trade system of the EU is among the most sophisticated financial incentives schemes we have seen to account for public goods. Such cap and trade ensures that companies have financial incentives to change business practices to reduce emissions. They are not seen as harmful agents who have to pay, but agents that can earn for improving the emissions. Due to this market, Tesla has earned \$6.5 billion between 2020 and 2023 by selling carbon credits, that is 19% of its profits in that period (L, 2024; Macrotrends, 2024). Such incentives are clearly working. Also, due to this market, fossil fuels are becoming less attractive compared with renewable sources, and CO_2 removal initiatives such as carbon capture are being incentivized.

To avoid any misunderstandings: using markets to protect public goods is not advocating for free markets, nor reducing public budgets. It is an argument for changing the way we put public money to use, leveraging the benefits of marketplaces.

Further, we can continue the market thinking for solving our legislative challenges. That is, we can offer those who create successful legislation financial incentives. This way, we can not only allow but incentivize new policy ideas to make their way into practice.

Currently, we pay politicians a fixed salary that is not impacted by their actual performance. But when it comes to CEOs, much of their compensation – much of it often in company stock – depends on the company's performance. We could learn from the private sector that the performance of legislation matters. We have a culture of expecting people's contribution to the political debate to be an altruistic one and a culture where all opinions count the same. This is undermining the drive for creating positive change and it kills the feedback loop where the insights that could make a difference get lost in the noise.

Further, we incentivize the brightest in society to focus pursuing a career in advanced tech companies, as these jobs have great pay and high social status. In turn, our institutions lose out on the talent that is needed to regulate markets for public interest.

Instead, we need to design a legislative process where all can engage themselves and creating social value translates into financial gains. Creating quality legislation is absolutely critical and is of high value to society. Thus, we should have strong financial incentives for those who create value for society through a decentralized, market-based system of governance. This would attract talent to engage with public policy, and insightful voices to gain more traction over time.

Merit Democracy is built on the idea that every person can easily be a part of the legislative process from the convenience of their home and computer and can expect a financial incentive proportional to the social impact they create. This would be a process where background and titles don't matter, where anyone can treat such engagement as a part-time political job.

EMPOWERING PUBLIC GOODS WITH (BIG) DATA

"Without data, you're just another person with an opinion."
—W. Edwards Deming

Underlying the principles of merit and accountability, as well as transparency is the reliance on **data**. As we explored in Chapter 2, use of data and experimentation is not only how science has flourished, but sophisticated big data and machine learning tools also gave rise to the most valuable companies of today. Can we use such data capabilities to create public goods?

Not only can we, but we must.

We must explore the potential of data in our legislative process, as well as in how we deliver public services. Using data, we can isolate the impact of a new law on the public goods we care about, we are able to claim its value, and we are also able to reward the work of the people behind it. Similarly, we can calculate the impacts of a product or service on our public goods, and we can reward or punish that company.

To properly leverage possibilities with data for delivering public goods requires significant changes. First, we need to collect even more data for public purposes. We then need to clean and store such data for its useful life. We need to link the sources to one another and enable various analysis methods on them. In the meantime, all this needs to be handled with transparency and observing privacy.

Data of the individual is entangled with how we take collective action. Our individual well-being and behavior are key inputs to the evaluation of our collective decision-making. We must be able to measure if some new service is addictive or if a new media outlet is promoting content with misleading facts. Instagram and YouTube will know how many hours into the night you were online. That's also relevant data for our policy-making. The more data we capture about our collective state, the better we can manage our goods.

Of course, such data capture very quickly creates concerns in many. The dark days of dictatorships come to mind. Much of our focus is on dealing with the dangers of data being exploited against our interest. Perhaps the fresh memories of Soviet deep state agents wire-tapping, combined with Snowden's reveal of how national security agencies track our communications, has fueled our fears. Abuse of data is a very real concern, and also indicates that the less we trust our governments the less we will be willing to share our data in any way, out of fear of it being against us.

Yet, big data is a key enabler of a better democracy. If we stop our governments from having and using it, we will be dealing with inferior tools up against pressing challenges. We cannot build visionary governance without a solid and powerful data infrastructure.

In a world where we allow all kinds of sophisticated tools of technology in our service as consumers we have the need to equip our governments with similar levels of technology. Based on data, we can create a government that attributes changes in public goods to companies' products and services, and to public policies.

We can use data powerfully to direct companies, while we avoid a big brother scenario, where our actions as individuals are traced, controlled, or analyzed. Using data in the public sphere does not translate to that dystopian vision, although there is a clear danger.

There is a catch 22 we need to break when it comes to government and data. If we trusted our governments, we would allow them to collect and use more data. But if we don't trust them, any use of data creates a backlash as citizens expect that to be against their interest. Building trust and cultivating deeper data practices could go hand in hand. Our governments would need to show willingness to reform, improve transparency, and provide us with more agency as it also takes initiatives on obtaining and processing data.

* * *

When I talk about the ideas presented in this book with various philosophers and economists, a point of friction is how we can protect our humanity when we start measuring and assigning value to things we care about. For many of us, what is measured becomes a part of the world of accounting, and loses its unexpected, unquantified, natural beauty. For others, attempts to quantify means reducing the value of a public good to a number.

I see the point of this concern in me as well. Nature is simply perfect, while no data models will ever reflect reality of the world perfectly. How in the world could we claim to protect it from ourselves, by measuring and regulating, for example, our footprint? How can we compare ourselves with its beauty and sophistication?

I believe we must acknowledge that our data attribution models will always be partial and imperfect, and at the same time this shall not discourage us from engaging with the process of creating and improving them. Like our legislation, our data foundations can and should always be improved.

We could find peace that nature can be observed through the lenses of numbers (Figure 5.4). Many patterns in nature find their explanations and modeling in mathematics, from plant growth to snowflakes. Observing the

Figure 5.4   Math can help us model and understand the nature.
(a) Fibonacci sequence is behind many patterns in nature from sunflowers to the shape of human ear. (b) The sequence starts simply with 0 and 1. Each subsequent number is the sum of the previous two.
Source: Sheng-lu Wu / Pexels.

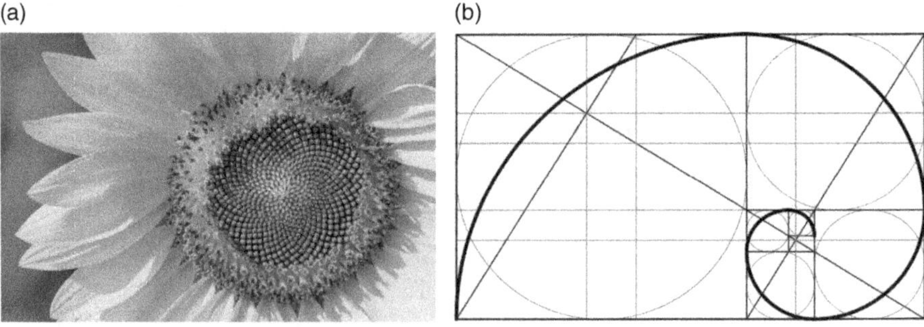

world, including mechanics of our societies through the lenses of data can help us understand patterns and affect them. Attempting to analyze how our legislation or products and services are impacting public goods is simply an extension of our culture of science and our need to understand.

Finally, a word on using AI to interpret our interactions and our world: I promote a democratic governance model that supports accountability and merit based on feedback loops. The idea is measuring the impact of legislation and the impact of products and services on our collective well-being established by certain metrics. The linking of impacts between such phenomena is not an easy task. This is where we can utilize AI and machine learning tools to build causational relationships.

With AI, currently we are dealing with black-box systems that create certain outputs without us being able to understand how the systems arrived at those solutions. The tools we build should give us the upper hand, with a thorough understanding of how it was trained. We should not give up our agency to an AI model. AI models such as LLMs can support our systems in various ways, but we must remain aware of the influence of technology and not delegate unless we have sufficient comfort and knowledge about their workings. Further, while AI can help assist us in creating for example legislation proposals to reach our collective goals, they cannot define our goals for us. Defining our goals and approving of new legislation shall remain in our power.

TRANSPARENCY BREEDS LEGITIMACY

"Transparency breeds legitimacy."

—John C. Maxwell

Further, Merit Democracy shall be fully **transparent**, while observing **privacy**. Full transparency is of course an ideal, as privacy also is. Nothing can be perfectly known, nor can we be perfectly private about everything.

What we could do, however, is to build the systems and processes that map out clearly the interactions that happen between persons, by capturing the most important interactions. While we want to apply privacy in terms of data collection to map the status of our society, we do not need to be private about the decision-making process. In fact, we want to be transparent about who argues which policies and be able to trace their influence during the whole decision process as much as possible. We shall not expect that all discussions can be forced to happen online, which shapes people's opinions about public matters. Yet, we can use some key principles of ensuring necessary information is shared and understood by all parties who promote certain viewpoints. And we can utilize a process of building arguments for or against a change in a bill that is fully transparent.

Some of the most vital interactions shaping politics today happen behind closed doors (or private electronic interactions), often with highly paid lobbyists. We cannot avoid people talking with whomever they want in private. However, just the sheer increase in the number of people joining the decision-making process will reduce the economic pressure from narrow interest groups. Even if we attracted 1% of the population to actively take part in the process of legislation, we would increase the number of decision-makers by a staggering 5000-fold, compared to an average of 500,000 citizens represented per representative. Decentralization of decision power makes it a lot harder for narrow interest groups to effectively lobby.

We can learn many lessons from the blockchain community on this. People discuss the future of Bitcoin and how to choose its developmental path. The decisions shaping many decentralized autonomous organizations (DAOs), or perhaps more properly addressed as wanna-be-DAOs, is shaped by online discussions as explored in Chapter 3. The coin holders with voting powers engage with one another under user-id's not disclosing their real world identities. They discuss matters with one another purely through online (private or communal or public) channels to make up collective decisions.

I believe the future of collective decisions should involve self-identified thought leaders (a new breed of influencers) whose identities are public to be transparent about their votes, and in return the public can see their policy success track record.

AN OPEN AND INCLUSIVE DESIGN

We may have all come on different ships, but we're in the same boat now.

—Martin Luther King Jr.

With **openness,** I argue for a platform that aims to engage people and make it very easy to get involved. We must find mechanisms to keep the barrier to entry low, both for individuals in the legislative process and companies in the public service delivery. You must have seen how a user-friendly tech product almost invites you to play with it. And then there are those services where registration is a hassle, and finding your way through is an adventure.

As argued earlier, getting involved actively in politics is very expensive: it demands one's full time from an early age for most people in politics today. Hence the term, career politician. If you are not an insider, and place most of your time in the political circles, or if you don't carry some aspects of fame that can benefit a political party, chances are you will not be allowed in, even if you have great insights to certain areas of public life and could contribute with creating beneficial public policy. We should make it very easy for everyone to utilize their expertise in the building of such policies.

Similarly, getting involved to create public goods, and reaping benefits of doing so is difficult, due to the high barriers to entry for winning public contracts. That is because the way we contract out public goods is through a public procurement process that focuses on risk minimization, and few large companies are specialized in winning those contracts because they have deeply experienced, teams and finances to work out the complex requirements to score highly in the public procurement process.

It does not need to be so. In the Merit Democracy, we need the execution of public goods to work through payments based on outcomes, where any company at any level of maturity in their journey can be a part of the process of contributing to public goods, and be remunerated for that.

Openness extends to inclusion and diversity – much debated topics these days. And they are also key for Merit Democracy. Let me use a recent debate to make my point.

I recently read about Aura Salla, a recent member of the EU parliament, who used to work for Meta until her election into a government position. The question is whether we can trust her with decisions concerning how we regulate media or tech companies. On one hand she has the insight and expertise, but on the other her real intentions are unknown.

Similar questions have been brought up concerning regulators and politicians who have been former businessmen and bankers. The problem is we cannot really know people's intentions.

Billy Tauzin, a former US representative from Louisiana, played a pivotal role in crafting the Medicare Prescription Drug, Improvement, and Modernization Act of 2003. This legislation prohibited Medicare from negotiating drug prices, a provision that significantly benefited pharmaceutical companies. Shortly after the bill's passage, Tauzin left Congress and became the president of the Pharmaceutical Research and Manufacturers of America (PhRMA), the industry's main lobbying organization, with a reported salary of $2 million per year (Zibel, 2019). It is difficult to argue that Billy had the best interest of the public in mind.

On the other hand, look at the case of Gary Gensler, the current Chair of the US Securities and Exchange Commission (SEC). He had been head of finance at Goldman Sachs before starting his career in politics. Many refer to him as the person who pushed for better and more stringent regulations to be implemented, proving the point that his expertise as a banker comes in handy as a regulator.

We live in a political system where we are required to place public trust in a person's intentions. We recognize that leaders are in close interaction and under the influence of powerful interest groups. Regulatory hijacking (or regulatory capture) is a term coined for regulatory bodies favoring interest groups as government representatives pursue individual interests. It is well documented. A 2019 study found 59% of representatives who left Congress ended up working lobbying for trade and business groups tasked with influencing federal policy (Public Citizen, 2019).

Nevertheless, relationships are complicated and we never really know someone's intentions no matter their identity. We can only see what, in reality, their actions are. In the name of neutrality we could bring people in charge who are new to an industry. But this has other problems including a steep learning curve. We cannot rely on someone's trustworthiness based on some of the identities they share with us. Both because this would be outright discrimination, but also because this would result in poor decisions in the long term, as identities are fluid and difficult to translate to one's principles and true intentions.

Our identities cannot be seen as limitations of our world views. A rich person could be arguing for a tax on the rich, while a poor one doesn't. There are government officials burning to support entrepreneurship, while there are also entrepreneurial spirits burning to create a better public life. Everyone has the ability to protect or harm the public goods we care about. It is through measuring and linking legislative processes to real world outcomes that we can finally understand who is contributing to what policy and how that affects us.

Hence, we must find mechanisms of governance where we differentiate one's identities in one realm of public to evaluate their arguments in another. This is not an argument about losing our judgments about one another in our private dealings. This is an argument about designing a system where discussing policy should be de-linked from the specific identities of its supporters. This way we can remain open to someone's contribution, no matter their background. As I will argue later, we can use someone's actual performance in contributing to policies that are beneficial to give them more voice, or equally, reduce their influence if they are not beneficial. This way, we remain objective and open, while still having ways to adjust to whom we give more influence.

Let us look again at how financial markets work for inspiration. The trading floor doesn't care who is buying or selling and sees them as contributors to allocating resources where they are needed, as well as contributors to establishing a price. Whoever you may be – and however much you may struggle with public speaking – if you are good at understanding the dynamics that make one company successful in its market, your trading signal makes a difference in the markets. Over time, the real world outcomes reward people on the trading floor. The way that world plays out decides who was right and wrong and rewards them accordingly. Diplomas, specific identities and good looks will not grant anyone the numbers.

Thus, openness and inclusion are key values of Merit Democracy. This means no matter one's background, experiences, origins, previous statements, or even criminal record, we shall find ways to give people a chance to not only voting, but also contribute in drafting a policy. Similarly, a company that was seen as a bad actor can change its business model and generate benefits. Instead of having to trust the individuals, leaders, or brands we can trust the process of the system and our measurements to allow all identities to be a part of the journey of contributing.

CHAPTER SIX

MERIT DEMOCRACY IN A BICYCLE

Now, I will dig into the mechanics of what I envision as a set of ideas worth exploring for our next democracy. Before I start to go deeper into those mechanics, it is worth reiterating that it is more important subject to experiment with different democratic models rather than sticking with one. And the most important parameters that a democracy needs to live up to, in my opinion, are quality and pace of decisions, and transparency and agency as covered in Chapter 1.

I named the model of democratic governance I believe in, *Merit Democracy*. The name stems from the idea of measuring and rewarding all contributions, to build a thriving social contract both in legislative process and how we execute on creating and maintaining public goods.

A democracy that lacks merit is one where decisions' impacts are not measured and the future prospects of poor decision-makers are unimpacted by them. It is also a democracy where money is delinked from social and environmental value, and where companies can create value for consumers and for investors while effectively extracting value from society and the environment.

We live in the latter one. But we can make the first one happen.

***

There are three important mechanical bits I will talk about in this chapter to describe what Merit Democracy looks like.

The **first** one is about **legislation** in Merit Democracy. This will be an iterative process of developing proposals and implementing them in order to observe the impacts on society. I will take you through the use of **prediction markets** to engage citizens where they can contribute their wisdom and expertise, as well as a **delegative (liquid) voting** process. This iterative process involves regular cycles during which we update our laws to improve public outcomes. Not only can everyone join via the convenience of their computer or mobile, but they are financially rewarded if they are able to create collective value. The legislative process evolves around challenges; every proposal is in response to one or more challenges, defined by measurable metrics. The process of legislation is preceded by a process of us defining our public priorities.

The **second** one is **delivery of public goods**. This is about redefining how we deliver public goods or the execution of government. The big idea is to leverage data and markets (private sector) to create public goods. We would link products and services impacts on public goods we care about and reflect those positive and negative impacts with dynamic price mechanisms. Just like CO_2 markets, we would have public values then create an efficient market around each of the public goods we care about and incentivize companies to change their business models to improve these public goods. This means pricing of externalities and making them internal with updates to these prices on an ongoing and iterative basis, in contrast to our current, random, one-off price regulations. The pricing of externalities helps guide the economy and companies to respect and defend our public priorities and overcome our collective coordination problem.

The **third** and last, but not least important, piece is about **setting priorities** for our societies. All legislation and execution of public goods happens as a result of addressing these priorities. We must know where we are going, and we shall grab and direct the society to the direction we want directly with as little friction and as few middlemen as possible. Such priority setting would be through an online, direct expression. We would each be invited to allocate our citizenship budgets across issues defined by measurable parameters and create new ones if we need to.

In writing this book, among other things, I've been inspired by Kate Raworth's *Doughnut Economics*. She packed in the ideas of social and planetary limits in a simple language and contrasted how traditional economics focusing on growth misses out on the simple limitations we have. To represent her ideas, she successfully utilized the visualization of the concepts in a doughnut.

When I thought of what could be a similarly a visual expression for Merit Democracy, I realized it is a bicycle (Figure 6.1). Perhaps Kate is a

Figure 6.1   Merit Democracy in a bicycle.

Source: Solvejg/Shutterstock

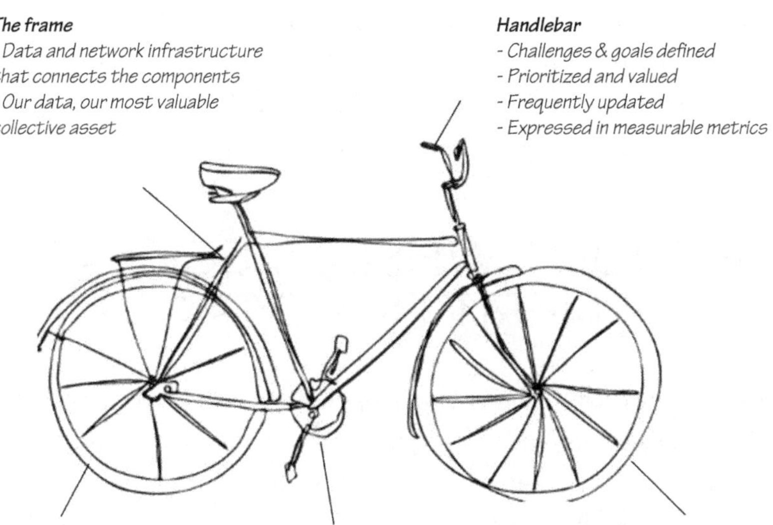

fan of doughnuts, as I am of bikes, and our brains do the rest. Nevertheless, I find a bike is a powerful tool to explain what I am about to explain with Merit Democracy.

The cyclical nature of law-making, which aims to solve the problems set forth, is expressed in the bike as the front wheel. Through each iteration, each turn of the wheel, legislative process moves us forward. The back wheel represents the execution of public goods. The turning of the back wheel also represents the iterative nature of defining the prices of public goods. The back wheel is interlinked with the pedal block, which represents the economy and all our work. The delivery of public goods happens through activities of companies collectively.

The handlebar represents our priority setting where we define the public goods we care about and where we price them. Just as we make subtle twists on the handlebar to keep our balance as we ride, we would keep changing our priorities, their definitions or values thereof. The handlebar sets direction: defining the public goods in measurable metrics enables both the legislative process and the execution process to tightly follow those priorities. Such priorities can be interpreted as both challenges to be solved, and opportunities for everyone to join and solve.

THE FRONT WHEEL: LEGISLATION IN MERIT DEMOCRACY

The legislative process (Figure 6.2) happens in the presence of well-defined, prioritized challenges (a.k.a. goals) in a community (city, nation). Each legislation proposal is a solution or move toward one or more of these goals. The definitions of challenges include their measurable goals, as well as current status and levels. More on this later.

The following steps make up the legislative process:

- A prediction market, where proposals are valued against the challenges they aim to solve.

Figure 6.2   Overview of the front wheel: the legislative process in Merit Democracy.
Proposals are prepared to solve challenges that have measurable metrics defining them, and a price that provides value of improvements in the metrics. A prediction market is used in order to facilitate development of proposals, where citizens directly collaborate with one another. Top valued proposals are taken to voting. The liquid voting process facilitates debate about the proposal, incentivizes participation and ensures representation. Proposals that are voted on become decisions, and their impact on the challenges is measured. Both participants in the proposal market and the delegates in voting get impacted by the proposal's eventual success. Proposal market graduation and voting continues for any given challenge until it is no longer a priority, in regular iterative cycles, for example, every month.

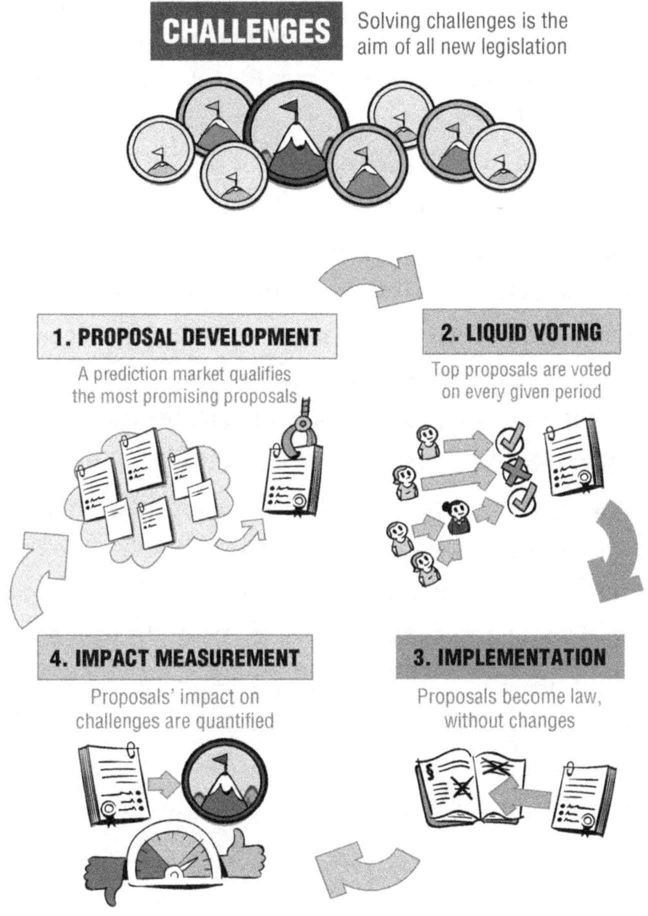

- A voting round, where citizens can choose between voting themselves or delegating.
- Transfer of top valued proposals from development to voting at certain frequency, f.x. once a month, where proposals voted positively move to execution.
- Measurement of proposals' impacts on the goals once in execution.
- Upon certain timeframe, proposals contributors receive rewards or retribution based on proposal's realized impacts.

Betting Can Save Our Democracy

You might not see betting as a valuable act. After all, betting often sounds close to gambling. Yet, betting is the essence of how we allocate resources – it is the backbone of financial markets as it invites informed decision-making. Betting, not surveys, is how we aggregate the information of everyone in the economy to define which businesses, technologies, and even countries are worth supporting. We do so by buying their equity, bonds, and currencies. Betting means putting your money where your mouth is, hence a well-established phrase.

Today, online betting markets exist for all sorts of things, from who will win elections or a basketball game, to when China will attempt invading Taiwan. I became fascinated with the potential of betting for its ability to bring about the crowd wisdom most effectively, as I studied the economic and psychological arguments why they do so.

Prediction markets (Figure 6.3) create contracts that pay a fixed amount if an event occurs, and then allow people to trade on the contract by submitting buying or selling prices in a manner similar to the stock market. Researchers have looked into how our brain works when we are responding to a question, say a survey, versus when we are committing ourselves and our resources into a future outcome (Jung, 2024). Two important dynamics are at play in prediction markets that set them apart from opinion polls: the first one is that in a prediction market, respondents

Figure 6.3   Prediction markets are already used to predict real world events, outside of the stock market.

Polymarket.com (a) and Futuur.com (b) are examples of prediction markets. There are predictions not only for election results or sports games, but for many kinds of information from global heating to AI developments.

Source: Futuur Inc / https://futuur.com/q/197462/which-will-be-the-top-ai-model-llm-in-generative-tasks-at-the-end-of-2024 / last accessed on January 7, 2025

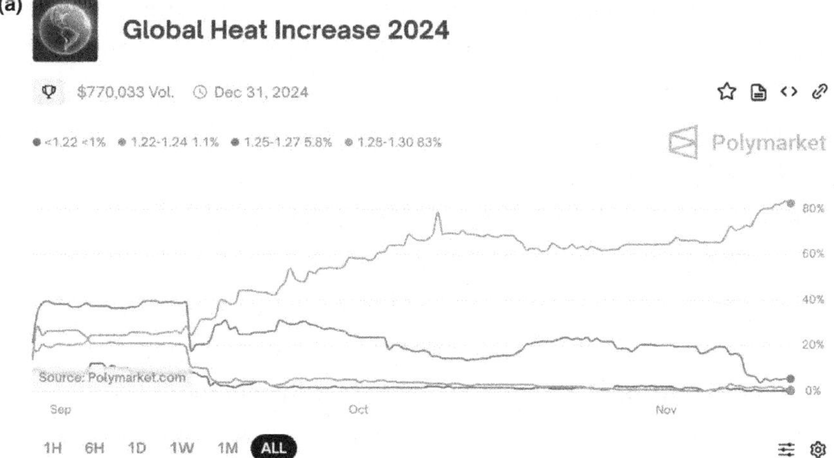

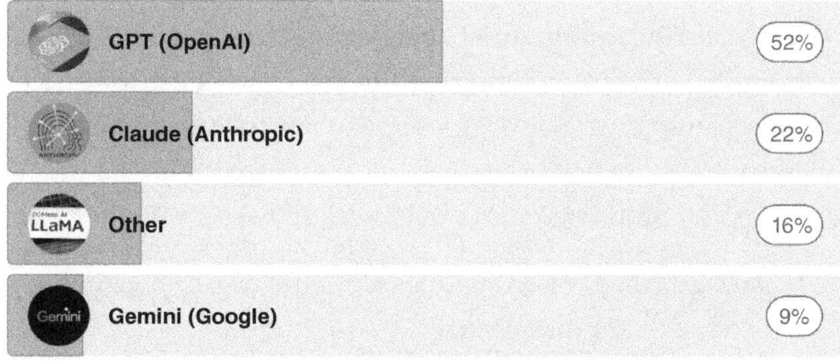

are incentivized to make an evaluation of their knowledge about an issue before they take a position, resulting in a reduction of noise, or less valuable information. Second, in surveys, humans being the social animals we are, tend to be influenced by social desirability bias. Even if unconscious, we are influenced by the answers we think we are expected to give rather than our true behavior.

Economists have already thought about the possibility of using markets to value ideas. Joshua Gans (University of Toronto) and Scott Stern (MIT) are economists specializing in innovation and management. In their presentation "Is there a market for ideas," they explore the possibilities of utilizing prediction markets for qualifying policies (Gans and Stern, 2008). Economist Robin Hanson is seen as an economist who has explored this field and helped establish the dynamics that make prediction markets work. The increasing and successful use of prediction markets outside of finance and sports with accurate estimates is the result of a maturing field.

Many of us associate markets and betting with greed. Yet what allowed investors to succeed has been their unique and consistent worldviews and thesis. The stories of Warren Buffet and George Soros show us that markets thrive when the feedback loops strengthen successful voices. In a world where investment decisions would be made with polling such successful voices would be lost in the noise. Yet, markets allow signals to grow out of noise and help gain traction. Markets are conversations that enable the valuable agents to grow over time.

Merit Democracy would utilize such market dynamics to improve our social contract. Today, our social contract is centralized in the hands of representatives. When decentralizing the power we must use successful market mechanisms that allow cultivation of our collective expertise. That is the function of prediction markets, where we would bet on the future success of policy proposals. Such mechanism addresses a few key issues:

- People get compensated for their time and engagement in line with success of their projections.
- People will self-select and get involved where they have key insights rather than spending time on issues they don't know much about. And from teachers to retail workers, we can all contribute with our expertise.

- The prediction market dynamics enable development of strong proposals and innovation to the top, as people are not worried about popularity but real life outcomes.

The "policy market" is created by challenges, which define the aim with clear, measurable metrics. Without the challenges there are no markets. The metrics of public goods (such as CO_2 emission reduction, or traffic congestion, or cases of depression or wealth inequality) will be linked to price indications that establish the value of improving the metric. The aim of the participants would be to solve the challenge in the best way possible by crafting the policy proposals and betting on them (Figure 6.4).

The most successful proposals would be taken, at a predefined frequency such as each month, to the next stage, where they are voted on. The reason to introduce voting on the most valued proposals is to avoid speculation: a group of people could bet on a proposal which stands to benefit them and not the greater group. And this benefit could exceed the loss they would make in the policy markets.

You might also say, why use the prediction market at all, instead of going directly into the voting stage? We could each submit a new proposal and see which ones become popular. This is actually very much the logic behind most online democracy portals. The problem here is the lack of engagement incentives, and random people expressing random opinions about random problems – and they don't stand to gain or lose anything from such engagement. On these platforms, proposals do not get shared ownership and developing a proposal ends up being an individual project of its initiator. Viewers of the ideas are not incentivized to make a bet; they have nothing to win or lose from expressing a positive or negative vote. Another problem, having too many proposals to vote on, and lacking incentives for the community to effectively engage, is acknowledged in the DAO space. One of the solutions debated in the DAO space is holographic consensus, where there is a prediction market prior to voting to predict which proposals would pass the voting stage.

Figure 6.4   Proposal development: First leg in legislative process. Legislative process would make use of a so-called "idea market". Proposals in the idea market to solve challenges can come from anyone. Citizens would "co-own" proposals by bidding on them with their Citizen Credits. When one is a co-owner, one can also vote for change of the content and one has incentives to make the proposal even better. Proposals' content opens up for more details and evaluations, once there are enough collaborators and interest a prediction of success. Proposals compete with one another in their predicted value to solve the challenge by attracting more citizens investing citizenship credits on them.

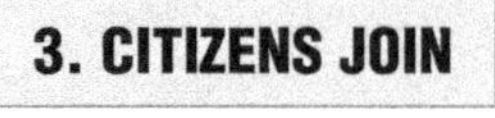

I believe that we need to take the prediction markets further in predicting not only that the proposals would pass the voting stage, but also that they would create the impacts we want. The combination of a policy (prediction) market combined with voting could address all the issues. On one hand we get the incentives to engage, and on the other, we get fewer polished policy proposals on which to spend our time, focus debate and vote on. Voting on a topic is an expensive exercise, so it is a good idea to limit number of proposals voted on from each of the markets.

The process of proposal building would take place across many ongoing challenges. Participants would look through the challenges to see which ones they can contribute to given their knowledge and experiences. In order to link the participants to the proposals, we would use a currency, what I would call Citizen Credits (CCs). One uses these credits to start proposals and buy into them, and can earn them if one participated in successful proposals. I will come back to the economy of the CCs later.

When a proposal is created, the participant creating it would commit some of their CCs into it. This is similar to tying up money in a company you start. By starting a proposal, you buy, for example, 50 shares, the maximum you can buy in any proposal, at an average price of 1, committing 50 of your credits. Others who believe this legislation proposal has potential to improve the challenge can now join the proposal. To do so, they bet some of their citizenship credits into the proposal by investing in it. Now, they have become co-owners of the proposal.

This means when proposals are created, the share price is low, for example, 1 share costs 1 unit. As more people buy into it, the price goes up. Buyers can decide how many of their credits they want to spend on this proposal, across all proposals in all markets. One could buy into a proposal that only a few have supported, and has a low price, while at the same time buy into another one that many thousands are co-owners of. A higher price of a proposal would indicate the belief by co-owners that the proposal is likely to pass the voting stage and that it will create desirable social impacts set out by the challenges.

When investing in expensive proposals, citizens would be making increasingly expensive bets, just like buying shares in a company with a high valuation. They will also have a smaller share and therefore less of an influence on changing the proposal. This means they will be incentivized to look for earlier stage proposals with strong potential, especially those they have a higher shareholding and influence upon.

The co-owners of the proposals edit the contents of the proposals. Proposals will start out their lives with limited information on them. As they get co-owned by citizens they get developed. We could design the markets such that a proposal starts with a rather simple template, a title and some key points of its enactments. And down the road, for example, once they reach one hundred co-owners, their template expands to where it now invites explanation of which specific legal text is linked, the hypothesis behind the changes expected, and perhaps even some economic modeling.

The changes in the proposal template can be initiated by any of the owners and are offered as a change proposal to all other owners. This is similar to a GoogleDoc edit suggestion feature, expanded with a vote. The co-owners of the proposal can have a short debate about the changes to the fields, with a resulting vote on the change within a limited timeframe, for example, 24 hours. If the majority of the votes go for accepting a change, it is realized, and the proposal is updated.

AI and LLM models are going to be instrumental in such a legislative market. They can help identify and list other similar proposals, they can help block creation of proposals that are too similar to one another. They can also help identify which current legal text the changes would make most sense to apply to. While we would not need to rely on the LLMs or AI in order to predict the future consequences of the proposals, citizens supporting or objecting to the proposals could obviously do their own research and use such tools.

One of the problems often pointed out with markets is shallowness, or lack of sufficient transactions to establish a meaningful price on the ideas at hand. One of the ways to overcome this issue is to introduce automated market maker mechanisms (Johnstone, 2013; Slamka, Skiera, and Spann, 2012). Instead of individuals setting prices on their proposals, the price setting of the proposal can be done through total shareholding of the proposal. Based on predefined market depth, the system can simply increase the prices as a function of the number of shares in the proposal.

I am quite well informed about the opportunities and design elements of such a prediction market because I have created a startup to facilitate citizen engagement through the use of prediction markets in 2010. My company then, Wedecide, ran prediction markets for public and private organizations with the design and dynamics I described above. It worked as intended, in joining people together into proposals, and aligning their interests with one another to work online to make the proposal better. What I did not have then was to make the decisions binding, and predictions being concluded in real world events. I stopped it in 2013.

One of the unwanted behaviors in such a market setting that I've experienced in Wedecide was people backing, then leaving, a proposal to earn the difference, and never really being keen on its actual content, but assuming it would gain attention and price. In other words, simply, speculative behavior. To reduce such behavior, one can place some kind of friction, which is also considered for financial markets and is known as Tobian tax (Kagan, 2022). If a user is selling a short time of period after buying, there could be an automatic tax, to return less credit (Figure 6.5).

The Economy of Citizen Credits

The concept of Citizen Credits is to mimic something we humans have done in our tribal past by respecting wisdom. We see the wisdom when we listen to someone, assessing their body language and voice and the

Figure 6.5   Short summary on the legislation market.
The legislation market would serve as a marketplace where citizens can use citizenship credits to bet on the ability of legislation proposals to solve collective challenges.

Reason to use markets for legislation

- Studies show that markets perform better than surveys in aggregating collective wisdom.
- Betting creates incentives for those with insights to engage.
- When betting, people are choosing (self-sorting) to areas where they feel more confident about their opinions or insights.

Co-ownership and co-authorship

- Idea markets enable co-ownership of an idea, in contrast to only vote-based editing.
- Co-ownership, just like in a cooperative or a partnership company, brings people together in the interest of their collective project.
- An internal vote among idea co owners based on shares can decide changes.
- Possible scoring of actual content contributions to be considered, for example by AI.

Pricing of proposals

- To overcome shallow market problems, market makers can be utilized.
- Increasing demand on a proposal increases prices.

Achieving success in legislation markets

- Concluding event that determines a legislation's success is determined through measuring its real life results.
- A proposal is successful if it is improving the metrics it aims to achieve.
- It is unsuccessful if its overall impact on all social metrics exceeds its benefits.
- Participants are implicitly also betting that the proposals at hand would be voted through.

Preventing speculation

- Participants may try to buy/sell to make money without real insights into proposals.
- A Tobian tax, or similar trading frictions can create incentives against such behavior.

Ensuring necessary content

- Proposals could require a certain kind of input to align all stakeholders, i.e. the exact legal text that would be changed.
- Such fields can be filled up over time by co-owners of a proposal as it receives more participants.
- Fields of interest could be hypotheses behind intended changes, reason to believe their impacts, modeling of economic impacts, implementation and roll-out plan.

Preventing duplications and overlap

- Proposals similar to one another can be avoided by requiring the differences to be documented.
- In the business world, we have created a whole industry of patent professionals in order to protect the value of inventing something new, which in return makes innovation investible for companies.
- Some kind of AI LLM models can assist in noting which proposals are similar, and prompting participants to explain differences.

Iterative process

- At every certain frequency (for example, every month) a certain number of most-valued proposals are moved to the voting stage.
- The price-signal serves as proposals' importance as well as fitness for receiving majority approval.
- The number and frequency is a matter of size and community, number of challenges worked on, and community resources set aside for governance.

confidence they induce in us. We also gain knowledge of them over time and build a reliable picture of their credibility.

We need a replacement for the natural assessment of credibility. We need some kind of score-keeping of wisdom, which lives and dies with the person. Such wisdom cannot be bought with money; one cannot buy CCs. They cannot be transferred from one to another. They are yours, and their use is linked to your success in participating in collective decisions.

In Merit Democracy, the developers of proposals would be rewarded by the number of their shares in the proposals. The rewarding would happen over a period of time that the public benefit of the proposal occurs, where the proposal co-owners receive a percentage of collective gains to society. Even an allocation of 1–3% of social gains can we worth billions of dollars when we are talking about reducing congestion or rate of chronicle disease development, or mental health issues, or crime at the national level. These gains would be distributed to the co-owners of the proposals, hence making the development of legislative proposals possibly a lucrative engagement, especially for people who really understand areas of valuable public concern.

The earnings would feed back into CCs. These credits can be used by those earning them to make more bets on new proposals, creating a virtuous cycle: those that have done well in predicting positive future outcomes of policies have more resources to do more of that. On the other hand, if you made bets that resulted in social losses, you would lose more of the CCs you bet.

The idea is that everyone would start with a set number of CCs, say 1,000. If you never use them they remain in your account. You can use them in order to invest in proposals. If you do so, you have the chance of gaining more CCs if your policy proposals succeed, creating future results in improving the metrics identified for the challenge they aim to fix. You may also lose them if you invest them in proposals that perform badly in creating the outcomes we want.

If you have earned some through successful proposals, you would have in excess of 1,000. That excess can be traded into money in our regular economy. Such transfer enables citizens to enjoy the benefits of participating in politics and even to make a living out of it (Figure 6.6).

Figure 6.6   The economy of citizenship credits in the legislative cycle.
All citizens would start with an equal, non-transferable Citizen Credits
that they can invest into legislation proposals. A virtuous cycle created
by feeding back positive insights that promote policies creating
desirable outcomes, while damping down negative participation in
proposals, which creates net negative impacts on the challenges.
Citizens can enjoy a substantial financial reward if their legislation they
back bear net positive impacts for the society, by converting the excess
Citizen Credits to cash.

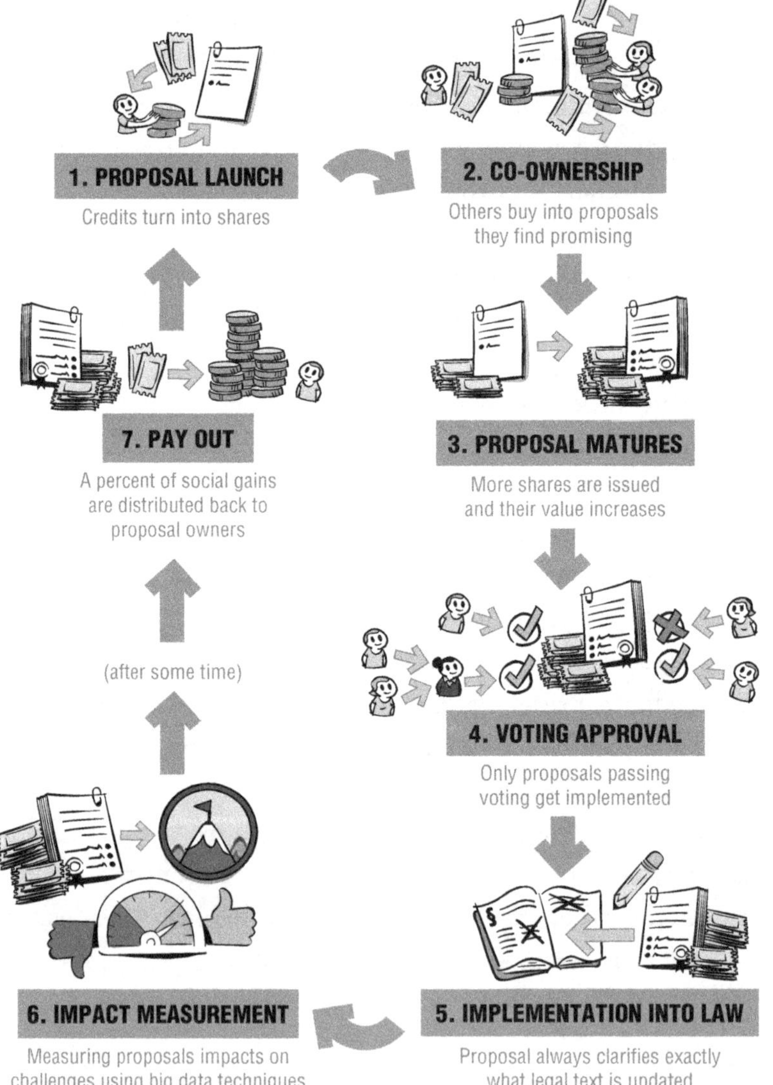

Losses and gains would be subject to some kind of taxation scheme. This is to bring everyone back to the standard of 1,000 over time. If you participated in successful proposals, but don't touch anything else for some decades, your gains will wear off. That is because we need incentives for participation, and the value of successful participation wears off over time, as the world changes, as does the participants' ability to make positive contributions. Conversely, we need to compensate those who have made some bad bets; they need to have new chances to engage. That would happen slowly over time to bring them back to the starting amount.

One other issue in this citizen credit economy is solving the problem of long-term outcomes. Say you've bet on a legislation proposal to help fix obesity. If we are observing the reduction of obesity due to a new policy, and we are observing the actual obesity level as our metric, it will likely take many years before effective policies show impact. How do we bridge the CCs allocated by successful bidders as they wait to earn out the long-term benefits of a good policy?

When we construct our challenges we might find metrics that are observable in short term, while linked to long-term outcomes as much as possible. However, often we will not be able to identify short term metrics for long-term outcomes we wish to create. In that case, we can use secondary markets (WallStreetPrep.com, 2024) to support the citizen credit economy. This means one can sell their share in a proposal to someone else at a price they agree on, while the legislation's outcomes are pending analysis. A secondary market can be constructed, because presumably there will be some early indicators that will become available while the ultimate long-term indicator of success is pending. Speaking of obesity, there may be a measurement on changes of consumption levels of sugar-containing products, or an increased amount of physical activity, which can prompt many to suspect the legislation is working as intended. Hence, there will be citizens who are willing to bet on the outcomes of a legislation whose measurement is pending, if another citizen wants to leave their shares to invest elsewhere.

Legislation in Merit Democracy will not be free of costs. Neither is running our governments today. We pay a high price for our political machinery, including a great deal of interest organizations, consultant hours, and public affairs (lobby) workers.

In Merit Democracy, in contrast, the amounts paid out to the citizens would be a function of the outcomes they achieve. As mentioned, these amounts would be a fraction of the overall value generated, and its funding would be driven by collective savings and prosperity and channeling a small taxation of those gains to remunerate the citizen credit economy.

Legitimacy Through (Liquid) Voting

A legislation market without voting would have an important design flaw: narrow interest groups could use all their credits to invest into policies that favor only them. As a result, they could lose citizenship credits but gain handsomely in their businesses at the cost of everybody else.

Voting is also a key part of the process to ensure legitimacy of the public decisions. A voting process ensures a proposal is debated, and everyone has the chance to speak up for or against it and vote on it. Even if we want market dynamics to incentivize citizens to engage, the one person one vote principle is rooted deep in our need for agency. We must have a clear, easy, and transparent manner in which to engage in the process of accepting and rejecting a proposal.

Just like the proposal development stage, this stage will have a fixed time period, for example a month. In this period people can vote for or against the proposal. Such a time frame allows for healthy debate to take place. The iterative nature also allows us to build routines around voting: instead of consideration of our social contract and changes to our policies being an extra activity in our regular life, it would become routine.

In order to ensure a high level of participation we would use online delegations. A liquid delegation system means that everyone is free to vote, but if they don't, their vote is represented by one or many representatives to whom they have delegated their vote. Citizens can choose several delegates based on each area of public policy and they can also move their delegations to new people any time they want, not waiting for elections. If an issue is important to someone then they can always vote for it themselves (Figure 6.7).

Since allocating time and attention to debating an issue costs us resources, perhaps most importantly our attention, we need to manage how many and which proposals are moving to the voting stage. If there are too many we risk not having enough attention or deliberation on them. If too few we risk not moving fast with iterating on our legislative agenda. The preceding process, where proposals are developed, allows us to prioritize them and mature them to make sure we are not debating random, unbaked ideas at the voting stage.

Since the voting on Merit Democracy would (only) take place online people can vote and debate the issues at hand flexibly from their own place and in their own time. By removing the representative bottleneck, we can have many more issues debated in parallel on the public platform, where many more than the small representative group would vote on the proposals. Currently, the pace of decision-making depends on the pace of one individual representing approximately 500,000 citizens. Even if we had an average of one out of 100 voting (and the rest delegating), we would already achieve a 5,000 fold increase in our capacity to engage.

We can utilize smart techniques to cultivate more awareness. When the voting period starts, as people are to cast their vote, we can require voters to provide their reasoning for why they vote the way they do. That reasoning can be rated by others, to formulate the main reasons

Figure 6.7 Dynamics of liquid voting in Merit Democracy.
The voting stage contains dynamics promoting fact fullness and citizen education. Citizens can set their delegation lines at any time and define them based on areas of concern. Before the voting period ends citizens can see the interim result, and have still the opportunity to cast vote their directly instead of delegating, or change their vote. Score-keeping of influencers over time is a crucial element in building feedback loops.

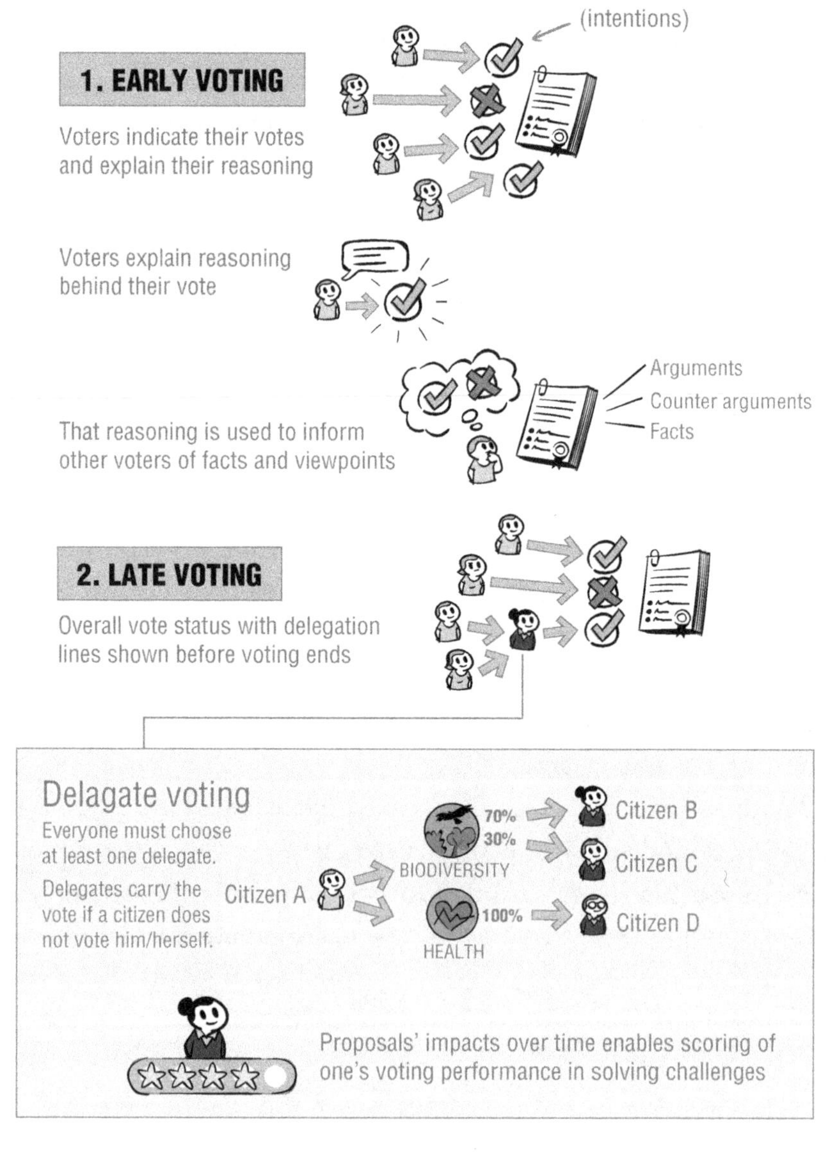

to vote and most relevant concerns. These can then be used to ensure the voters that vote in the opposite direction see the most important arguments against their position before they vote. This can ensure a minimum level of awareness on the voter base.

If the prediction market is a phase where experts are to thrive, voting is the stage for communicators to do so. They do not need to be specialists. Strong communicators, arguably today's politicians as well as journalists, can act as the new breed of "thought-leaders," or inspired by the term cultivated on social media, as "influencers." They would use video or other forms to explain the legislation to their audience. Their securing of followership would be through securing of delegation lines.

In order to engage sufficient talented communicators, we would need to create financial incentives for the online delegates, or influencers. Since the legislation's performance is measured, we can link those to each influencers' own voting patterns, and rate their accuracy in accepting (and rejecting) legal proposals. An influencer's score would increase if they are advocating against a proposal, which gets approved in a vote anyway, but then performs badly. Equally, their ratings would improve if proposals they promote do perform well.

The communicators' remuneration could be based on two things: number of delegations they carry and rate of achieving success with their votes. We could assign a budget toward influencers as a recurring monthly budget, where a lump sum amount is shared among the total number of delegations one has carried. This is somewhat inspired by Spotify model: The available budget for musicians doesn't increase or decrease if people are listening to music more or less, but the total monthly subscription revenues are divided to musicians based on how much their music is played. In order to reflect the time delay of proposals' success, we could make a bonus based on actual performance of the proposals – with a downside of withholding future (delegation) payouts if they did not perform well.

Securing majority votes could be the pathway to passing new legislation. But it doesn't have to be: we can increase the level of approvals we need to a higher percentage. The higher the rate of approval, the more difficult it will get to pass new legislation. At the same time, given we are opening up the process to everyone, a lot more creativity and expertise will be available to fine-tune proposals and represent interests to get to higher levels of approval. It may well turn out that two-thirds majority becomes the new standard for approvals in a system of Merit Democracy (Figure 6.8).

Figure 6.8   Short summary on liquid voting.

Voting ensures legitimacy, awareness, and secures rejection of proposals not acceptable to the majority.

Reasons to use liquid voting

- One person one vote and minimum of majority votes provide legitimacy to decisions.
- Enables high rate of participation, combining self vote and delegation.

Time frames

- Legislation proposal moves from prediction market to voting.
- Initial period without votes but only deliberation.
- In the next period, voting is permitted, while overall vote is not visible to prevent a too small minority from influencing overall vote outcome.
- Interim result of voting becomes visible while citizens can still vote.
- Upon voting deadline, delegation lines carry the vote for those who did not vote themselves.

Delegations

- Everyone has to pick at least one delegate.
- Everyone can vote directly whenever they want.
- If not voting directly, one's delegate's vote counts as theirs.
- Multiple delegates with freely assigned representation weight (for example, person A vote carries 30%, while person B carries 70%) for each issue area (for example environment, health, etc) permissible.

Anonymity

- One's vote would be anonymous by default.
- Delegating persons will have access to knowledge to the representing person's vote.
- If one wants to remain anonymous, they can reject obtaining any delegations, or relay delegations to others.

Financial incentives

- Communicators, a.k.a. influencers, play an important role for engagement in the voting stage.
- A total monthly budget to be divided among delegated votes casted.
- A market is created for communication work: if too many involved, payout per person drops, if too few, higher payout.
- Influencers' score in terms of their vote achieving success would be displayed clearly.
- A bonus or penalty can be applied based on the influencers' votes' realized performance.
- Unlike representatives, delegates are assigned per issue area, and delegation lines can be revoked at any time, for example due to changes in one's view in terms of the delegates' values or knowledge of the subject.

Awareness of facts and arguments

- Access to voting could require a minimum understanding of information and arguments against one's position.
- Such arguments are cultivated by the community over time as they vote, where voters provide arguments for why they vote the way they vote.

Necessary majority

- A simple majority is the minimum we can try.
- The system could also work with higher levels of majority requirements, i.e. two-thirds or even higher.
- Higher majority requirements would slow down decision making, while allowing more fine tuning of policy proposals to cater for the interests of the losers from new policies.

Measurement as Underlying Enabler

The legislative process I took you through starts with defined challenges. Prediction markets are used to develop proposals that can respond to the challenges. A voting stage enables deliberation effort and legitimate decision-making. When we implement the legislation we track its performance. The performance feeds back to the ability of citizens engaging in the legislation market as well as the track record of the communicators at the voting stage.

This process could not work without measurement of legislation's outcomes. Without such measurement we cannot conclude the legislation markets, and voices supporting or rejecting a proposal, would not receive a conclusive judgment. In the private sector, it is the reality of the performance of a company that makes entrepreneurs or investors thrive, not their ability to make big speeches about why they are right. Thus, linking legislation to real life results is a crucial part.

Sometimes we hear politicians talk about economy in measurable metrics. GDP growth, inflation, and unemployment are pronounced in that rhetoric. Even if these were our collective priorities (which they aren't) what we don't know or measure are the impacts of decisions taken by a politician on those priorities. We might experience a high inflationary environment and blame our politicians. What if this is a result of climate change or COVID-19, or result of the decision made six years ago by previous leader? Our ability to judge a leadership is seen in light of objective criteria of their undertakings.

The leap we need to make is to clear: we need to use the latest technology to link each and every public policy decision and intervention into impacts on the public goods we defined. We need to learn and improve how we govern.

When we measure outcomes of proposals, we need to not only measure the impact on a single challenge, but actually on all the challenges. We cannot afford that a policy that solves a challenge in one area cannot worsen one in another area. When we express our common goods in many dimensions, for example, in 100 or 1,000 measurable KPIs, and assign them a certain value, then we also shape the space in which we evaluate the proposals. They need to create net-value across all the metrics we measure, weighted by the value assigned to each. In order to focus the problem solving on the specific parameters of the challenge, we can make the market dynamics such that legislation's positive impacts on non-intended metrics can be discounted.

Making such data-driven analyses is not easy or straight forward. But thankfully, we can make it work with existing technologies, and especially so as those improve. Our ability to quantify the world has increased exponentially in past two decades. The amount of data we produce globally was estimated 5 billion gigabytes in 2003, and in 2023, it was estimated to be 120 trillion gigabytes. That's a 25-fold growth in 20 years, and about 66% annual average growth. More importantly, our data analysis tools have truly revolutionized how we live and continue to do so. There are numerous big data analysis techniques that enable us to make not only correlational but causal analysis. Methods like Granger causality, propensity score matching, regression discontinuity, and more sophisticated models like Bayesian networks (Hassani, Huang and Ghodsi, n.d.) are techniques available to us.

Tech companies show us the way with data capabilities. As Shoshana Zuboff has explored in her book *Surveillance Capitalism*, companies innovate and develop methods to better understand our needs and behaviors and use them to target us with products and services. This was the picture some 5–10 years ago. Now that we are in the midst of the AI revolution, all of the tech will become even more powerful.

What would happen if we were able to use social data in order to understand implications of public decisions on our collective priorities? Further, what would happen if we were able to use data in order to link the impacts of products and services on our collective priorities? What if such measurements received funding to the tune of hundreds of billions of dollars, enabling us to understand our collective space anew?

Data enables power. Through data we can design destructive weapons, platforms that can change our behaviors to act or consume in various ways. Currently, we use almost none of that power for our collective actions. In the future we shall not only use our data for shaping our policies, but also own it, and manage it as an invaluable public asset.

Envisioning a Policy Market to Overcome Loneliness

In Denmark the culture of associations is striking. Getting off work at 4pm, most people have a rich social life, dedicating themselves to the cause(s) they enjoy. From sauna clubs to music bands to permaculture, people engage in activities though non-profit organizations where they regularly volunteer, creating platforms for rich, non-transactional interactions. Perhaps, this has been a key to Danish success of happiness. And the government has been supporting them with public contributions, although it did not quantify their value.

Unfortunately for Denmark, such voluntary engagement association life is in decay, in line with reduced support from government, and increasing pressure for young people to make ends meet. According to Danish health researchers' report in 2021, loneliness has become the biggest health issue in the country. The anxiety and stress caused by it causes more death than alcohol or cigarettes, or dining habits, or even, physical activity.

There is an increasing body of literature that now concerns itself with the importance of people having (meaningful) interactions. Happiness researchers find that one of the most important factor is engaging with people around, whom one might call "acquaintances" (Qvist, Henriksen and Fridberg, 2018).

"How can we create more meaningful social engagement?" could be the title for a new challenge. We could measure how much time people spend in the presence and company of others and the quality of gatherings through surveys. We could take a step further and use some mobile and communication data for this purpose. We can also observe health consequences, through interactions with the public health system, and if needed, further by collecting data through smart applications. Any data collection would be known by citizens and would employ methods ensuring privacy of data.

What does a village in Greece, one in Japan and one in California, the United States, have in common? Three villages have impressed researchers in terms of the longevity of their residents' lives. These villages produced some of the oldest people on earth, earning them the name of "blue villages." Not only were they living long lives, they were also engaged and productive members of their tribes.

Researchers delved into genetics. They looked into what people ate. Their exercising habits. The Californians ate whole grains and fruits, the Greeks at a lot of vegetables, while the Japanese consumed a lot of legumes and seaweed (Asher Longevity Institute, 2024). They all ate healthily and did regular exercise but this wasn't the surprising element. What made a special impression on researchers was that there were frequent and tight gatherings. All members in the villages felt they belonged to the group, and further, they've contributed in important ways, despite their age. They cared for one another and did favors for one another. They felt they made a difference.

In the Netherlands, experiments showed that a policy incentivizing students and the elderly living under same facility was beneficial to both.

It reduced cost of living for both, elderly could help chores such as cooking while the young help them with other tasks and keep them company (Humanitas, 2024).

I believe that people can benefit from living in housing arrangements where they regularly come in contact with one another. As I am writing this book, I am in the process of building a tiny house in a communal village, in Danish "bofellesskab" of 16 tiny homes. Each home is a self-sufficient home, but one that is not very large. Besides being ambitiously sustainable, the community aims to create quality of life without requiring much material wealth, by bringing people of different backgrounds and ages together, who share a vision of such communal and sustainable living. We would expectably eat together a few times a week and share hobbies and some infrastructure such as greenhouses and perhaps even a sauna.

Such co-living spaces, where one has their private home, albeit usually smaller than regular private homes, supplied with common spaces where one spends time in the company of others, are on the rise. New long-term co-living villages have been established in Denmark in recent years, showing demand. Yet they make up a very small percentage of homes. The real estate market subtly operates against them: shared spaces are not counted toward one's purchase, making the estate look more expensive than it is.

My proposal to overcome the challenge of loneliness would involve a policy change creating financial incentives for co-living in terms of housing taxes, as well as changes in the building permits, to favor building more co-living units as a percentage of new housing developments.

The early indicators showing the success of this policy would be existing homes converting into co-living spaces. I am rather sure our first policy will not be the optimum one. Yet we need creative thinking unleashed in all sorts of areas of our lives. Each challenge we propose in our policy markets is an opportunity to unleash radical new thinking.

The policy markets will then enable experts pricing the policies based on body of research that convinces them it is the policy that yields desired results. Most young people are not specialized in anything. But they become experts in whatever area of finance they delve into as they research their way in order to make a living. This is where prediction markets can help us move forward and leave behind the populism trap.

THE BACK WHEEL: DELIVERY OF PUBLIC GOODS IN MERIT DEMOCRACY

I described in Chapter 4 the history of public delivery. Whether delivered through government employees such as teachers or nurses, or delivered through contracts with the private sector, many public services are continued without linking them to impacts we want to generate.

The future of our social contract not only needs reform in legislation, but also in how we deliver public goods. We can and must use the data and market thinking here to realize changes we need.

At the center of my proposal is a data exercise, similar to what I have described in estimating the impacts of legislation, in order to estimate the impacts of products and services. Once we estimate them, we provide the financial cost and benefit to the companies creating them (Figure 6.9).

Money–Value Alignment

The solution we need must align "money" with "value" that is holistic upon all transactions, that is adding the value borne by society to the value of the consumer (Figure 6.10). This means, in economic terms, internalizing externalities.

As I covered in Chapter 1, so long we (only) measure "value" by what each of us want, individually (as consumers), we cannot focus on delivering

Figure 6.9   The back wheel of service delivery.

It is recognized that companies' goods and services sold to customers have external impact to societal challenges. Companies' products and services' impacts are measured up against all relevant metrics, and generates a net pay into the company, or a pay out. For such measures companies share their operational data with public authorities, who have the necessary capabilities to undertake such measurement. Companies learn over time how to change their products and services to create better impacts and improve their businesses.

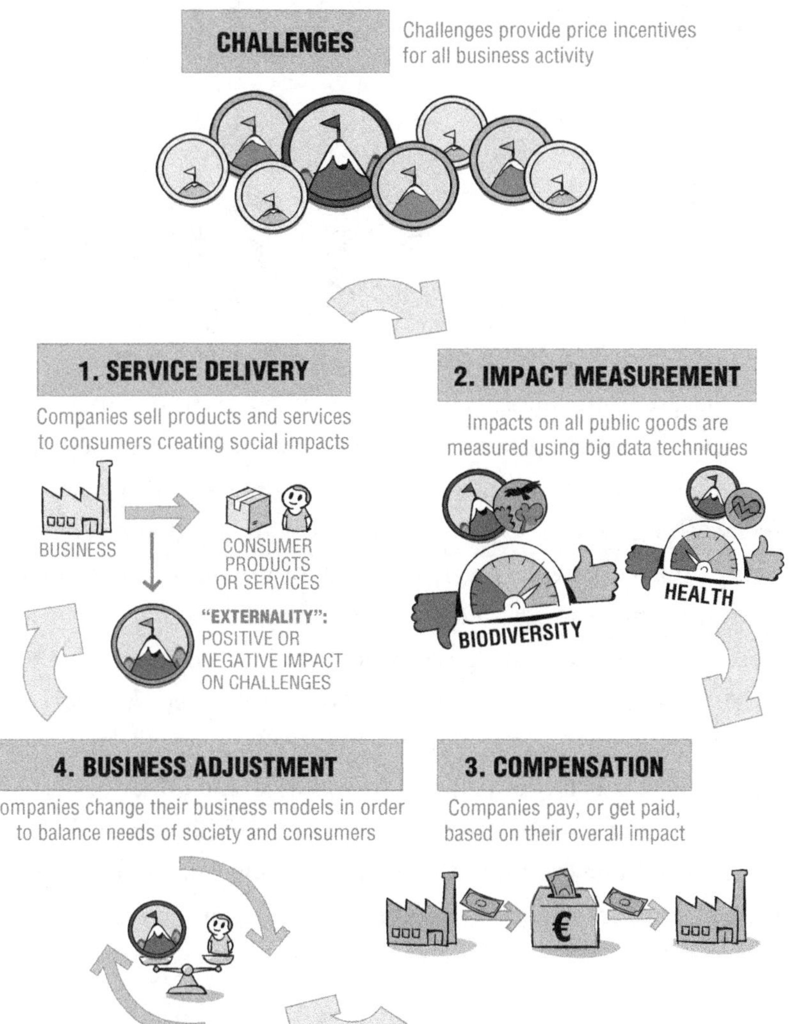

Figure 6.10   The need to account for externalities of products and services.
Money only represents consumer value today, since there is no way of monetizing creating environmental or social benefit . . . until we start measuring companies' products and services impacts on planet and society and link it back to their financial interests.

impacts that we want collectively. The individual incentives in each transaction inevitably position us as consumers and deprives us of our citizen's economic hat. "Consuming according to our values" ends up in a misery of greenwashing as well as hopelessness due to the free-rider problem, observing others not being as sensitive about the values we care about and undoing the impacts we created by suffering ourselves.

Thus, bringing about change must be a coordinated effort as at the heart of the matter is a coordination problem, and hence we need a social contract to reflect the value. We can align the earning of money with the interest of humanity where we start accounting for value: in the books of businesses, deep in our accounting definitions and systems. This is a good place to intervene since value creation is financially acknowledged first when sales, profits, and taxes are recorded in companies' financial statements. It is also a good place, because companies are superbly logical in prioritizing their financial results and acting on incentives to improve them.

We can add a section to companies Profit and Loss statements – the statement where companies' activities are summarized in a financial language (Figure 6.11). It shows sales, costs contribution margins, investments, and so on. A new section to be added would express "financial gains and losses due to non-direct (external) activities." In this section companies would start seeing their impacts on various social and environmental

Figure 6.11   We need companies to account for their externalities – positive or negative – in the future.
The future Profit and Loss statement would include economic impact values that the company has generated or detracted from society as a reward or punishment. EBESI (earnings before environmental and social impacts) would be equivalent to today's Earnings. That would prevent companies from realizing consumer-driven gains from a new technology that means society and the planet are facing losses.

THE NEW P&L INTERNALISING EXTERNALITIES		
	This Period	Last Period
Revenues		
Cost of goods sold		
Gross Profit		
Fixed cost		
Other operating income		
Other operating expense		
NEBITDA (Narrow Earnings Before Interest, Taxes, Depreciation and Amortisation)		
Depreciation and Amortisation		
Interest		
Taxes		
Narrow Earnings (aka Earnings in old definition) = EBESI		
EBESI (Earnings Before Environmental and Social Impact)		
Environmental Impact		
Air quality		
BioDiversity		
GHG emissions		
Social Impact		
Mental Health		
Labor Market		
Traffic Congestion		
Earnings		

Good old company profit and loss

New section to the P&L with all society and environment impacts in $$ - just like CO2 metrics, and their impact on each of these metrics will provide them with either money coming in or going out.

The overall impact value of a company then will be based on cross-relating all of the companies' activities with all of the public metrics we care about. Next to EBITDA, which stands for "Earnings Before Interest Taxes Depreciation and Amortization," we could start hearing EBESI: Earnings Before Environmental and Social Impacts. Such a new financial term making its way to the Profit and Loss statement would take the concern for environment and society away from the desk of the marketing and investor relations department, where sustainability and ESG reporting usually lives. Instead, with such financial relevance, the concerns would land right on CEO's and CFO's desks.

This can work in a setting similar to businesses receiving and reporting their value added taxes (VAT) every quarter. Instead of simply reporting their VAT payments, businesses would now also receive a report on their impact on various metrics. Through such monthly updates, businesses can see how they affect various social metrics and through which interactions. A gaming company may find out that they improve creativity especially with first few hours per week exposure, while on the other hand, worsen social skills with too long exposure. A scooter share company may find out they contribute to the goal of reducing car use and related public consequences in the outskirts of a city, while it has more negative consequences in dense urban areas for reducing general use of the area by older people due to perceived threat.

Just like tax collection or national security, the task of calculating the impacts would be the job of public authority, and this makes it the most important public authority of the future. This implies organizations whose main goal criteria is to understand the underlying drivers of influences and causes to public goods. Any data-driven conclusions would be expressed with some "level of confidence" that we are familiar with from statistics. The more we figure out a social phenomena's drivers in terms of its connection to other public goods, legislation, products, and services, the more confidence we would gain in our models.

This comes in the acknowledgment of success of the finance-driven organizations and economies we created. If we want change, the language we use must change where power lies. Sustainability and impact must become concepts in the language of finance, and a direct and core part of value generation, expressed in money and profits.

Unleashing New Business Models

Let us go back to the story of Tesla, the company that drove adoptions of electric vehicles, and made Mr Musk the richest man. It was the regulations involving deep tax incentives in the Nordics that drove Tesla's sales in the company's early days. Norway provided free pass from congestion charges sales tax, and offered free parking, making it first market where Tesla gained serious traction. In Denmark, one could pay one-third for a Tesla compared to a regular car thanks for generous Danish legislation making the EVs free of otherwise very high car surcharges. As mentioned earlier, other CO2 quotas and regulations gained the company $7bn 2020–2023, 20% of its profits.

Incentives set by governments are crucial in driving markets and new business models. The carbon emissions market – despite its low pricing of carbon emissions so far, and only levying it on select industries – has shown how pricing externalities can be an important driver of business. What we have seen with companies aiming to improve their emissions is only the tip of the iceberg.

Many other publicly beneficial companies, however, do not get paid for their impact. Meet Danish startup Tiimo and its founders Helene and Melissa. Tiimo is an app that helps neurodivergent persons dealing with everyday life through scheduling of tasks and reminders, especially those suffering from attention deficit, ADHD. I've met them early in my journey with Donkey Republic in an incubation center. Their app is improving the lives of tens of thousands of individuals around the world. The Tiimo App, mostly used through a smartwatch, helps the users keep on schedule and establish routines. Yet, like many other entrepreneurs, the social value they create does not get paid by society.

A US-based startup, Akili, has even developed a game with the aim of helping young people with attention deficit. Their game, EndeavorRx was designed to train young individuals with simultaneous motor challenges, targeting neural systems that strengthen attentional control over time. They even obtained an FDA approval – the first game to do so – as a prescription treatment for attention deficit after clinical studies.

Yet, in our economy, having such great positive outcomes does not pay. In return, many of the most famous games are linked to negative outcomes for the players. Violent video games such as Grand Theft Auto have been suggested to increase aggression over time, while decreasing empathy and prosocial behavior (Goldbeck and Pew, 2024). Games designed to be addictive to improve play time (with extensive reward systems such as World of Warcraft) have also shown to increase levels of depression and anxiety, and players neglecting real life responsibilities and relationships (Kirby, Jones and Copello, 2014).

Social media platform exposure has also been shown to cause some mental health issues, due to feelings of inadequacy and low self-esteem, and in other cases, anxiety caused by fear of missing out and cyberbullying (Vogels, 2022). Many researchers now show how we get addicted to our screens thanks to various social media platforms' addictive design. Absent financial incentives measuring and paying for citizens well being, businesses turn to what makes them money, and addiction pays.[1]

We can create an economy where social and environmental factors we care about are priced, and products and services stand to make or lose money by how they influence them. When we priced CO_2, it gave way to companies like Tesla to benefit and prosper. If we price mental health, others like Tiimo and Donkey Republic might do the same.

In an economy, where all externalities are linked to financial outcomes, we unleash the creativity and innovation of the business world to help us create the society and environment we long for. In such an economy, a growing business would mean contributions to our social goals, either directly creating them, or by paying for their damages.

With some imagination, we can foresee major changes happening in various areas of the economy if we are able to establish such links and set appropriate prices by linking the financial implications of externalities to companies.

- (Social) Media: we could have media outlets who move their business models away from keeping readers' eyeballs on whatever provocative news they can find, and value more what we would publicly want from media, things like critical thinking skills and factualness.
- Transport: we can imagine free bike share with car share, cargo bikes ebike leasing and carpooling being subsidized to reduce car trips and ownership, making cities much more livable with reduced noise, congestion, pollution, and stress.
- (Mental) health: health professionals focusing more on the causes of bad health, from trauma that needs to be resolved to lifestyle changes. Therapy would become more affordable and commonplace. We can imagine an increased level of businesses for all sorts of activities with the aim of bringing people together, from cooking and dancing to meditation and yoga classes.
- Housing: We can foresee changes in the construction industry to consider not only low cost and heat efficiency but also social consequences, spending time with others, as well as broader environmental and health consequences of materials.
- Dating/Family: dating apps would have new incentives to prioritize relationships that benefit our long-term well-being.

The world is complicated and becoming more so. Products and services have unintended consequences for our lives. We cannot reward or penalize them upfront based on our hypotheses. We must iteratively experience how various (and evolving) business models impact our metrics and keep a dynamic way of placing taxes on them and rewarding them. We must remember that both business models and technology, and our social and environmental priorities, are moving targets. Therefore, we cannot assume a new set of regulations can lastingly put us better off. The impacts of products and services can also vary based on the place and people they are present – we cannot simply assume what worked in one place and at one time will work here and now.

How to Fund Public Goods

You may be worried about how to pay for all the public goods. If we start paying businesses from public pockets you may be afraid we will run out of money in no time.

The good news is that we can design the public goods as "markets" that do not require tax-payer money.

Sounds too good to be true? Well, let's look into how the CO_2 markets work: by setting a level of emissions quotas toward companies, this market establishes a price of CO_2, not by paying for emissions reduction from public budgets, but by making the high emitters pay for their negative impacts.

We can simply look at the delivery of public goods as a marketplace: there are companies that improve our metrics of public goods, and those that worsen them. What we simply need to do is to establish the prices on the metrics to make businesses really care for them. That can be done by implementing quotas, or by simply declaring the prices of impacts (Figure 6.12).

Such intervention does not need to cost the state anything. It can simply change the way a business succeeds over the other, without drawing the money out of the economy or creating expensive frictions.

Take congestion as an example. We can model when and how cars create congestion and on which roads. We have already implemented congestion charges in some cities, which make it expensive to use certain roads at certain points in time. Now imagine that the money raised by

Figure 6.12 Leveraging markets for impacts.
Markets for various public goods can ensure that
companies that contribute get paid while those
harming the metrics pay in. A fund serves as a balancer
for each challenge.

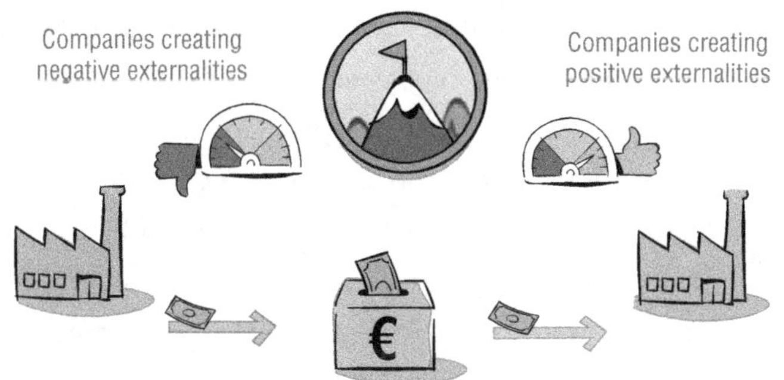

Companies pay into impact fund in proportion of their combined external impacts

congestion-increasing businesses (the car economy) is going to pay for those initiatives that reduce congestion. That can include all alternatives to cars: from bike sharing to carpooling.

If we treated congestion reduction as a market as we do CO_2 emissions, we would both levy charges to contributors to congestion and we would use those funds to support alternatives. Many new business models would thrive because they would receive public funding for their positive impacts. These services would become more affordable and available.

We can go further and introduce the idea to even more measurable metrics that improve our quality of life linked to transport: particle emissions and traffic accidents have serious public health consequences that can lead to markets just like congestion. Public space is yet another one, where most of our urban public space is currently taken up by roads and parking lots.

In essence, we can make impact markets for certain verticals, for example a Mobility Impact Market, where those bearing negative impacts can pay in, and those creating positive impacts are paid. The attribution is, again, of key importance and attainable thanks to possibilities of big data today. Currently, cities try to deal with such challenges without using effective tools. They deploy a lot of public money in running public transport based on a logic of funding inputs, but without incentivizing public transport operators to innovate to find ways to attract more people to their vehicles.

When dealing with local public goods, such as congestion, space and noise and particle pollution, we really need to convince a small group of people – residents of a city – to set a fair price for these. The challenge is usually the lack of sophistication and lack of resources to deal with such a smart mechanism. However, thanks to increasing availability of tools to collect and analyze data we can today run small markets for public goods effectively, moving funding away from companies worsening the goods, and moving them to companies improving them.

I don't mean that we do not need to spend any public money on creating the goods we want, other than what is raised by detractors in a market setting. Not at all. I believe we should support these (impact) markets for public goods with public funding raised through ordinary taxes. My claim is that we have many products and services that are currently undertaxed (think cars, social media platforms, harmful games, or dating platforms) and simply documenting their impacts and levying effective prices on them will cover some if not most of the funding we need in order to provide proper incentives for businesses to really care about creating impacts we need (Figure 6.13).

Envisioning a Mobility Impact Market to Overcoming Car Dependency

An impact market could help us transform urban mobility. Currently most cities across the United States and Europe and the world have many more car trips than the citizens would like (European Investment Bank, 2025). But we

Figure 6.13   Short summary on impact markets.

Impact markets can incentivize companies to adjust business models away from negative externalities to helping create public goods.

Reasons to use impact markets

- Companies are rational and focused on.
- improving profitability, hence linking any impacts to bottomline is necessary.
- As CO2 markets show, this is an effective way to steer companies to innovate and change business models.

Overcoming narrow impact focus

- Only focusing on low emissions or similarly single dimensional impact ignores impact on other issues.
- A net impact to be attributed based on effects on all externalities.

Outcome attribution

- Social and environmental data along with companies' operational data to be used in modeling impacts.
- Not only 1st order impacts, but also 2nd, 3rd and nth order impacts would be attributed to relevant goods and services.
- Behavioral change is complex and cannot be estimated based on models; instead, look at the trends and link them to goods and services.

Pricing the impacts

- Each impact category would be linked to metrics, whose changes are also priced.
- Companies' impacts in the metrics are reflected in their quarterly reports with public authorities and become a part of their P&L.

Measuring authority

- Public authorities are to run the measurements, similar to tax authority, thanks to their ownership and legitimacy of dealing with public data.
- This is in contrast with the current model with accounting firms providing guidance for CSRD and ESG.

Funding of impact markets

- While companies contributing the positive impacts will get paid, those with negative impacts will pay in.
- There can be positive or negative net financial impact on public budgets.
- Public budgets can be defined to provide net positive payments towards the impacts, where needed.

Contrast with CSRD and ESG reporting

- CSRD and ESG reporting assume impacts going forward without taking into account complexity of a society and environment, ignoring many 2nd, nth order effects.
- Reports are based on companies' own data, which is limited and mainly addresses the supply side, leaving the behavioral impacts on the consumers out of the equation.
- Impacts are not priced, and not translated into companies' profitability.

have a situation where most households have already committed to a car, and where public transport isn't convenient enough and bikes are not safe.

One of the key enablers for reducing car dependency is removing the infrastructure that they take as given and is usually subsidized in terms of free or low parking fares, and use of roads – our public space. While removing car infrastructure, cities that build infrastructure for bikes have seen ridership rise in great figures, as safety is key for cyclists.

Negative incentives for car ridership work but often generate political frustrations that limit their use. So, the idea is not just punishing the modes that create negative impact, but also supporting the modes that are the socially desirable alternatives – to the extent they help. The Mobility Impact Market is thus a framework where the impact of a trip on congestion, public health, emissions, and space affects its affordability and availability. That is when cars pay in for the negative consequences, we use that money, transparently, to financially support the trips that are improving the provision of those public goods.

This means we would have much more funding available for incentivizing use of bikes, whether individually owned or shared, cargo bikes, car pooling, public transport, and also what is on the horizon: autonomous vehicles.

A trip by an ebike from a suburb to the city today does not receive any financial incentive, while it is clearly socially preferable to you making the trip by car. The car trip would have taken away from everyone in terms of time, space, noise, pollution,[2] emissions, and so on. An impact market would fund companies who make such alternatives viable. Whether a bike share, leasing company, or one that helps citizens document their trip on their own bikes, would receive funding from the impact market (Figure 6.14).

The impact market would need to assess the behavioral change created by the introduction of its various targeted subsidies. Through various data sources, such as mobile phone data and data from the vehicles, it would be possible to estimate over time the modal transport behavior of residents (i.e. how much they use the different modes of transport). By doing so, the impact market can isolate the behavior change introduced by the financial incentives.

An important use case for impact markets is to manage the urban transport behavior when autonomous vehicles become widespread. We

Figure 6.14   An overview of select externalities related to transport industry.
The social value of various transport modes is rather well researched. Public health benefits of active modes (walking and biking) are clear and usually forgotten or underestimated in transport policy, while social cost of cars in terms of (anxiety of) accidents, noise, and air pollution is also often omitted.
Source: Donkey.bike based on research by COWI, Eurostat, OECD. https://op.europa.eu/en/ publication-detail/-/publication/9781f65f-8448-11ea-bf12-01aa75ed71a1; https://www.itf-oecd.org/ good-go-assessing-environmental-performance-new-mobility.

	Congestion €/km Time delay costs to society	Public health €/km Effects of activity, accidents and air pollution	CO2 emissions Gr/km	Space m2/passenger For avg daily commute
Bike	0 €	1.3 €	17 Gr/km	2 m2
Train	0 €	0 €	66 Gr/km	0.7 m2
Scooter	0 €	–0.3 €	107 Gr/km	1.5 m2
Car	–0.35 €	–0.12 €	162 Gr/km	50 m2

want fewer car trips in the city centers, so we would need to make it expensive for cars to enter city centers through congestion charges. On the other hand, we want such vehicles to assist us for the trips from home to a public transport hub. Thus, we could pay an autonomous vehicle company for their "first-mile" service, helping residents get to train stations. These would be trips out of the city centers, and they would help residents switch to public transport for the whole trip instead of using a car.

Impact markets would enable us to set specific subsidies for trips given a (start or end) place, time, and vehicle type, and we can iterate these subsidies in short intervals, for example every three months, in order to adjust to changes in the market. We can test out what kind of new vehicle type and service is creating the behavioral changes we benefit from and scale them as they work.

By not only taking money away from cars and being upset that people don't use inconvenient form of (traditional public) transport, we would create transparent ways of pricing our social goods, show how the different trips impact them, and allocate the funding where they work to help us create a transport behavior and economy that fulfills social goals.

Envisioning a Media Impact Market to Overcome Click Bait Culture

There's been much talk about media regulation to overcome fake news. More generally, there has been an unsolved question about how the public authorities should govern the media, if at all. Many are concerned about free speech.

First, let us talk about free speech. It seems we have overcome our fears of limiting free speech when it comes to the consumer economy. You cannot write on the package of your chocolate 200g if it actually only weighs 100g. Or, that the ingredients have to be what you declare them to be. Further, a claim about organic needs substantiation. No, we are not free to say whatever we want when companies sell their products and services.

And let us talk about the economy of the media industry. It used to be that public funding was a substantial component of media revenues – besides advertising. In Denmark, government funding still covers about one-third of all media revenues, the rest being consumer revenues and advertisement.[3] In the United States, about two-thirds of news media revenues are from advertising (Holcomb and Mitchell, 2014).

What if we accept that not all content has the same value for society, but some content is more valuable than others? Just like not all food is as healthy as other food, not all media content is as good for us. We would need to agree on the metrics of value from media. Let us assume that we managed to define those as factfulness and critical thinking. These are important skills for citizenship, after all, and in general are good for us in our everyday lives. Could we then set up an impact market, where media outlets and distributors stand to gain and lose financially, based on their effect on these metrics? I think so.

The media impact market would acknowledge that various media outlets have an impact on the metrics we care about. It would manage this impact by charging a fee to those media outlets that worsen citizens' factfulness and critical thinking, while providing financial support to those that improve those.

In order to measure the impacts on those it could use a directly elected media board, whose job would be to design surveys that help measure factfulness and critical thinking skills. These surveys would be presented to media viewers as they are exposed to various channels with simple questions. All media channels would need, by law, to accept the media board's surveying of their readers. The surveying could happen through a digital protocol (an API) so that the outlets do not have control over when and how these are shown, or how they are responded to.

Once we have enough data, we can start to make statistically significant causal inferences on how various media platforms impact the skills of their readers over time. And with that we can place financial incentives for platforms to do a better job on those metrics. Such intervention would challenge the click bait media on the side of content creators that currently focus on attracting the eyeballs and keeping them at the cost of creating false perceptions of the world. It would also challenge social media platforms in order to find ways to change their media distribution.

The content and outlets that do not care about their impacts will face higher impact taxes, while those that improve will receive financial support that enable them to provide services increasingly free of ads and reader revenues. Such an impact market built on data can properly address the challenges of our media, that is also digitally empowered (Figure 6.15).

Figure 6.15   Illustration of a hypothetical media impact market.
Metrics such as factfulness and critical thinking skills can be established as public goods relevant for media. We can measure the impact of exposure to various media to these metrics, and use these impacts as basis for financial incentives.

Fund settles balances among companies based on their impacts on citizen factfulness and critical thinking skills

THE HANDLEBAR: TAKING OWNERSHIP OF OUR CHALLENGES

If I asked people what they wanted, they would have said faster horses

—Henry Ford

Those that have ever worked with innovation, startups, design, and tech likely know this: it is a difficult task to stay with the problem. Our brains are wired to jump into solutions when we are speaking of a problem. Yet, it is important to stay with the problem, and describe it well, if we are to find the best solutions.

In my first startup, called Wedecide, a citizen engagement platform, we ran campaigns to gather citizens of a town, members of associations, and employees of a corporation in order to solve a challenge online. We investigated how open versus focused innovation processes compare, where the latter involves a specific set of goals to be achieved. Goal orientation and introduction of background and constraints can actually foster creativity compared to undefined goals.

Companies have been running innovation challenges over the past 15 years. From Netflix to Unilever, many companies have experience with such processes and established some best practices depending on their intentions. In any case, the innovation process starts with clear guidelines and communication. For both our legislative and public service efforts to succeed we need to define our challenges well. Such a definition will require measurable goals, expressed in some kind of metrics, such as average traffic congestion in minutes in a given time and place, or unemployment rate for specific target group in given area.

I sympathize with the healthy anger displayed with voters in the United States and European countries by voting for extreme left and right wing parties. I believe they feel frustrated due to lack of agency. The most important tool for agency would be for the citizens to decide what their collective problems are, in relative terms, and assign them value.

Merit Democracy is about enabling people to define their future. As mentioned in the Chapter 1, agency must be one of the core features of democracy. In the sections above, I described how we can construct a new, decentralized legislative function, and then how we can deliver public goods through impact markets, linking products' and services' impacts to the parameters we care about. In both of these reforms, at the core was markets acting on achieving improvements in what we define as our challenges.

We shall define these challenges collectively, online, in a transparent and decentralized manner. We would ask people to define our social problems and assign budgets to them in order to enable markets to take care of the rest.

We hear of direct democracy experiments where there is, for example, a citizen ballot to discuss a proposal, such as legalizing marijuana. Such initiatives happen without first identifying what problems they try to solve and clarify the importance of that problem compared to others. To be fair, almost any legislation will have impacts on numerous areas of public concern, and thus we would map how a proposal impacts all of the challenges we have at hand. Similarly, when we reward a company for its service, we shall not look only at its impacts on a single dimension but on all dimensions we care about. Nevertheless, new solutions should be in response to commonly acknowledged goals, otherwise we are like.

Once we have set up measurable goals as challenges we then need to prioritize the challenges. How can we prioritize our challenges in a decentralized manner? In the consumer economy, the products and services we buy more of achieve higher revenue, driving more resources and investment to those companies. Can we simply do the same, and aggregate our wishes for public goods?

One way of doing so would be through aggregating our public preferences for various public goods by extending a digital public budget wallet to each one of us, and allowing us to allocate our wallet into the goods we want more of. This wallet is one where you are each assigned an equal amount. We then place this budget onto programs we want to support. The relative placement of our citizen budgets in aggregate help determine the weight we will assign to challenges.

The issues and metrics we define as public goods can be anything that is measurable. They shall not be predefined by some experts, as SDGs are. Such predefined concepts are surely helpful in inspiring us but working with predefined and expert-dependent goal setting can diminish the agency we need to have. We could decide reducing crime as the top problem to be solved, instead of, for example, reducing loneliness.

When we define public goods, there is a general, moral, existential calling: we are actually defining what is meaningful for us collectively, which is what should make it more likely that we survive. We are creating realities we believe would make us more sustainable as a species. There are no rights and wrongs but preferences in the goal setting.

Look at the competition between Europe and the United States. For a long time, Europe has prioritized its citizens' welfare more than United States has. In terms of social care, healthcare, free higher education, higher minimum wages, various other protections made the European feel safer and more protected than American counterparts. The business-friendly environment in the United States seems to have prioritized accumulation of capital in few hands, and less protective regulations for consumers and long working hours. While Europe prioritized its diverse cultures and maintained a high level of local (national) control over the federal level, the United States has enjoyed a true single market. One of the outcomes of the US reality has been the birth of large and innovative companies, especially tech companies.

A recent report by Mario Draghi (Draghi, 2024) concerning the future of Europe's economy names the development of critical technologies by

European companies as a public good. From Draghi's perspective, critical technologies making a state more powerful in its exports and spill-overs in the global scene is a public good.

It will be difficult to argue which public goods matter more. We need competitive economies and stay strong in a world with strong voices and values that clash with ours. We also need to maintain trust and care for one another and our environment. We need to care for not only the next few years, but the next few generations. There are no rights or wrongs, but bets into the future for the longevity of our species. Our societies are to make compromising choices about what public goods we want to invest in over other public goods. The more deliberative, transparent, and diligent we can make those choices, the better chance we have in deploying our collective wisdom and avoiding the trap of few like-minded people having a group bias, and echo-chamber, as we see with our representative system (Figure 6.16).

City, National/Federal, Global

In Chapter 1, I discussed the idea that public goods have certain geographic or legal boundaries that they apply to. These boundaries are sometimes quite clear due to legal jurisdiction: for example, improving national security for a country clearly defines what geography is of concern. When we talk about reduction of congestion, it makes most sense to apply it to a metropolitan city level, as most commutes do not involve longer stretches.

Clean air can be a tricky one, as the winds can easily make a city suffer from pollution in a neighboring area. Healthcare is also tricky: much of what happens at a city level defines how healthy we live, and the city assumes much of the cost of health-related positive and negative consequences. But some of the costs and benefits concerning health occur at the national and federal level.

Security is also both a local, national, and even a global issue: we expect cities to keep streets safe by providing sufficient lighting and policing for example, but national policies around provision of welfare, social housing,

Figure 6.16   The handlebar in the Merit Democracy helps align us on our challenges.

Citizens set up challenges collectively. During qualification, random surveys can serve as qualifiers for popular challenges to move to voting. A government authority will be needed to step in for providing method and basis for measuring the proposed social/environmental metrics. Citizens allocate their (equal) citizen budgets onto challenges at any given time and thus aggregates overall priorities across the group. This enables assignment of financial value to the improvements in the metrics in the challenges. A well-funded challenge will pay out more in legislation and in service delivery.

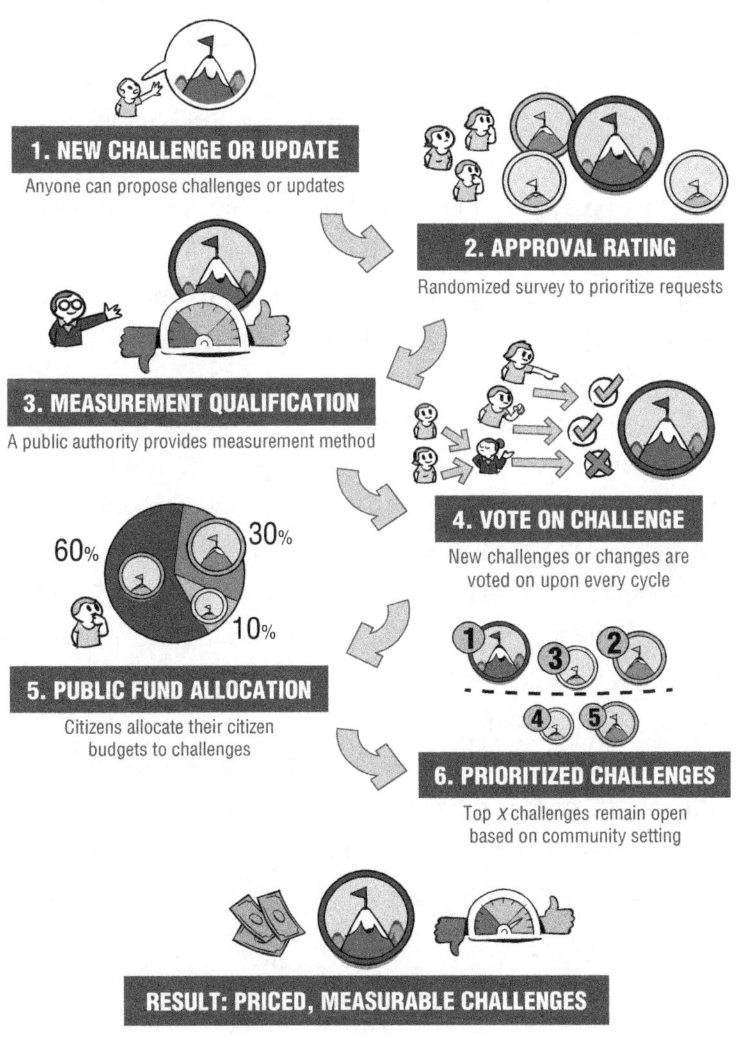

justice and incarceration, drugs etc., all play a role. It is also a global issue because smuggling happens across borders, and an arms race across continents make us concerned about our livelihoods, with the hanging threat of nuclear weapons and biological warfare.

The way forward in terms of allocation of budgets to public goods, seems most sensibly split into four levels: city level, national/state level, federal level, and global. Each of the four can be imagined as distinct social contracts. In one city we may want provision of more public goods, which might mean steeper prices for the goods, and possibly also higher taxes. Moving away from that city, and to a new city, we leave one social contract, and enter another one, with new budgets and priorities.

That is not too dissimilar from what we live in today: when we move to a new city, we face a different tax regime, and different ways of handling public goods. Our trash might be sorted in one place and not the other. Car parking fees may be different and so possibly is the minimum salary. What we don't have today is transparency over which challenges the group prioritizes, how much budget is assigned to improving each metric, and finally our own capacity to directly change the allocation of resources into one challenge versus the other.

As you may deduce here, the future of democracy should eventually be extended to everyone on the globe in order to effectively address the global challenges. The beauty of the ideas here are their scalability over larger groups of people. We shall work around some of the design parameters in order to adjust it to accommodate 10 billion people globally instead of the 5 million people in our metropolitan area. That may mean many more challenges are allowed to remain open concurrently, and challenge revisions can happen faster.

If we are to look at where we start reforming democracy we are likely to find it easier to start at the national and city levels. That is because we already have strong enforcement available, and the benefits of these goods will accrue to us in this limited jurisdiction. Focusing on a global problem like climate change in a small jurisdiction like our city often creates a back-lash in the form of free-rider problems: we don't want to take on painful measures unless others do it too (Figure 6.17).

Figure 6.17   The nature of who stands to benefit or lose from provision or absence of public goods defines the scope of the group that needs to govern.

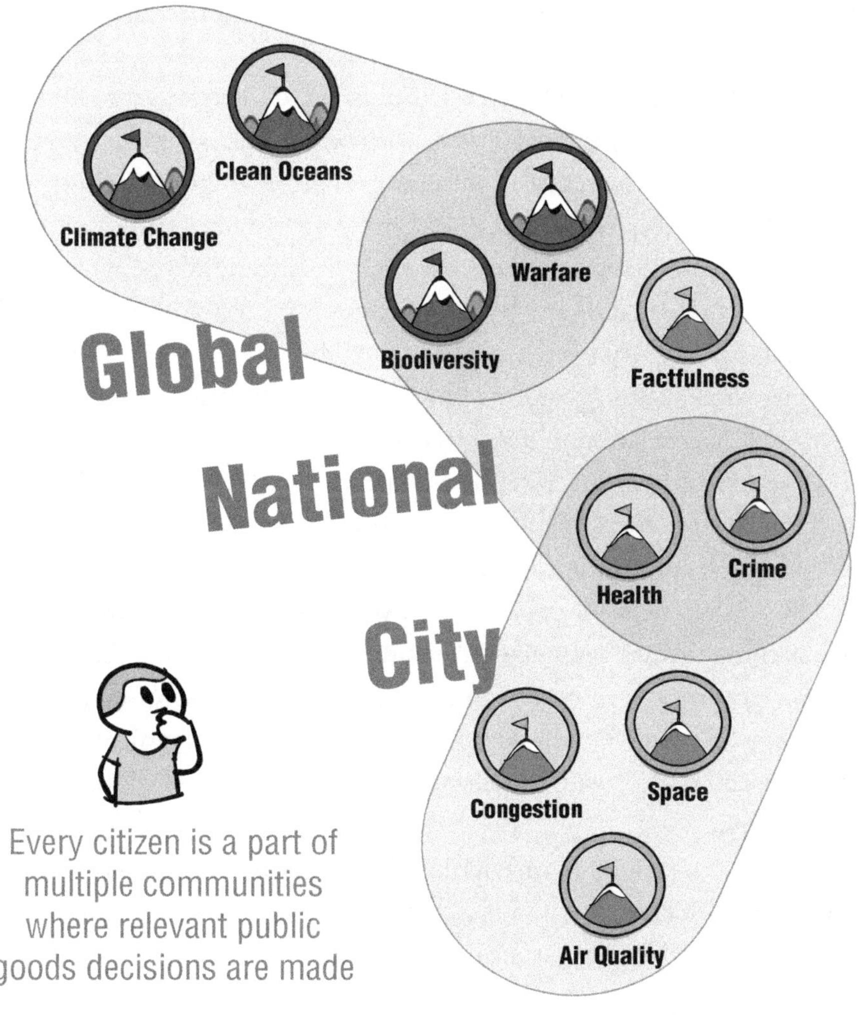

THE BIKE FRAME: ROLE OF STATE IN MERIT DEMOCRACY

We have painted the picture of Merit Democracy as a bicycle. We define challenges we want to solve (the handlebar), run iterative legislative cycles resulting in new laws (the front wheel), and set prices for the goods we want the economy to work on delivering (the back wheel).

What is then left for governments to do? Are we not going to have any institutions?

Merit Democracy is about creating strong, decentralized institutions that rely on direct personal interactions where necessary, to maintain directness and transparency as much as possible. It is about creating institutions born into systems that are driven by flows and controls written in code, and are hence objective, easy to read, visualize, and interact with.

The main institution in Merit Democracy is the frame of the bike holding it all together. That is defined mainly as the set of rules and processes that the whole platform works with, written in software code just like we have written a constitution that governs how we *should* behave.

The most important asset of democracy will be the social data and learnings we generate. The learnings are what we find out when we run the iterative legislative and service delivery cycles, when we start to understand how various laws, products, and services impact our public goods, and start intervening with new rules and pricing of the externalities.

For governance to be possible we need lots and lots of data and to put them to effective use. Without having access to data-driven learnings, we cannot deal with understanding the complexities of society and environment.

Collecting, cleaning, safeguarding, anonymizing data where needed, and creating the necessary causal relationships using the data will be key tasks to be performed by a state institution.

You may say, there are many areas of government that are naturally monopolistic and need to be delivered by the government agencies. This is true for national defense, police services, building of infrastructure, approval of market functions such as drugs or factory sites. These could remain under the control of various governmental authorities. The appointment of the people who are in charge of them and approval of budgets could happen online through a democratic voting process. Such appointments could possibly include supervising boards. Thereby we can overcome the idea of one president or prime minister who holds power over everyone. Instead of working with four-yearly appointments, we could appoint and let go of government heads when necessary.

Issues that require secrecy and confidentiality are tricky to handle in a democracy that aspires to be as transparent as possible. Military command and the intelligence office may need to be the areas where transparency is limited. However, we can assure that citizens are always aware of the kind of programs running, their purpose, and status. We could appoint supervisory functions in order to audit practices versus reports so that public will is not exploited.

Surely, any kind of design of state building will not be free of pain and expensive mistakes. A real attempt to reimagine democracy will also bring up new questions not previously thought about. The description of Merit Democracy is meant as an inspiration, because we are lacking inspiration for our path forward.

When I talk and debate about these visions for an alternative future of democracy and the ideas in this book, which I magically introduced to most of the dinners I attended in the past few years, I face concerns and criticism, as there should be. Let's have a look at those.

CHAPTER SEVEN

REASONS TO REMAIN CAUTIOUS

We are not faced with a crisis in society, not a crisis in nature, but a crisis of the modern framework itself, which requires us to rethink the way we view the relationship between humans and the world.

—Bruno Latour

It is perfectly true that there is no path forward if we simply continue to debate capitalism and socialism, or if we see the ecological crisis as a question that can be solved within the framework of either.

—Bruno Latour

I like Latour's invitation for us to confront our dichotomies. One such dichotomy we experience in popular culture is about reversing human progress. Looking at how modern society has failed to cater for some important human needs, for example, belonging and community, and further, the GDP growth-focused consumerism-driven economy that has been ignoring environmental and social limitations makes many skeptical as to whether humanity is making any real progress after all, in an intergenerational and civilizational sense, in securing the sustainability of the species. For them, many human inventions are unnatural, and what seems like progress is actually harmful to nature and thereby humanity.

Latour reminds us: we are nature. What we do next is the natural flow of evolution. There is no sense in reverting to another time when nature was more natural than it is now. We must think forward, instead of romanticizing how things could have been at a point in the past. Science and technology are not bad things. Money is not a bad invention, nor are microchips or methods enabling AI, or nuclear technology.

But our capacity to coordinate becomes critical as our ability to make mistakes in the evolutionary learning process becomes exponentially more costly. We must move forward but we cannot do so if we do not learn how to govern ourselves without destroying us.

We all know Churchill's famous quote: "Democracy is the worst form of government, except for all the others that have been tried." His message is a humbling one and invites us to pragmatism about which solutions can help us attain a more sustainable future for humanity. There are good reasons to believe some form of democracy is the way forward, but the shape and form democracy can take is up to us. There are pitfalls that may well render what I've introduced, Merit Democracy, a decentralized and direct governance form based on data and markets, dangerous and dysfunctional. Nevertheless, I believe not testing out new forms of democracy, as our very old technology is slipping to irrelevance, is even more dangerous. Next, I will investigate pitfalls and how we can deal with them.

DIGITAL LITERACY AND ACCESS

You might have seen this already with the introduction of personal computers and smart phones. Some people are not used to writing emails. Others have difficulty dealing with the user interfaces. I felt like an old man at 40, when I had my first interaction with Snapchat.

When we make people interact with others through computers – or any kind of digital means – we will boost the voice of those that are familiar with, even born digital, and at the cost of those who struggle with it. Some people work all day online, others with their hands. That should not put them at odds.

I've seen many well-intended government policies that are concerned about inclusion. However, often the efficacy of such policies is not measured, and we can often spend a lot of attention or resources to prevent a bad story in our political environment where stories are what drives popularity and power. Look at how we are not even allowing digital voting for national elections in many states due to concerns about vote security, where we often lose hundreds of thousands of votes in the process by making it – often intentionally – harder for people to join the process. We often require antiquated options of payments for public services, such as opportunity to pay for your parking in cash, creating high costs for little in return.

Inclusion and the interface of the next democracy systems we use can be a part of the metrics we are working toward optimizing. Besides making the platforms intuitive, we can establish libraries, where people can be taught by others how they deal with the system, step by step. Lack of digital literacy for not adapting to a digital democracy sounds like not writing down laws because there are citizens who cannot read.

LOSING THE PERSONAL TOUCH

We are social animals who need human touch and interaction. We are not made for looking at screens for long periods of time.

Indeed, I believe we should have policies that encourage more people to live in smaller communities, where regular, unplanned, and spontaneous connection with others is a part of daily life. I believe that when we create a better democratic system, it will ensure policies are in place to incentivize living in more socially rewarding settings for all.

Yet, when we talk about governing ourselves, where our numbers exceed 100,000, we have trouble using in-person formats. For the reasons covered in Chapter 1, our democratic institutions run into mud when we limit the exercise of our citizenship to voting once every some years for another person to represent us with great social distance between us and the representatives.

In Merit Democracy, I foresee that we will have many in-person interactions where we discuss politics and engage ourselves in it. Such live events, from dinner tables to events in town halls and libraries, can be a part of what we incentivize with public money as we find out informed and engaged citizenship is of value, and so is also experiencing community.

Unlike today, those in-person discussions and interactions we have will have a very concrete way of becoming reality, through a few touches on the screen.

LIMITS TO MEASURING

There are two kinds of rejections of what I propose here by implementing prices for externalities, with the aim of changing the way markets currently work in ignorance to public benefit.

The first one is about simply rendering the measurements unnecessary, or even harmful, for attempting to measure what really matters. "How do you measure love?" I heard from an economist, who objected to the idea of quantifying public goods.

The other critique I heard is also from another economist friend, who suggested that pricing goods, such as use of natural resources, creates the perception that we can exploit them by simply paying the cost. Therefore, she rejects the idea of measuring and pricing public goods. Many valuable public goods have a kind of value of their own, that is not compromiseable, and measuring and pricing goods inevitably makes them exchangeable (with money), according to this view.

While I think I understand the fundamental objection, I find myself on the side of favoring measuring, or at least attempting to measure, things that we care about. Further, I believe we constantly make difficult choices and compromises, both as individuals and also societies, even though we totally lack clarity on the value of public goods. Absence of an integration of public goods into our economic and monetary systems makes societies more vulnerable, not less.

After all, what we don't measure, we cannot focus on. Even if we do not want to trade them with a given price, we cannot even know they are being harmed or diminished if we don't measure.

One of those things where measurement becomes very difficult is when discussing life and death. At a policy class at UC Berkeley, we were presented with a number of collateral deaths of innocent people justifiable in order to take out a person high up on the danger list. I still remember being deeply saddened by the idea of such warfare and the question itself.

At the same time we have to, and already do, take life and death decisions in public policy. In countries where healthcare is a public good, there is a clear question around what cost can be born to society in helping a patient prolong their life. We use measures like HALE (Health Adjusted Life Expectancy) and QALYs (Quality Adjusted Life Years) in order to assess when it makes sense to spend more public money to try increasing the chances of someone's survival, and when it does not.

Besides questions around the ethical aspects there are of course many technical challenges, and challenges to our privacy that has to do with measurement.

How well can we attribute effects to various contributors of a social phenomenon? The world is highly complex. If someone is suffering from depression, how can we assess the contributors to that, be it social media or housing situation, or job market and conditions?

The world of marketing gives some hope in terms of attribution. Thanks to the generous budgets we have allocated to ensure our products reach customers we have developed complex tools that enable companies to allocate attributes of their sales driven by certain channels from search-driven website visits to influencer marketing and word of mouth thanks to brand recognition.

Rich datasets meeting complex analysis tools enable us to create parametric equivalents of groups of people, in an effort to control for effects we want to isolate. We are able to isolate effects of other drivers of a cause by modeling their historic impacts forward. Similar to all coding, big data analysis is also quickly becoming a domain where AI can assist. Machine learning tools like neural networks and random forests are highly effective in detecting non-linear, complex interactions between variables. They can help us form new hypotheses of causes between phenomena and enable us to make fast, real-time analyses. Such fast analysis is important in a construct such as Merit Democracy, where companies and legislation contributors need quick feedback from the social platform in order to adjust their activities.

Google, for example, offers the CausalImpact package that uses time series models to determine whether a specific event (new legislation, introduction of new product or service) caused a shift in observed outcomes. Propensity Score Matching (PSM) is a common technique to assign attribution to causes to an event, especially when randomized controlled trials are not feasible. PSMs estimate causal effects by creating causal effects by creating balanced comparison groups with similar characteristics. There are other tools and methods available and the data analysis field is becoming increasingly powerful.

I think most of the challenges around measurement are met once we agree that no measurement will ever be perfect. Further, our efforts to measure and understand the world will keep getting more sophisticated as the world we aim to govern also becomes more complex. We shall find peace in the process of improving measurements, instead of expecting to achieve a model that finally delivers perfection.

And while no measurement will ever be perfect we shall also see that not measuring or ignoring the impacts of laws or products and services on public goods do not make things any better. Doing some of the work is better than doing none. Actually, getting started on this path will be a huge step forward and probably half the job. Once we set our minds into executing on such a framework, human ingenuity will take over to address the challenges that are more technical in nature.

WE SHOULD FOCUS ON DEGROWTH

Our economic growth, without considering the externalities, if continued, is going to harm us. This is not only true due to climate change, but also other environmental threats such as biodiversity loss, nitrification of soil and so on. It is also true in terms of social suffering the growth focus causes when we don't consider factors like mental health and belonging in our well-being. The result of the latter is increasingly traumatized individuals, feeling lonely and depressed, and seeking comfort and agency in conspiracy theories.

Kate Raworth's *Doughnut Economics* provided a strong foundation in framing the debate on harms when we exceed planetary and social boundaries. With various emission reduction goals in place around the world all economists seem to agree that the need for respecting the idea of long-term planetary boundaries shall be respected.

I believe that the idea of Merit Democracy – pricing of public goods, and attributing the effects on public goods to companies' products and services – can provide a better alternative to "degrowth."

What if we do not need to stop growth, but redefine growth as becoming more sustainable? Going back to the money-value alignment discussion, if money represented sustainability would we worry about having more of it? I think not.

As long as we can align the value of money with what we collectively care about, having more money and wealth collectively would represent more human sustainability. A net positive. I believe we get lost in the growth vs. degrowth discussion as for many growth symbolizes a way forward and generation of wealth, while for others it symbolizes destruction and long term suffering at the cost of a temporary and superficial pleasure. The first group must accept the redefinition of money to include social and environmental factors if we are to continue with growth. The second group needs to consider where the alternative, degrowth, is to take us as conscious living beings whose most-inner drive by definition is to increase the sustainability of its species.

FIGHTING THE ENEMY
IS PRIORITY

The geopolitical situation that the United States and Europe find themselves in, with the threat of other powerful states with completely different value sets such as Russia and China, might make it difficult to focus on public goods, especially those that require global coordination, and those that cost us in the short term with long term benefits.[1]

The US policy of providing cheap fossil energy to maintain low energy prices at the cost of not reducing emissions is a good example, but there are others such as pollution and overfishing in oceans. The race to the bottom to beat the enemy may seem unavoidable.

The coordination problems persist in all groups where a few are to win at the cost of the group as free-riders, if we do not have proper governance structures preventing them from doing so.

Global coordination is the hardest form of coordination to secure. There are periods in which such coordination was easier, such as just after the Second World War, and the decade following collapse of the Soviet bloc. Today, there is a credible enemy to the Western values with the autocracy of certain states, that making "give aways" or bearing costs for global goods while the enemy can benefit from them, is a less acceptable situation.

Nevertheless, we can focus the principles of Merit Democracy to build up capacity for our governance of public goods, at federal/national and city levels. The argument that "we cannot talk about reforming democracy right now, we are busy dealing with the enemy" does not hold: reforming democracy IS the way to become stronger. External threats are not only dealt with using hard weapons. In fact, the United States won the Cold War not because its weapons were more destructive. It did so because its cultural creativity inspired others. Its films and music told a compelling story.

The story of the west and its old-fashioned democratic ideals does not inspire any longer. The American Dream doesn't work. Similarly in Europe, it is difficult to see how future generations should get excited about their prospects. Life has become increasingly expensive and our agency to change the course of our public life seems weaker. The decline of democracy in the past 15 years has happened for good reasons. It is not delivering.

Fear has always been used by those who want to maintain the status quo. Especially fear toward external enemies proves to be a valuable tool to keep the authority of a regime that needs legitimacy. Sure, there are external pressures and threats. But we cannot hide behind the fear of threats in facing our obvious need for reforms, and we can start executing on reform at local and federal levels.

The way to win the global war is to make democracy really work at home and to inspire the rest. We do not need to force it onto others, but we also need to be strong to defend ourselves and our values when needed. At some point, we will come to terms with finding long-term solutions in governing ourselves globally.

PRONE TO MANIPULATION

Would we be at heightened risk of manipulation if people have a direct vote on the future of legislation? And what if they price public goods that don't make sense?

With manipulation in governance, I refer to the use of deceptive, dishonest, or unethical tactics by politicians to influence or control public opinion and decisions to achieve specific goals, often at the expense of the well-being of the general population.

We have a great deal of manipulation in Western (and other) democracies around the world. Such manipulation occurs both through legal forms such as campaign finance and lobbyism, and also by corruption and regulatory highjacking. Thus, when we ask for a system to resist manipulation, we should simply compare how it performs compared to the status quo.

Much of what goes wrong in democracy today has to do with lack of proper incentive alignment. Politicians' incentives are not aligned with those they represent, experts lack incentives to engage, communicators' incentives are to gain attention at all cost. To overcome the incentive alignment problems, Merit Democracy introduces a few mechanics in its legislative process:

- Legislation proposal development is rewarded by how much they are enabling improvements on the problems they are aiming to solve.
- In the voting stage, collecting delegations is rewarded similar to followership in social media, with the caveat that those that are receiving online representation will receive a score based on how well the legislations they supported (and objected to) have fared in reality.

Thanks to the widening of the voter base, it will be harder for the lobbyists to buy votes for their interests in the Merit Democracy. Instead of one representative carrying 500,000 votes, we could aim for an average of one person out of 100 to vote on a given decision. A broader base of voting on a given issue means buying votes will become 5000 times more expensive.

Certainly, now and then, someone with a large following could pursue legislation which serves their self interest, and lead their community to believe that. Yet by doing so they would harm their credibility, which is linked to the performance of what they supported and always remains a part of their profile.

PRIVACY AND DATA SAFETY

Some are concerned that if we have too much of our public life on digital platforms then we become vulnerable. They'd rather see the votes crossed on paper and people meeting one another in person to have a real debate.

First, we are already vulnerable to digital attacks of many sorts. From satellites to power plants and military assets, much of our life and infrastructure is reliant on digital access and control.

Second, blockchain technology has shown that we can make systems that are safe and reliable while also being transparent. There are already clear pathways in securing digital systems including blockchain services such as bitcoin, against future quantum computer attacks.

Estonia is a good example in terms of a state digitizing its information. The country is not only one of the leading nations where almost all public services are available digitally; it also has highly effective public data exchange platform (X-Road) enabling data handling among public authorities and also with private sector (Hirdaramani, 2024). While enabling such data exchange, the country also secures privacy of citizens and information, and integrity of its data using blockchain technology.

If we are to create a strong welfare society we will need a strong data foundation. We will need to collect more data for public purposes, and process and analyze a lot more of it. The principles behind GDPR is a good starting point for securing our fundamental privacy rights. We will need to maintain a healthy debate about improving and strengthening where needed, and also removing constraints where it is not necessary or offers a bad compromise.

Ensuring privacy and security of data are not challenges that cannot be overcome with adequate focus and investment. It has been done and we can do much better. Arguing against a data driven social welfare backbone due to concerns of privacy and safety are not sufficiently weighing the very real and already materializing dangers of remaining in the dark with our valuable time and resources, and losing out to the influence of tech companies who are effective in utilizing data to tap into the consumers in us.

TRAPPED IN SILOED THINKING

We cannot afford to tackle one issue at a time. Where there are multiple urgent topics to be dealt with, we cannot merely look into biodiversity or mental health or inequality or climate change. We need to tackle topics concurrently.

A market setting where multiple public goods are listed and priced would perfectly allow for that. If a legislation improves some goods, but worsens others, we would look at the net effect to evaluate the outcome. Similarly, if a company is resolving issues in one area while worsening others, we would not simply look at the positives, but the overall result.

By linking legislations and products and services to our public priorities, we create the marketplace where human ingenuity and capitalism can work to our benefit. We can see games that improve attention skills, social media that enhances self-security and belonging, and innovative mobility companies that minimize cars in cities.

If we see that some of our priorities get addressed, at the cost of other priorities, we can always adjust the prices. If we are experiencing companies finding ways to trigger the results by using some kind of shortcut without really fulfilling the ultimate goal, we can update the method with which we measure.

Merit Democracy is a design that addresses many issues pressing us at once:

- Defining and valuation of public priorities, providing agency, and transparency.
- Iterative, transparent, fast-paced legislative process.
- Citizen engagement secured through adequate financial incentives.
- Quality of legislation enabled by markets rewarding qualified inputs.
- Business incentives aligned with humanity via translating their impact on society and environment directly into financial value in their bottom line.

EXPERIMENTATION IS WELL WORTH THE RISKS

The law never is, but is always about to be.
—Benjamin Cardozo, 1921

I've been an avid listener of Sam Harris's *Making Sense*. For a while, Sam asked his hosts a set of questions at the end of his podcasts, including what would be "the one problem" they'd like to solve. The answer from guests usually varied between climate, media, and warfare. What made me stop and smile was the answer from Jack Dorsey, founder of Twitter. He said he would solve public governance. I had a big smile on my face when I heard this. I agree.

We take our current form of democratic organization as too much of a given. People don't even think about any other way than the current form when speaking of democracy.

We always knew that laws need to change, with time. That is true for how we govern ourselves, as it is true about everything else. The pace at which we need to change our laws also must accelerate to adapt to the pace of change out in the world.

The problems related to major changes to the current shape of democracy are of a second order compared to the harms of a system that doesn't provide policy that makes the people better off, moves too slowly, is not sufficiently transparent, or does not allow sufficient control by its subjects.

Our current governance systems are in trouble. And the system does not have self correcting measures to lift itself from the difficult moment. Thus, we need a new approach, a renewed focus and attention and resource to innovate governance.

Whatever we try to replace our current system of governance with will run into problems of sorts, if not at first, then over time. It is not so interesting to claim that there will be problems. What is interesting is to figure out what is worth spending our energy on experimenting with. Thus, our future governance should have an ongoing agenda for internal reform, how the governance technology itself improves. Our current democracies make changes to the democratic organization, if anything, harder than other kinds of policy changes, as many such decisions require a higher percentage of votes and do not become an important agenda item in our crisis-ridden democracies where even forming governments is a challenge in many countries.

The challenge to continuously reform the governance mechanism could be seen as a "meta challenge" in Merit Democracy. Such a meta challenge aims to improve the democratic process, and keeps experimenting with new processes, settings and ways of doing things to continue progress on this front.

A data- and market-driven approach can be applied effectively to deal with our collective goods problems. They represent hope for the future of governance. They can help overcome the divide of the left vs. right, growth vs. degrowth.

By now, you may be thinking that we have no chance of any of this becoming a reality, and therefore a waste of time.

In the next and last chapter, I discuss the path to change.

CHAPTER EIGHT

THE MISSION AHEAD: BEND NOT BREAK

*Knowing what's right doesn't mean much unless you do
what's right.*

—Theodore Roosevelt

I borrow the chapter title, Bend not Break, from a podcast of Daniel Schmachtenberger with Nate Hagens. The term "Bend" refers to the capacity of civilization to adapt and respond to the complex challenges it finds itself in, without major catastrophic consequences, while "Break" means severe catastrophes as a major threat to human civilization. It seems one of the two will be necessary in the near future.

It is May 2019 and I was at a mobility conference in London. The speaker was Robin Chase; she founded ZipCar (a leading car sharing provider) in 2000. She was now leading a not-for-profit called NUMO with the aim of bringing possibilities of new mobility to help cities to be sustainable and just. Toward the end of her informative, passionate, and impressive keynote speech focusing on the severe challenges lying ahead due to climate change, she stopped abruptly. There was a black slide.

The audience of around 500 venture capitalists and entrepreneurs was tensely quiet. Robin moved on to say that the science pointed us toward major catastrophes in the coming decades if we did not change course. She said she would give two options for which people needed to raise hands based on what they believed was more likely. The first one is that we could not change course sufficiently and the world would run into a major catastrophes within the next two to three decades, where a substantial proportion of lives would be lost and the tragedy we experience would be comparable to the Second World War. The second option is we would be able to take the necessary measures to avoid such large scale conflict and course-correct how our markets operate.

Then, she asked people to close their eyes. She did not want people to see one another and be influenced by others' thinking. Then she asked for hands to be raised if people believed we were headed for option one or two. Importantly, the question was not what people preferred of course, but what we were headed toward.

Eyes were shut. Quietly, some hands went up. Then other hands went up.

I lifted my hand for the second, optimistic scenario. But I could not help but open my eyes slightly to see who lifted their hands up for the first one. To my dismay, I saw a large majority of hands up for the pessimistic camp, over the optimistic camp. Robin said she saw about 80% hands up for the pessimistic scenario. Further, she said she had been asking the question at a number of conferences where she delivered a keynote, with a similar ratio. "The scary part is" she continued "you are not the average citizens – you are in fact *shaping* the world." She was right. Had we already given up?

I don't think we have. But we are deeply disillusioned about the potential of our current governance structures to lead us out of the mess we are in. Many who are rich are trying to chase impact investments so their capital does some good along with decent returns. Young and bright people I meet often do not even think about working for the government because of its slow moving, hopeless state. Instead, many seek jobs in companies promising impact – focused on the business prospects enabled by some technology. Many are still going after the big paycheck, even if they are now and then questioning how their startup, consulting or investment job is not necessarily helping the world. A smaller group is working on building the parallel future-proof governance mechanisms around the system on the back of financial successes of bitcoin, and following crypto services.

We are divided in many ways: growth vs. degrowth, technology vs. simplicity; business focus on business vs. on impact; small vs. large government. What we lack is a large majority of people sharing an exciting, common vision about the future that unites us. An alignment around the strong state was the case following the Great Depression when the state-led economic growth created a path forward for a few decades over the privately owned, monopoly power ideology from 1930s through 1960s. This was also the case for a half century, from the 1950s until the 1990s, when the capitalistic bloc fought the communist bloc with strong shared values placed on personal freedoms, democracy, ownership and markets.

Now, increasingly, the whimsical sales pitch of neoliberal stories from the 1990s that turned into a tech enabled neoliberal "tech will save us" story is looking hopeless. And worse, we simply lack strong visions for the future to unite us around a conversation that excites the most of us.

Reimagining democracy and state, based on technologies proven to be powerful, is the way forward.

It means redefining the value of money to include social and environmental goods in how we price things. It means opening up policy making to everyone who can make a difference, and doing so in smart ways to facilitate the wisdom of the crowds using market principles. It means data-driven feedback loops to observe how our laws are solving our challenges and iterating them. It means giving people direct access to defining collective challenges and pricing them as market makers. It means tapping into opportunities offered by use of data and markets, which we until now have associated with means to make money and exploit the consumers, and not with building a new state. But these technologies are not bad as such, they are simply not yet deployed to serve our collective benefit.

CHANGE FROM WITHIN

In Merit Democracy, I've talked about two kinds of governance shifts: that in legislation and in delivery of public goods.

Let me start with the kinds of actions we can take to attain them, starting with the delivery of public goods. Cities, states, and federal governments can set up experiments to this end, depending on the public goods of concern. We can set up what I like to call **impact markets** that connect the buyers of the impact (primarily the government) and the providers of it (companies through their products and services).

Rewarding companies for positive externalities is already possible with the current legal frameworks. Giving away money for desired public impacts can happen through new "impact funds" belonging to the public authorities. Informed citizenship and better public health could be focus areas for the federal governments, motivating media and (preventative) health services. Local governments can also try setting up impact markets with focus on local goods such as reducing congestion, improving air quality, or creating more green spaces and trees in dense urban areas.

Paying for positive effects is easier to sell to businesses relative to taxes. This is why introducing a carbon tax in the United States didn't really happen, while the Inflation Reduction Act with the giveaway to the sustainable energy alternatives was so much easier.

You might say cities and states do not have much funding available to take on such new actions. And that is correct, especially as we keep taxes relatively low for the richest. The way to pursue impact markets could be to run pilots to reward the positive impacts at first. But in the long run, the aim would be to create self-balancing impact markets where the funding for positive impact is generated from those impacting the goods negatively. Private capital from foundations can help support implementing such impact market constructs, setting up pilots, and proving the concepts.

When setting up impact markets we could have politicians and public officials initially do the work of defining the metrics that the impact market pays for. While the long-term perspective is to have citizens define directly which public goods matter, and how much they matter, that can be treated as a separate module.

In making this happen there is of course the task of mapping how products and services affect the metric of interest, doing the big data collection work. Public authorities have some of the data they need, but in many cases more data collection will be needed to improve the accuracy of assessments. Among other sources authorities can request data from businesses themselves in order to assess their impacts. With the existence of rewards for positive impacts, many businesses will happily share their data.

In the longer run, we would need to make legal changes in order to force businesses to report their data, perhaps increasing the data reporting requirements beyond a certain size in order to evaluate their impacts. With such impact markets in place, we can start to see the sensitivity of businesses' reactions in various areas, from media to education, housing, labor practices, transport, and much more.

We will need to work on simplifying the ways in which the government can collect and process data for the benefit of citizens in a transparent manner. We shall not repeat the scandals following Snowden's reveal of NSAs surveillance practices with hidden government data collection and analysis. The agenda here does not need any secrecy; quite the opposite. The impact market needs to be highly transparent in order to help businesses see how they can create value by triggering the desirable impacts. The aim should be to make everything about the data analyses transparent so long as we don't compromise privacy. We can share data sources, data flow, the algorithms used in cleaning and analyzing the data.

Working on a data infrastructure as the backbone of the state will necessitate major state capabilities. For this, we could imagine a project similar to the Manhattan Project. We know that tech companies have much of the talent we need for building this key pillar, the data frameworks and impact assessments for a new social contract. We should be wary of outsourcing these tasks to private businesses, as this is the core function of the government in the future. Just like we do not outsource the congressional budget office, or our regulatory commissions, we cannot just outsource our core competency.

Perhaps the bigger challenge is about changing the way we legislate. I believe that there are public leaders who share the view that democracy cannot continue operating as it has and that it needs to evolve. They are rare, but the trajectory of challenges we see, and increasing awareness of the lack of fresh ideas could make more decision-makers take bold bets and try new ideas. As is the case with the city of Ghent, there are leaders who accept the possibility of losing power and sacrifice their positions for the sake of ideals. Any inspiring models and learnings can spread quickly to attract others in the midst of the need to move forward.

In order to establish a more objective legislative framework we first need to start defining measurable metrics and baseline values that each piece of legislation intends to achieve. We could do this at any level of public authority. Further, we can start tracing the new legislation's impact on its success criteria and other important measurable public concerns. This effort will potentially also trigger the need to collect more data, and improve big data competencies.

There is some acceptance for the idea of using data-driven and iterative learning loops (build/analyze/learn) in order to continuously improve on legislation. An OECD (2024) report, and Finland's leadership on the topic are promising. These can surely help politicians approach the topic with more acceptance instead of continuing with our *"forecast better and consider changes when we see fire"* approach.

Once we start having an objective measurement of success of a legislation's impact on its intended metrics we will have a new realm of possibility to rate legislators: instead of looking at their popularity to deem their success we can rate the success rates of their legislation! Such objective scoring of politicians can help break through loyalty to party lines, and incentivize politicians to focus on positive impact over popularity of legislation, and assume the role of championing and explaining why certain decisions are necessary.

Another interesting initiative will be to engage citizens not only by allowing them to comment on legislative proposals, but financially incentivizing them by betting on the future outcomes of legislation as discussed earlier. We can allocate them special credits (a.k.a. citizen credits) to engage, so their material wealth does not create an imbalance. As explained in Chapter 6, we can allow citizens that contribute to positive legislations to receive a small percentage of the social gains. Could that not enhance not only engagement levels but also improve the quality of the conversation?

We can introduce frequent and strictly online referendums for legislation, where citizens are free to use delegates to vote on their behalf or vote directly. Through the liquid voting process, we can establish a new breed of influencers who could campaign to attract delegations. In return, they could receive a payout for delegations they carry as well as the real life outcomes of the legislations they advocated for. In such a setting we can attract talent that is today working with influencer marketing of consumer goods, and click-bait journalism, to instead target reviving the conversation about citizenship in creative and lively forms.

Finally, we can create direct access for citizens to identify and value the public goods, and link our public budgets and programs to these. Providing the connection between government programs and challenges we prioritize would bring a lot more clarity to the ordinary citizens about why we spend public money the way we spend it, and also provide the motivation to spend more by raising taxes. Once citizens feel in charge of defining public priorities, we can once again make governments the platforms where people seek change instead of buying some sustainable consumer product.

With each of these initiatives, we can test how they affect what we set out to be a good – or better – democratic system; one that delivers better quality decisions, faster, transparently and enables agency.

In summary, the following initiatives can pave transformation toward the Merit Democracy:

- Setting up impact markets and rewarding and penalizing companies for their impacts, starting at local (city) governance, and/or focusing on narrow verticals (media, transportation, etc.).
- Clearly framing the goals from a given legislation and measuring the real impact legislation has on its goals.
- Setting up iterative legislative process where there is less focus on upfront analysis but quick updates to initial versions of legislation based on learnings of its impact.
- Providing a mechanism for citizens to bet on the future success of legislative alternatives.
- Creating opportunity for citizens to create and work (online) on legislative proposals to solve particular challenges, and collect (significant) rewards if their contribution actually helps solve those challenges.
- Allowing citizens to vote on legislations on a digital platform with automated delegations, fueling the debate for/against legislation, with mechanisms to reward engagement, for example, through rewarding thought leaders.
- Providing a platform for citizens to aggregate their priorities for social challenges that are measurable and can be the basis of governmental focus on both legislative and executive agendas.

DIGITAL-BORN ALTERNATIVES

In his book, *The Network State*, Balaji Srinivasan talks about how inefficient the government as we know it has become and that it fails to address important issues such as economic insecurity. His suggestion is to go all in with building new nations with digital foundations for their governance and decentralization of decision power.

Indeed, bringing about change from within can seem hopelessly slow, or even impossible. If governments do not take the steps toward experimenting with new ways to make democracies stronger, are there any alternatives outside of the system?

Many decentralized autonomous organizations (DAOs) seem like an interesting alternative, as Balaji also seems to think. They have two interesting enablers: (1) promising amounts of wealth among its communities thanks to the rise of value of bitcoin, and (2) born digital organizations, where there is high willingness to test out (digital) innovations in governance. For these reasons, DAOs are quite interesting platforms for experimentation.

So far, governance and decision-making processes in DAOs have remained rather simplistic. In most DAOs, coin holders have voting power linked to their holdings. In most DAOs, while all members (read coin holders) can propose new ideas for platform decisions, they lack interest in pushing collective agendas without supporting their private interest. This is a similar problem to that we see with the participatory budgeting processes and needs to be addressed. Time will tell if and how DAOs will treat the question of decentralized governance as a key issue. Currently, most of them focus on competing with one another in terms of product innovation and specific features, and are still rather centrally governed despite ambitions or declarations of decentralization.

Nevertheless, I believe DAOs can prove resourceful in shining a light for the future of governance. Focus on better governance models may prove an important bet in qualifying long-term winners over focus on features.

This is especially so with the increasing ease of building code thanks to AI, putting more emphasis on the decision hierarchy and process over executive capabilities among competing DAOs.

You might be doubting the significance that DAOs could have on our world and economy. They may do so by providing inspiration through new governance models if they continue to try out new models and keep gaining momentum as well as providing well documented learnings. They will also increasingly have a footprint in our economy and compete with the traditional organizations.

Already an increasing number of DAOs have a real world footing, that is, what they aim to govern and control is not only in the digital space. Power-Ledger is an energy trading DAO. RealT enables real estate development. Perhaps most innovation is happening in the financial sector: platforms like Aave and Compound are creating a financial borrowing platform.

Whether or not DAOs can lead the way to innovative governance models is a pending question in my mind. But they at least constitute real potential.

BUT WHAT CAN I DO?

With great power comes great responsibility.

—Voltaire

I cannot remember the exact words, but I had a discussion with Julian Assange about how he ended up taking on the challenge of bringing global justice through transparency with WikiLeaks. My recollection of the discussion was that one's awareness and understanding of the present problems defines the level at which we engage with it. If we cannot relate to the issues of democracy, or feel solutions are beyond our imagination or control, we cannot act. Conversely, grasping the issues and the interlinkages makes us each responsible for taking action in the unfolding drama.

Each of us can do a lot. The fact that you cared enough about the issue to read this book and think about alternative paths for democracy is a great start. We need to create the conversation around governance crisis as the metacrisis, over and beyond the symptoms of it, from inequality, loneliness, mental health, deterioration of oceans and land, biodiversity, our inability to prevent climate change, and so on.

You might say, focusing on one of these issues is more important than public governance. We can find a community that focuses on the issue, and it is easier to engage in that issue than others. Climate change is the obvious one, but biodiversity, security, mental health crisis, loneliness, inequality – you can pick any one from the cocktail. Unfortunately, though, each of us picking our fight in the siloes of issues will not bring about the new governance solutions we need.

Just like the paperclip problem, focusing on one issue at a time can easily make the other issues worse. Focusing on green technologies to reduce carbon emissions could end up having dire consequences on biodiversity and agriculture. It could also worsen the already historic high wealth and income inequality – shaking further the foundation of society and bring us to the brink of civil unrest.

Thus, we need to pay more attention to the governance problem itself than the attention we pay to the individual issues. Further, we need to start allocating budgets and efforts toward developing effective solutions to governance.

The good news is that there are a lot of idealistic, smart, and generous individuals who are willing to take on the effort. Many of them are trying to make a difference by working for an impact company, or an impact investor, or as a consultant on impact projects, yet are finding out the impact is not happening. I meet such people every week. They intuitively agree with me that the issue of governance is at the core, and tackling it as investor or employee or consumer is insufficient.

The other good news is that there is quite a lot of concentrated wealth out there in this time of great inequality. Much of it belongs to people who are keen to improve the world. They are public about their intentions to make a difference and seek new ways to do so. And they can help fund the initiatives to pave the way for much needed experimentation around governance.

Salesforce CEO, Marc Beioff tells us that the system has led to profound inequality, that we need a new capitalism (Hunt, 2019). Klarna founder, Niklas Adalberth in Sweden is open about his meaning crisis when becoming a billionaire, wanting to use his wealth to create positive social and environmental impact (Darrah, 2019). Ray Dalio, founder of Bridgewater, posted on LinkedIn in 2024 his concerns about the brewing difficulties in society, and that even his rich friends are not happy (Dalio, 2024). George Soros has long worked on democratic initiatives through Open Society Foundation and warns against the danger of authoritarian highjacking of the current form (Central European University, 2021). (Sir) Ronald Cohen wants to change capitalism where companies bear the positive and negative fruits of their impact (Cohen, 2020). The Bill and Melinda Gates Foundation is dedicated to innovating for public benefit. The list is long.

One thing the foundations and the ultra rich cannot do alone is to bring legitimacy to their interventions. That needs broad public support. Without a broad conversation on democratic governance challenges and engagement from citizens, philanthropic aid can create unintended, reactionary consequences. While the rich could fund initiatives, the credibility of such initiatives would need to come from the provision and commitment of resources into projects based on the transparent and democratic processes of the foundations who manage them.

Learning from the DAOs, one concrete way to take on the challenge could be creation of a foundation with the aim of generating learnings for the future of government. Such a foundation could provide decision-making power to any citizen joining the community. Its projects could be executed in partnership with researchers who study the consequences of various democratic governance initiatives. Public authorities and other entities with democratic claims (DAOs, associations) could apply for joining initiatives to experiment with new types of governance. The results can be communicated effectively by social media to bring us closer to wide-accepted governmental reforms.

We don't know where the best hotbeds of future democracy experiments will be. They might not necessarily come from the global north or west. Mobile payments (from one mobile device to another) became mainstream in Europe and the United States between 2015 and 2020. Before then, it was a hassle to pay someone for their used chair on Craigslist, or paying back a friend who had paid for your weekend trip. But this technology was used widely almost a full decade prior, in Kenya with MPesa. I've seen it for myself. It was the very small business transactions where cash payments were most difficult, especially in those small buses, called matatu, where moving one's body often was difficult enough, let alone getting your hand into your pocket to deal with the cash. The experiences from MPesa helped rest of the world catch up, especially on the regulatory side.

Similarly, it may well be possible that the experiments shaping the future of democracy as we know it start elsewhere. Taiwan's experiments are a good example. Countries outside of Europe and the United States can leapfrog in exploring better methods if they can overcome institutional or cultural barriers to trying out radical new ideas. The problem has been that in the past half century our institution building efforts in the developing world have focused on mimicking what existed in Western democracies. Now that we know that our solution isn't that good after all, we might want to change gears and fund learnings that are different.

The political movements for reforming democracy cannot afford to remain local or national as the movements after the 2010 economic crisis have been. The conversation for modernizing democracy shall be a global conversation. Even if the experiments are local, the learnings can bring inspiration to all institutions across the globe. We should fund and communicate democratic experiments globally, enabling a lively exchange among public authorities to tap into the potential of new methods. The tools and settings we use will be adjusted to cater for each setting, but the learnings will be shared.

GETTING POLITICAL

First they ignore you, then they laugh at you, then they fight you, then you win.

—Mahatma Gandhi

While we cannot plan it, we need to have ideas about how the whole political system may transition as we gain learnings about new forms of democracy. We cannot simply assume that any new democracy experiments (such as use of prediction markets) proving high engagement and outcomes in one place can make them popular in another place.

Politics often occurs behind closed doors, but it also listens carefully to what is popular. If we have created a popular idea that democratic reform is possible with totally new tools showing promising results, some political parties will eventually listen and adapt. The experiments with PiratenPartei in Germany in early 2010s showed that 30% of voters considered voting for the party for its promise of direct democracy. More transparency and agency are very appealing promises, especially if we have shown in various scenarios that the platforms we intend to use can deliver. In the case of PiratenPartei, the movement did not have the resources to develop various products and tests. When in government they could not live up to expectations. But they had significant influence on how other parties viewed the importance of citizen participation.

Similarly, other political movements in Southern Europe following the 2010s that emphasized cutting the distance between the voter and politics with direct influence have not delivered but showed their promise was very attractive. History shows that the suggestions of Merit Democracy in this book are not inherently left or right. Parties promoting more direct forms of engagement ended up being on either of the sides. While in Germany it was mostly left leaning citizens who voted for the pirates instead of the greens, in Italy and Spain, direct democracy (cutting out the elite middleman) became more of the promise of the right. The ideas of this book can be endorsed by both sides in their own ways.

Further, parties can try the voter reaction to the ideas state/national, or city level. It could be some state governors or city mayors adopt them first, to then bring them to the federal level.

Perhaps you are worried about the two-party system in the United States blocking the path for any movements on the fringes. It is true that the focus on the median voter in the US system makes it harder for fringe ideas to move to the center of the political agenda. However, single issue candidates can also make a difference: they can generate high levels of voter interest and make a deal with the party that is doing best in accommodating the issue at hand. Imagine an independent candidate running with the promise of implementing democratic reforms, including measurement of legislative success. If they manage to raise significant voter interest, that could become a part of the winning party agenda. In this sense, Americans could find some peace with the relevance of independent candidates. They may divide votes, but also offer an invitation for the mainstream parties to buy into their efforts and align priorities.

This is also how various political issues moved from being fringe issues to the mainstream in Europe with its multi-party parliamentary systems. From green transition to immigration, parties in the center embodied new policies to defend their majority positions. And governance openness and innovation are not completely new subjects. The rising attention from the 2010s on the issue gave birth to new political parties in Europe. For a while, reading the political sentiment elsewhere, many political parties invested in engaging citizens better with online platforms.

Reforming government and engaging citizens better are high on Europe's political agenda. Like in some nation states, the legislative process at the EU level is open to public feedback through a simple platform.

Despite limited usage due to lack of incentives and commitments to follow through the received feedback it is better than where we were 15 years ago. More recently attention has moved to creating citizen panels. As discussed in Chapter 3 citizen panels have important limitations. Nevertheless, one point remains highly relevant in Europe: governance needs reform and have more direct citizen participation. Citizens are not happy with the status quo, which is policy being made behind closed doors.

If we manage to learn globally, from various experiments of democratic reform, then it will be increasingly easy to shift the reception of these ideas in political parties – new and existing – and get them to become part of our systems.

* * *

What we need is political and grassroots interest, local experiments, and globally shared learnings that government can look very different in the future.

We need the support of various movements, from the likes of Occupy to climate activists who focus on the various symptoms of failing governments, to build a broad citizen base. We need business leaders to support reform of government for it to assume a stronger role in public discourse and to shape markets instead of the rhetoric of businesses bringing about impact through self-regulation. We need tech talent to deploy digital technologies for modernizing governance with data. We need academia to study and evaluate what is working. And we need the funding to enable experimentation and learnings.

Once we have some nations or blocs using new governance technologies, such learnings can spread quickly to inspire others. We have seen trends gaining traction quickly and globally, from Occupy to MeToo.

We stand in a time where democracy's failure is increasingly evident, and like the moment after Second World War that enabled formation of new global institutions, we can quickly find ourselves in a moment of opportunity where new institutions can be born. We live in a hyper-connected world, and the pace of change is therefore commensurately faster. Therefore, we need to get ready to seize the opportunity with relevant visions and learnings.

With better governance we will see countries and federations starting to thrive. This will be felt in the quality of life, and the videos and stories will influence minds well beyond their borders.

Not only will the changes be felt in quality of life but also strength of their economy. Successful governance will enable inventions without the existing fear of regulation. Investing in critical technologies, the countries that manage better governance can quickly amass the power to build future-proof industries. They will be stronger when it comes to military power and in their ability to better withstand external threats.

ONE DAY IN NOT SO DISTANT FUTURE

Caroline was excited: she found a cofounder and an investor for starting her business. She had been entrepreneurial before but this was the first time she would really start something. As a 28 year old who studied social care, she thought this was the right idea at the right time: housing for the elderly, and for students as well as short-term stays, and a community space with various activities.

She figured there were a lot of resourceful and older people between 65 and 80, who wanted social life around them, and who also wanted to give back with various talents and experiences, while university students moving to town could get affordable housing and meet new people in the neighborhood. She had also stayed in a co-living establishment recently and had seen how such a community could be of interest for people looking for a more limited period of housing.

It was the right time because she saw that New Mexico was placing an increasing amount of public money into preventative health with loneliness being one of the key issues. She figured she could trigger at least one-third of the necessary rental fees from the health impact market if she could run the project as she imagined. At the same time, affordable housing is a key issue for students and the financial pressure is creating a lot of stress and anxiety among young people. She figured that by having activities such as meditation, xi-gong, yoga, and free dance, she could bring calm to the young folks while establishing a vibrant community. Also here, she realized there was a lot of money available in the impact market for mental health, especially for 18–25 year olds.

One of her father's friends, Robert, who had done well as an economics researcher who later made a side career as an (online and part-time) politician, would be her main investor. Robert was the perfect match because he had really understood the economy of preventative healthcare. In his time at Berkeley as healthcare economist, he had seen the link between meaningful personal connections and health. He had led one of the landmark policy proposals that changed the landscape of healthcare in the United States: he invested early and coauthored a piece of legislation that introduced new approaches in medicinal education and practice that went outside of the traditional focus on the various body systems. The legislation he led enabled a new breed of professional health practitioners to focus on preventative care with a holistic approach to the patient's environment, home, friends, and more. Inspired by the legacy of Gabor Mate's work and research, this legislation was finally a big success. After five years of its implementation, not only was there less treatment and lower costs, but the patients' self-reported life satisfaction was much better. Thanks to positive social impacts of the legislation he co-authored, Robert now enjoyed life as a multi-millionaire.

Caroline's father, Miguel, met Robert at a conference about health politics. The two found inspiration in each other's work and kept in touch.

Miguel was also a contributor in the holistic healthcare legislation, but his interest was more on exploring fresh ideas on exploring how creativity connected to health. He had been an activist growing up, and after the adoption of Merit Democracy he became an avid communicator on the inequality reduction acts. It took many pieces of legislation over a decade to see the laws reducing tax avoidance, increasing tax levels on not only capital income but also wealth and inheritance, and tightening the conditions around intellectual property rights. He was well respected for his advocacy explaining how inequality related to worsened health and violence. He even received the "Top 100 communicators for oversees tax avoidance bill" prize where he had collected almost 30,000 online delegations.

Growing up in New York City, Miguel, learned early how to sell. He started his e-commerce business selling craft beer as a teenager. He then became a successful influencer, first for beers then for health drinks. He understood well how to craft videos – often with a note of dark humor – that could get more clicks. He made good money, and his future looked bright in his early thirties when he struggled with depression and sex addiction. After a couple of years that involved many retreats, including some psychedelic retreats, and therapy sessions, he found himself in New Mexico. He no longer found meaning in selling stuff but wanted to contribute and give what he could. With the introduction of Merit Democracy, he also found meaning joining the debate. He learned about economy and politics from his edge-of-desert home. And soon enough he was producing videos that were receiving hundreds of thousands of views, and even considerable delegations for key legislations.

Miguel was also the reason that Robert decided to move to New Mexico: after a lively visit, the two families enjoyed one another's company and soon enough Robert decided to buy up some old traditional farming land, and turn it into a biodiversity haven – a dream he had for a decade. Thanks to the new federal impact market price set up for biodiversity creation, this dream was now really affordable. His land would feature buffalo grass and cottonwood trees, perhaps even willows if he could manage it. His business plan relied on reforestation taking place within a decade, and he could finance 70% of the funding from the bank. He also really liked Caroline's idea relating to co-living space, it made sense. And if it worked well in the city, where she would start, he thought he might one day do another version of it, a co-living village with tiny homes, in his land of biodiversity.

Like many others, Robert was a worried about crime on his land. And this section of the border to New Mexico proved a popular entrance for drug trafficking. While the issues with this seemed more settled in the past five years, it would be a nightmare to imagine settling on his land a short decade ago due to the policing and conflict. But Robert took a bet: he decided to believe in the power of good governance and that things would keep getting better.

Recently, Mexico has ramped up its use of data-driven policy making, and started effectively pricing products and services public externalities some decade ago. It seemed to help the country's unemployment situation and along with it the crime rate. Now, the country is about to fully integrate with the global direct governance platform.

Robert turned on his vision pro glasses to view the global governance website that now defined the future of about 60% of the global population with the inclusion of India. Before putting it on he took out to the porch while sipping his coffee. It was a cool, early spring morning. The sun rose perhaps a half hour ago and the dew on the tall grass across the land sparkled, swaying gently in the soft breeze. He noticed a rabbit jumping a few hundred meters away toward the river, the same one he thought he saw some weeks before. This time, it seemed to have a few more jumping around. It brought a deep smile.

Now inside the mask he looked for challenges to be solved. Global inequality was one of those that got much traffic. And even though many of the valued proposals he valued were voted against he felt a deep sense of purpose being here. In his youth none of the progress of the last twenty years would have been imaginable. His favorite act was spotting early proposals by people whose track record would convince him they were on to something important.

And now, there. He just noticed that a wild proposal that was gaining early traction for the challenge addressing reduction of global inequality: one that would mean passports would become a thing of the past within two decades, and allow anyone to travel and settle anywhere they wanted to. He read on. It was well thought through and had various compensation mechanisms. But much work was still needed, and it would probably not achieve the high threshold for majority votes it would need.

Nevertheless, Robert felt inspired. Taking another sip of coffee and breathing in his barren land view and the rising sun, he started humming his favorite youth song along with the beats from the speaker:

Imagine there's no countries. It isn't hard to do-oo. Nothing to kill or die for. And no religionnn, too. Imagine all the peooooople. Living life in peeaaaaace. MM-mmmmm. You may saaaaay, I'm a dreamer. But I'm not the only one. I hope someday you'll join us, and the woooo-ooorrlllllddddd will be as one.

NOTES

Introduction

1. Famous technologists such as Larry Page and Peter Thiel think we should delegate public decision making to an AI system. Martin Jacques, a British academic and author of *When China Rules the World*, has argued that China's model of governance is fundamentally different from Western democracy but has proven to be highly effective in delivering results. Daniel A. Bell, Canadian scholar, praises Chinese governance for its planning and long termism.
2. The original quote belongs to Madeline Albright. She said "citizens are speaking to their governments using twenty-first century technologies, governments are listening on twentieth century technology and providing nineteenth century solutions."

Chapter 1

1. Term coined by Daniel Kahneman. Thinking Fast and Slow. System1 is the mode where brain doesn't have to think and can make a snap judgement driven by prior associations.
2. https://www.theguardian.com/news/2018/nov/29/why-we-stopped-trusting-elites-the-new-populism.
3. https://www.economist.com/graphic-detail/2020/01/22/global-democracy-has-another-bad-year.
4. Another example is the much needed congestion charge policy for Copenhagen. The city started experiencing heavier traffic in the 2010s and the government proposed a congestion charge in 2014. It made good sense; many Copenhageners

do not own cars, and commuters could use public transport instead. The suggestion was dropped due to media outcry.

5. Human instinct shows how people are able to smell the chance of future disease by engaging in a genetical analysis. As per the experiment, we find a smell increasingly attractive if the chances of us giving birth to an unhealthy child is lower.

6. Laurie Renee Santos is a cognitive scientist and Professor of Psychology at Yale University. She researches and teaches in the science of human well-being.

Chapter 3

1. The US presidential election is a special simple plurality system, where even a majority of votes does not guarantee winning the election. It has an additional layer of Electoral College, which is not evenly distributed, where underpopulated states receive a higher power in determining election outcome.

Chapter 4

1. As behavioral economics have well explored, individuals are – unlike companies – influenced by *present bias* (favoring immediate gratification), *status signaling* (buying to impress others), and by *loss aversion*.

Chapter 6

1. But it is not only bad: some other studies (Winstone et al., 2021) showed that social media can also enhance feelings of social connectedness – especially among those in social isolation.

2. EVs also create particle pollution through tires and brakes, which is shown to cause cancers. In fact, because of the higher weight of EVs, their particle pollution levels are similar to that of combustion engine vehicles.

3. The media funding from Danish government is distributed to media outlets through an annual funding application. The ministry provides their judgment on social benefit of each outlet to decide what they shall receive. As per the main ideas in this book, this is an outdated and ineffective form of public spend in reaching goals.

Chapter 7

1. As of the final review of this book, it is early days of Trump's new administration, and as a result of the new administration's activities in its first month, the values of the United States and Europe may be further apart from one another than it seemed before.

REFERENCES

ABC News (2018). Leave No Dark Corner. https://www.abc.net.au/news/2018-09-18/china-social-credit-a-model-citizen-in-a-digital-dictatorship/10200278. Accessed 19 December 2024.

Acemgolu, Daron and Robinson, James, A. (2006). *Persistence of Power, Elites and Institutions*. Working Paper 12108. Cambridge, MA: National Bureau of Economic Research. https://www.nber.org/system/files/working_papers/w12108/w12108.pdf. Accessed 18 December 2024.

Acemgolu, Daron and Robinson, James, A. (2012). *Why Nations Fail: The Origins of Power, Prosperity, and Poverty*. New York: Crown Publishing Group.

Alvaredo, Facundo, Garbiniti, Bertrand and Piketty, Thomas (2017). On the Share of Inheritance in Aggregate Wealth: Europe and the USA, 1900–2010. *Economica*, 84, 239–260. http://www.piketty.pse.ens.fr/files/AlvaredoGarbintiPiketty2017.pdf. Accessed 18 December 2024.

Asher Longevity Institute (2024). Living to 100? The Science and Skepticism Behind Blue Zones' Longevity Secrets. https://asherlongevity.com/healthy-aging-longevity/living-to-100-the-science-and-skepticism-behind-blue-zones-longevity-secrets. Accessed 6 January 2025.

Bartels, Bernhard (2022). Impact instead of risk: paradigm shift in ESG ratings necessary. https://www.scoperatings.com/ratings-and-research/research/EN/172410. Accessed 21 December 2024.

Beyer, Rebecca (2022). A Global Look at the Connections Between Happiness, Income, and Meaning. https://www.gsb.stanford.edu/insights/global-look-connections-between-happiness-income-meaning. Accessed 18 December 2024.

Bhargava, Vikram R. and Velasquez, Manuel (2020). Ethics of the Attention Economy: The Problem of Social Media Addiction. *Business Ethics Quarterly*, 31(3), 321–359. doi: 10.1017/beq.2020.32.

Bolton, Doug (2016). The reason Steve Jobs didn't let his children use an iPad. https://www.independent.co.uk/tech/steve-jobs-apple-ipad-children-technology-birthday-a6893216.html. Accessed 18 December 2024.

Bostrom, Nick (2002). Existential Risks. https://nickbostrom.com/existential/risks. Accessed 6 January 2025.

Bostrom, Nick (2019). The Vulnerable World Hypothesis. https://nickbostrom.com/papers/vulnerable.pdf. Accessed 4 January 2025.

Brosnan, Sarah and de Waal, Franz, B. M. (2012). Fairness in Animals: Where to from Here? *Social Justice Research*, 25 (3), 336–351. doi: 10.1007/s11211-012-0165-8.

Central European University (2021). Soros: AI Instruments of Control Pose "Mortal Danger" to Open Societies. https://www.ceu.edu/article/2021-06-18/soros-ai-instruments-control-pose-mortal-danger-open-societies?utm_source=chatgpt.com. Accessed 6 January 2025.

Centre for Mental Health (2018). Anxiety, Loneliness and Fear of Missing Out: The impact of social media on young people's mental health. https://www.centreformentalhealth.org.uk/anxiety-loneliness-and-fear-missing-out-impact-social-media-young-peoples-mental-health/?utm_source=chatgpt.com. Accessed 4 January 2025.

Clearly Cultural (n.d.). Power Distance Index. https://clearlycultural.com/geert-hofstede-cultural-dimensions/power-distance-index. Accessed 4 January 2025.

Cohen, Ronald (2020). *Impact: Reshaping Capitalism to Drive Real Change*. London: Ebury Press.

Cohn, Alain, Maréchal, Michel André, Tannenbaum, David, and Zünd, Christian Lukas (2019). Civic honesty around the globe. *Science*, 365 (6448), 70–73. doi: 10.1126/science.aau8712.

companiesmarketcap.com (2024). Largest Companies by Marketcap. https://companiesmarketcap.com. Accessed 19 December 2024.

Dalio, Ray (2024). Pick A Side And Fight For It, Keep Your Head Down, Or Flee. https://www.linkedin.com/pulse/pick-side-fight-keep-your-head-down-flee-ray-dalio-53fpe. Accessed 18 December 2024.

Danmarks Nationalbank (2022). Effects of borrower-based regulation on housing demand. https://www.nationalbanken.dk/media/a4xaosy0/effects-of-borrower-based-regulation-on-housing-demand.pdf. Accessed 6 January 2025.

Darrah, Kim (2019). Klarna cofounder Niklas Adalberth's Norrsken Foundation launches €100m impact fund. Sifted. https://sifted.eu/articles/klarna-norrsken-impact-fund. Accessed 6 January 2025.

DeCelles, Katherine A. and Norton, Michael I. (2016). Physical and situational inequality on airplanes predicts air rage. *PNAS*, 113 (20), 5588–5591. doi: 10.1073/pnas.1521727113.

De Jong, Piet (2012). The Health Impact of Mandatory Bicycle Helmet Laws. https://www.cycling-embassy.org.uk/sites/cycling-embassy.org.uk/files/documents/health_impact_helmet_laws.pdf. Accessed 6 January 2025.

Draghi, Mario (2024). The future of European competitiveness. https://commission.europa.eu/topics/strengthening-european-competitiveness/eu-competitiveness-looking-ahead_en#paragraph_47059. Accessed 6 January 2025.

Ebrary.net (n.d.). Rolling Back the State? Fiscal Squeeze, Thatcher-Style. https://ebrary.net/86801/political_science/thatcher_squeeze#137. Accessed 6 January 2025.

Economist Intelligence (2023). Democracy Index 2023. https://www.eiu.com/n/campaigns/democracy-index-2023. Accessed 18 December 2024.

Economist Intelligence (2024). Democracy Index: conflict and polarisation drive a new low for global democracy. https://www.eiu.com/n/democracy-index-conflict-and-polarisation-drive-a-new-low-for-global-democracy. Accessed 18 December 2024.

EPRS (n.d.). Average duration and number of concluded ordinary legislative procedures. https://epthinktank.eu/2024/06/04/european-parliament-facts-and-figures/ep-facts-and-figures-fig-19/?utm_source=chatgpt.com. Accessed 4 January 2025.

ESG News (2024). MSCI Study Finds Higher ESG Ratings Lower Cost of Capital for Companies. https://esgnews.com/msci-study-finds-higher-esg-ratings-lower-cost-of-capital-for-companies. Accessed 18 December 2024.

European Investment Bank (2025). Public transport: 64% of Europeans ready to make the switch for environmental purposes. https://www.eib.org/en/infographics/adopting-more-environmentally-friendly-means-of-transportation. Accessed 6 January 2025.

Faqir-Rhazoui, Youssef, Arroyo, Javier, and Hassan, Samer (2021). A Scalable Voting System: Validation of Holographic Consensus in DAOstack. *Proceedings of the 54th Hawaii International Conference on System Sciences*. https://scholarspace.manoa.hawaii.edu/server/api/core/bitstreams/d0686298-aa64-4f41-aa7c-ff4b379d0c87/content. Accessed 19 December 2024.

Fast Company (2024). How these towns are successfully fighting the 'Airbnb Effect.' https://fastcompany.com/91111637/towns-fighting-airbnb-effect. Accessed 18 December 2024.

Feinstein, Brian D. (2010). The Dynasty Advantage: Family Ties in Congressional Elections. *Legislative Studies Quarterly*, 35 (4), 571–598. doi: 10.3162/0362980 10793322366.

Foley, Edward B. (2024). Decreasing the Political Polarization of the American Public. *American Bar Association*. https://www.americanbar.org/groups/public _interest/election_law/american-democracy/our-work/decreasing-political-polarization-american-public. Accessed 6 January 2025.

Fracassi, Cesare, Khoja, Moazzam and Schär, Fabian (2024). Decentralized Crypto Governance? Transparency and Concentration in Ethereum Decision-Making. https://papers.ssrn.com/sol3/papers.cfm?abstract_id=4691000&utm_source= chatgpt.com. Accessed 4 January 2025.

Galloway, Scott (2024). How the US is destroying young people's future. TED Talks. https://www.ted.com/talks/scott_galloway_how_the_us_is_destroying_ young_people_s_future. Accessed 4 January 2025.

Gans, Joshua and Stern, Scott (2008). Is there a market for ideas? https://www.ftc. gov/sites/default/files/documents/public_events/first-annual-microeconomics-conference/stern.pdf. Accessed 23 December 2024.

Garrett, Anna (2018). Cost-benefit of cycling infrastructure. Cycling Embassy of Denmark. https://cyclingsolutions.info/cost-benefit-of-cycling-infrastructure. Accessed 6 January 2025.

Geiselberger, Heinrich (2017). *The Great Regression*. Cambridge: Polity Press.

Girard, Charles (2021). Lessons from the French Citizens' Climate Convention. https:// verfassungsblog.de/lessons-from-the-french-citizens-climate-convention. Accessed 6 January 2025.

Goldbeck, Lauren and Pew, Alex (2024). Violent Video Games and Aggression. National Center for Health Research. https://www.center4research.org/violent-video-games-can-increase-aggression/#:~:text=In%202017%2C%20the%20 APA%20Task,linked%20to%20criminality%20or%20delinquency. Accessed 6 January 2024.

Govtrack.us (2023). Statistics and Historical Comparison. https://www.govtrack.us/ congress/bills/statistics. Accessed 4 January 2025.

Govtrack.us (2024). Advanced Search for Legislation. https://www.govtrack.us/ congress/bills/browse?sort=-current_status_date#enacted_ex=o. Accessed 19 December 2024.

Graber, Diana E. (2021). Facebook Knew Instagram Could Be Damaging to Teens. *Psychology Today*. https://www.psychologytoday.com/us/blog/raising-humans-in-a-digital-world/202109/facebook-knew-instagram-could-be-damaging-to-teens. Accessed 18 December 2024.

Hagens, Nate and White, D. J. (2017). GDP, Jobs, and Fossil Largesse. https://www.resilience.org/stories/2017-11-30/gdp-jobs-and-fossil-largesse. Accessed 19 December 2024.

Hansen, Christian (2018). Uffe Elbæk i opgør med den private ejendomsret: Ingen skal eje sin egen jord. https://www.bt.dk/politik/uffe-elbaek-i-opgoer-med-den-private-ejendomsret-ingen-skal-eje-sin-egen-jord. Accessed 18 December 2024.

Hassani, Hossein, Huang, Xu and Ghodsi, Mansi (n.d.). Big Data and Causality. https://dora.dmu.ac.uk/server/api/core/bitstreams/b940c1bd-a90a-4c2c-a55d-a4d1c1f814b1/content. Accessed 6 January 2025.

Heckmanequation.org. (n.d.). Invest in Early Childhood Development: Reduce Deficits, Strengthen the Economy. https://heckmanequation.org/wp-content/uploads/2013/07/F_HeckmanDeficitPieceCUSTOM-Generic_052714-3-1.pdf. Accessed 6 January 2025.

Hirdaramani, Yogesh (2024). Estonia's X-Road: data exchange in the world's most digital society. https://govinsider.asia/intl-en/article/estonias-x-road-data-exchange-in-the-worlds-most-digital-society. Accessed 6 January 2025.

Hokkanen, Lari and Seppänen, Jaakko (2017). Evidence-based approaches and experiments – Towards progressive policymaking? SITRA. https://www.sitra.fi/en/articles/evidence-based-approaches-experiments-towards-progressive-policymaking/#_edn14. Accessed 6 January 2025.

Holcomb, Jesse and Mitchell, Amy (2014). Revenue Sources: A Heavy Dependence on Advertising. https://www.pewresearch.org/journalism/2014/03/26/revenue-sources-a-heavy-dependence-on-advertising. Accessed 23 December 2024.

Horton, Chris (2018). The simple but ingenious system Taiwan uses to crowd-source its laws. *MIT Technology Review*. https://www.technologyreview.com/2018/08/21/240284/the-simple-but-ingenious-system-taiwan-uses-to-crowd-source-its-laws. Accessed 6 January 2025.

Humanitas (2024). https://www.humanitasdeventer.nl/wonen/humanitas-woon-studenten. Accessed 6 January 2025.

Hunt, Ben (2019). To My Fellow Billionaires …. Epsilon Theory. https://www.epsilontheory.com/to-my-fellow-billionaires. Accessed 6 January 2025.

International Energy Agency (2021). Global corporate R&D spending of selected sectors as a share of revenue, 2007–2019. https://www.iea.org/data-and-statistics/charts/global-corporate-r-and-d-spending-of-selected-sectors-as-a-share-of-revenue-2007-2019. Accessed 19 December 2024.

IPCC (2023). *Climate Change 2023 Synthesis Report.* https://www.ipcc.ch/report/ar6/syr/downloads/report/IPCC_AR6_SYR_FullVolume.pdf. Accessed 6 January 2025.

Johnson, Paul and Stark, Graham (1989). Ten Years of Mrs Thatcher: the Distributional Consequences. *Fiscal Studies*, 10(2), 29–37. https://onlinelibrary.wiley.com/doi/10.1111/j.1475-5890.1989.tb00107.x. Accessed 6 January 2025.

Johnstone, David (2013). A Simple Automated Market Maker for Prediction Markets. In *The Oxford Handbook of the Economics of Gambling*, L. Vaughan-Williams and D. S. Siegl (eds.), 542–559. doi: 10.1093/oxfordhb/9780199797912.013.0028.

Joyce, Fay S. (1984). Mondale Program Would Raise Taxes $85 Billion by '89. https://www.nytimes.com/1984/09/11/us/mondale-program-would-raise-taxes-85-billion-by-89.html. Accessed 18 December 2024.

Jung, Min (2024). Prediction Markets: The Next Big Thing? https://www.prestolabs.io/research/prediction-markets-the-next-big-thing. Accessed 23 December 2024.

Kagan, Julia (2022). Tobin Tax: What it is, How it Works, Examples. https://www.investopedia.com/terms/t/tobin-tax.asp. Accessed 23 December 2024.

Kahnemann, Daniel (2011). Thinking Fast and Slow. Farrar, Straus and Giroux.

Kainulainen, Sakari and Juutinen, Anna-Mari (2017). Nuoren elämäntilanteen hahmottaminen 3X10D-mittarilla. https://unlimited.hamk.fi/hyvinvointi-ja-sote-ala/nuoren-elamantilanteen-hahmottaminen-3x10d-mittarilla. Accessed 23 December 2024.

Kaplan, Marty (2009). How Would the Right Know It's Wrong? https://archive.learcenter.org/wp-content/uploads/2018/10/100509-How-Would-the-Right-Know-Its-Wrong_-_-HuffPost.pdf. Accessed 18 December 2024.

Kerber, Ross (2024). CEO-worker pay gap has narrowed to 268: 1, but that won't last. https://www.reuters.com/sustainability/ceo-worker-pay-gap-has-narrowed-2681-that-wont-last-2024-08-14. Accessed 18 December 2024.

Kirby, Amy, Jones, Chris and Copello, Alex (2014). The Impact of Massively Multiplayer Online Role Playing Games (MMORPGs) on Psychological Well-being and the Role of Play Motivations and Problematic Use. *Int J Ment Health Addiction*, 12, 36–51. doi: 10.1007/s11469-013-9467-9.

Kohavi, Ron and Thomke, Stefan (2017). The Surprising Power of Online Experiments. https://hbr.org/2017/09/the-surprising-power-of-online-experiments. Accessed 18 December Ager 2024.

L, Jennifer (2024). Tesla Hits Record High Sales from Carbon Credits at $1.79B. https://carboncredits.com/tesla-hits-record-high-sales-from-carbon-credits-at-1-79b. Accessed 23 December 2024.

Lin, Kai-Yin and Schank, Jeffrey, C. (2022). Small group size promotes more egalitarian societies as modeled by the hawk-dove game. *PLOSOne*. https://journals.plos.org/plosone/article?id=10.1371%2Fjournal.pone.0279545&utm_source=chatgpt.com. Accessed 6 January 2025.

Longley, Robert (2021). What Is Neoliberalism? Definition and Examples. ThoughtCo. https://www.thoughtco.com/what-is-neoliberalism-definition-and-examples-5072548?utm_source=chatgpt.com. Accessed 6 January 2025.

Macrotrends (2024). Tesla Net Income 2010-2024 | TSLA. https://www.macrotrends.net/stocks/charts/TSLA/tesla/net-income. Accessed 23 December 2024.

Marsh, Chris and Robinson, Simon (2021). ESG and Technology: Impacts and Implications. https://www.spglobal.com/marketintelligence/en/documents/451-esg-and-tech-dckb-report.pdf. Accessed 21 December 2024.

Masterton, Gary and Evans, Nicholas (2024). Do we fully understand the impact of cosmetic surgery on our NHS and are we planning for the increased burden? *Journal of Plastic, Reconstructive & Aesthetic Surgery*, 88, 500. doi: 10.1016/j.bjps.2023.11.044.

Maté, Gabor (2022). *The Myth of Normal*. New York: Penguin.

National Press Foundation (2022). 21 Types of Political Spin You Should Know. https://nationalpress.org/topic/21-types-of-political-spin-you-should-know/?utm_source=chatgpt.com. Accessed 4 January 2025.

OECD (2021). Recommendation of the Council for Agile Regulatory Governance to Harness Innovation. https://legalinstruments.oecd.org/en/instruments/OECD-LEGAL-0464. Accessed 23 December 2024.

OECD (2024). Regulatory Experimentation: Moving ahead on the Agile Regulatory Governance Agenda. https://www.oecd.org/content/dam/oecd/en/publications/reports/2024/04/regulatory-experimentation_fc84553c/f193910c-en.pdf. Accessed 23 December 2024.

Oosterbeek, Hessel, Sloof, Randolph and van de Kuilen, Gijs (2004). Cultural Differences in Ultimatum Game Experiments: Evidence from a Meta-Analysis. *Experimental Economics* 7, 171–188. doi: 10.1023/B:EXEC.0000026978.14316.74.

Palladino, Lenore and Karlsson, Kristina (2019). Towards Accountable Capitalism: Remaking Corporate Law Through Stakeholder Governance. https://corpgov.law.harvard.edu/2019/02/11/towards-accountable-capitalism-remaking-corporate-law-through-stakeholder-governance. Accessed 18 December 2024.

Piketty, Thomas (2014). *Capital in the Twenty-First Century*. Translated by Arthur Goldhammer. Cambridge, MA: Harvard University Press.

Public Citizen (2019). Revolving Door Class of 2019: Nearly Two-Thirds of Former Lawmakers With Jobs Outside Politics Land in Influence Business. https://www.citizen.org/news/revolving-door-class-of-2019-nearly-two-thirds-of-former-lawmakers-with-jobs-outside-politics-land-in-influence-business. Accessed 6 January 2025.

Pulu, Tibi (2024). Scientists Put Over 100 Experienced Astrologers to The Ultimate Test — The Results Are Embarrassing. *ZME Science*. https://www.zmescience.com/science/news-science/astrology-debunked-2024-study/?utm_source=chatgpt.com. Accessed 6 January 2025.

PYMNTS (2023). Sixty Percent of US Consumers Live Paycheck to Paycheck – That Could Change in 2024. https://www.pymnts.com/economy/2023/2023-year-pay-check-consumer/#:~:text=Persistent%20inflation%20and%20increasing%20prices,to%20pay%20their%20monthly%20bills. Accessed 18 December 2024.

Qvist, Hans-Peter, Y., Henriksen, Lars Skov and Fridberg, Torben (2018). The Consequences of Weakening Organizational Attachment for Volunteering in Denmark, 2004–2012. https://www.vive.dk/en/publications/the-consequences-of-weakening-organizational-attachment-for-volunteering-in-denmark-2004-2012-3vy32dxy. Accessed 6 January 2025.

Rania, Francesco, Trotta, Annarita, Carè, Rosella, Migliazza, Maria Cristina and Kabli, Abdellah (2020). *Sustainability*, 12 (9), 3854. doi: 10.3390/su12093854.

Ravilochan, Teju (2021). The Blackfoot Wisdom that Inspired Maslow's Hierarchy. https://www.resilience.org/stories/2021-06-18/the-blackfoot-wisdom-that-inspired-maslows-hierarchy. Accessed 18 December 2024.

Rehal, Viren (2024). Understanding the Tragedy of the Commons. https://spureconomics.com/understanding-the-tragedy-of-the-commons. Accessed 6 January 2025.

Reich, Robert (2015). *Saving Capitalism*. New York: Alfred A. Knopf.

Rhee, Robert J. (2017). A Legal Theory of Shareholder Primacy. https://corpgov.law.harvard.edu/2017/04/11/a-legal-theory-of-shareholder-primacy. Accessed 18 December 2024.

Salotti, Jean-Marc (2022). Humanity extinction by asteroid impact. *Futures*, 138, 102933.

Sather,, Andrew (2021). R&D Spending as a Percentage of Revenue By Industry [S&P500]. https://einvestingforbeginners.com/rd-spending-as-a-percentage-of-revenue-by-industry. Accessed 19 December 2024.

Simpson, Ian (2022). How did New Zealand get proportional representation? *ElectoralReformSociety*.https://www.electoral-reform.org.uk/how-did-new-zealand-get-proportional-representation. Accessed 6 January 2025.

Slamka, Christian, Skiera, Bernd, and Spann, Martin (2012). Prediction Market Performance and Market Liquidity: A Comparison of Automated Market Makers. *IEEE Transactions on Engineering Management*, 60 (1), 169–185. doi: 10.1109/TEM.2012.2191618.

Social Finance UK (n.d.). Reducing reoffending in Peterborough. https://www.socialfinance.org.uk/work/reducing-reoffending-in-peterborough. Accessed 6 January 2025.

Socialmediavictims.org (2024). Facebook Whistleblower: Frances Haugen. https://socialmediavictims.org/facebook-whistleblower-frances-haugen. Accessed 6 January 2025.

Soros, George (2009). https://www.youtube.com/watch?v=DFyfYBcbbac. Accessed 18 December 2024.

Statista (2024). Denmark: Ratio of government expenditure to gross domestic product (GDP) from 2019 to 2029. https://www.statista.com/statistics/318639/ratio-of-government-expenditure-to-gross-domestic-product-gdp-in-denmark. Accessed 18 December 2024.

Statistics Denmark (n.d.). Economic Model ADAM. https://www.dst.dk/en/Statistik/ADAM. Accessed 23 December 2024.

Stein, Jeff (2017). A staff survey shows just how broken Congress is. https://www.vox.com/policy-and-politics/2017/8/8/16112362/congress-survey-broken-yikes. Accessed 18 December 2024.

Stoller, Matt (2016). How Democrats Killed Their Populist Soul. https://www.theatlantic.com/politics/archive/2016/10/how-democrats-killed-their-populist-soul/504710/?utm_source=pocket_saves. Accessed 21 December 2024.

Stonehage Fleming (n.d.). The impact of wealth on family relationships: managing expectation. https://www.stonehagefleming.com/insights/detail/the-impact-of-wealth-on-family-relationships-managing-expectation#. Accessed 18 December 2024.

T&E (2020). Uber pollutes more than the cars it replaces – US scientists. https://www.transportenvironment.org/articles/uber-pollutes-more-cars-it-replaces-us-scientists. Accessed 18 December 2024.

Tax Policy Center (2023). Historical Highest Marginal Income Tax Rates. https://taxpolicycenter.org/sites/default/files/statistics/pdf/toprate_historical_6.pdf. Accessed 19 December 2024.

The Conversation (2022). The origins of human society are more complex than we thought. https://theconversation.com/the-origins-of-human-society-are-more-complex-than-we-thought-179137. Accessed 19 December 2024.

The Economist (2023). What are the chances of an AI apocalypse? https://www.economist.com/science-and-technology/2023/07/10/what-are-the-chances-of-an-ai-apocalypse. Accessed 19 December 2024.

TheGlobalEconomy.com (2022). Ukraine: Military spending, percent of GDP. https://www.theglobaleconomy.com/Ukraine/mil_spend_gdp/?utm_source=chatgpt.com. Accessed 6 January 2025.

The Guardian (2021). From the archive: Brazilian butt lift: behind the world's most dangerous cosmetic surgery – podcast. https://www.theguardian.com/news/audio/2024/jun/26/from-the-archive-brazilian-butt-lift-behind-the-worlds-most-dangerous-cosmetic-surgery-podcast. Accessed 18 December 2024.

The World Bank (2008). Brazil: Toward a More Inclusive and Effective Participatory Budget in Porto Alegre. https://documents1.worldbank.org/curated/en/778301468019774995/pdf/401440v10ER0P01sclosed0March0302008.pdf. Accessed 6 January 2025.

Thierer, Adam (2020). Amidst "Techlash," Many Americans Still View Technology Industry in a Positive Light. https://www.discoursemagazine.com/p/amidst-techlash-many-americans-still-view-technology-industry-in-a-positive-light. Accessed 18 December 2024.

Ting, Wang Leung (2017). Nepotism or meritocracy? Explaining the rise of career politicians. https://blogs.lse.ac.uk/politicsandpolicy/explaining-the-rise-of-career-politicians. Accessed 18 December 2024.

Tooze, Adam (2021). Has Covid ended the neoliberal era? https://www.theguardian.com/news/2021/sep/02/covid-and-the-crisis-of-neoliberalism. Accessed 18 December 2024.

UK Government (2024). Stubbing out the problem: A new strategy to tackle illicit tobacco. https://www.gov.uk/government/publications/stubbing-out-the-problem-a-new-strategy-to-tackle-illicit-tobacco/stubbing-out-the-problem-a-new-strategy-to-tackle-illicit-tobacco. Accessed 4 January 2025.

UNEP (2021). Rebuilding the ozone layer: how the world came together for the ultimate repair job. https://www.unep.org/news-and-stories/story/rebuilding-ozone-layer-how-world-came-together-ultimate-repair-job. Accessed 4 January 2025.

visualcapitalist.com (2024). Ranked: The 50 Most Valuable Companies in the World in 2024. https://www.visualcapitalist.com/ranked-the-50-most-valuable-companies-in-the-world-in-2024. Accessed 19 December 2024.

Vitalik.eth.limo (2021). Moving beyond coin voting governance. https://vitalik.eth.limo/general/2021/08/16/voting3.html. Accessed 19 December 2024.

Vogels, Emily A. (2022). Teens and Cyberbullying 2022. Pew Research Center. https://www.pewresearch.org/internet/2022/12/15/teens-and-cyberbullying-2022. Accessed 6 January 2025.

WallStreetPrep.com (2024). Secondary Market. https://www.wallstreetprep.com/knowledge/secondary-market. Accessed 6 January 2025.

Wang, Laura Friis (2023). "Depressing" analysis: Danes' trust in politicians has fallen significantly. https://www.information.dk/indland/2023/10/deprimerende-analyse-danskernes-tillid-politikerne-faldet-markant. Accessed 18 December 2024.

WHO (2023a). Road traffic injuries. https://www.who.int/news-room/fact-sheets/detail/road-traffic-injuries. Accessed 18 December 2024.

WHO (2023b). Tobacco. https://www.who.int/news-room/fact-sheets/detail/tobacco. Accessed 21 December 2024.

Wigle, Reda (2024). A shocking number of Gen Zers, millennials have been dumped over their zodiac sign: Here's when to quit — or commit. *New York Times.* https://nypost.com/astrology/shocking-number-of-gen-zers-millennials-dumped-over-zodiac-sign-heres-when-to-quit-or-commit/?utm_source=chatgpt.com. Accessed 6 January 2025.

Wikipedia (2011). "Fifteen Million Merits." https://en.wikipedia.org/wiki/Fifteen_Million_Merits. Accessed 19 December 2024.

Wikipedia (2016a). "Hated in the Nation." https://en.wikipedia.org/wiki/Hated_in_the_Nation. Accessed 19 December 2024.

Wikipedia (2016b). "Nosedive." https://en.wikipedia.org/wiki/Nosedive_(Black_Mirror). Accessed 19 December 2024.

Wilkinson, Richard and Pickett, Kate (2010). *The Spirit Level: Why Equality is Better for Everyone.* London: Penguin.

Winstone, Lizzy, Mars, Becky, Haworth, Claire, M. A. and Kidger, Judi (2021). Social media use and social connectedness among adolescents in the United Kingdom: a qualitative exploration of displacement and stimulation. *BMC Public Health* **21**, 1736. doi: 10.1186/s12889-021-11802-9.

Zibel, Alan (2019). Revolving Congress: The Revolving Door Class of 2019 Flocks to K Street. https://www.citizen.org/article/revolving-congress. Accessed 23 December 2024.

Zipper, David (2023). Self-driving cars would be a climate disaster. https://www.fastcompany.com/90846919/self-driving-cars-would-be-a-climate-disaster. Accessed 4 January 2025.

INDEX